THE FILMS OF AKI

THE FILMS OF AKI KAURISMÄKI

Ludic Engagements

Edited by

Thomas Austin

BLOOMSBURY ACADEMIC

NEW YORK · LONDON · OXFORD · NEW DELHI · SYDNEY

BLOOMSBURY ACADEMIC
Bloomsbury Publishing Inc
1385 Broadway, New York, NY 10018, USA
50 Bedford Square, London, WC1B 3DP, UK

BLOOMSBURY, BLOOMSBURY ACADEMIC and the Diana logo are trademarks of
Bloomsbury Publishing Plc

First published in the United States of America 2018
Paperback edition published 2020

Cover design: Eleanor Rose
Cover image: Photographer, Malla Hukkanen © and courtesy Sputnik Ltd

Library of Congress Cataloging-in-Publication Data

Names: Austin, Thomas, 1966- editor.
Title: The Films of Aki Kaurismaki: Ludic Engagements /
edited by Thomas Austin.
Description: New York, NY: Bloomsbury Academic, 2018. | Includes
bibliographical references, filmography and index.
Identifiers: LCCN 2018033044 | ISBN 9781501325380 (hardback) |
ISBN 9781501325410 (epdf) | ISBN 9781501325403 (eBook)
Subjects: LCSH: Kaurismèaki, Aki, 1957—Criticism and interpretation.
Classification: LCC PN1998.3.K384 F55 2018 | DDC 791.4302/33092—dc23 LC record
available at https://lccn.loc.gov/2018033044

ISBN: HB: 978-1-5013-2538-0
PB: 978-1-5013-6316-0
ePDF: 978-1-5013-2541-0
eBook: 978-1-5013-2540-3

Typeset by Integra Software Services Pvt. Ltd.

To find out more about our authors and books visit
www.bloomsbury.comand sign up for our newsletters.

To Charlotte, the love of my life

CONTENTS

Part III
PERFORMANCE

LIST OF FIGURES

LIST OF CONTRIBUTORS

Thomas Austin is Reader in Media and Film at the University of Sussex. He is the author of *Hollywood, Hype and Audiences* (2002) and *Watching the World* (2007), and co-editor of *Contemporary Hollywood Stardom* (2003) and *Rethinking Documentary* (2008). His latest research is on representations of migrants and refugees in the cinema of Fortress Europe.

Henry Bacon is Professor of Film and Television Studies at the University of Helsinki. He headed the Academy of Finland research project A Transnational History of Finnish Cinema, the results of which were published in *Finnish Cinema – A Transnational Enterprise* (2016). Among his publications are the monographs *Luchino Visconti – Explorations of Beauty and Decay* (1998), *Audiovisuaalisen kerronnan teoria* (Theory of Audiovisual Narration, 2000), *Elokuva ja muut taiteet* (Film in Relation to Other Arts, 2005) and *The Fascination of Fictional Violence*, 2015. He has also written extensively on the history of opera.

Ulrike Hanstein is Lecturer in Film Studies at the Friedrich-Schiller-Universität Jena. She has held academic positions at the Bauhaus-Universität Weimar, at the Hochschule für Musik und Theater Leipzig, and was a fellow at the Getty Research Institute in Los Angeles. She is the author of a book on the melodramatic film aesthetics of Lars von Trier and Aki Kaurismäki (*Unknown Woman, geprügelter Held: Die melodramatische Filmästhetik bei Lars von Trier und Aki Kaurismäki*, 2011) and co-editor of an anthology on media history entitled *Re-Animationen* (with Anika Höppner and Jana Mangold, 2012).

Pietari Kääpä is Associate Professor in Media and Communications at the Centre for Cultural and Media Policy at the University of Warwick. His work has focused on the intersections between transnational and ecocritical media studies. He has published several books on Finnish cinema, including *The National and Beyond: The Globalisation of National Cinema in the Films of Aki and Mika Kaurismaki* (2010) and *The Cinema of Mika Kaurismaki* (2011). Other books include *Transnational Ecocinema: Film Culture in an Era of Ecological Transformation* (2013) and *Ecology and Contemporary Nordic Cinema* (2014). Kääpä has also edited special issues of *Interactions* and *Studies in Documentary Film*. His latest book *Environmental Management of the Media* is due out in 2018.

Panos Kompatsiaris is Assistant Professor of Art and Media at the National Research University Higher School of Economics in Moscow. He holds a PhD in art theory from the University of Edinburgh and has published on the politics of art, media representation, creative labour and cultural institutions in academic journals, magazines and exhibition catalogues. His first monograph *The Politics of Contemporary Art Biennials: Spectacles of Critique, Art and Theory* (2017) explores the strategies of legitimizing contemporary art's critical potential in Europe through an ethnography of large-scale perennial exhibitions in the context of the rise of the post-2010 protest movements against austerity and neo-liberalism.

Angelos Koutsourakis is University Academic Fellow in World Cinema at the University of Leeds. He is the author of *Politics as Form in Lars von Trier* (2013) and the co-editor of *The Cinema of Theo Angelopoulos* (2015). His next book, *Rethinking Brechtian Film Theory and Cinema*, will be published in 2018.

Michael Lawrence is Reader in Film Studies at the University of Sussex. He is the author of *Sabu* (2014) and the co-editor, with Laura McMahon, of *Animal Life and the Moving Image* (2015) and, with Karen Lury, of *The Zoo and Screen Media: Images of Exhibition and Encounter* (2016). He is currently completing a book called *The Bollywood Version: Transnational Adaptation in Popular Hindi Cinema*.

Andrew Nestingen is Professor of Scandinavian Studies at the University of Washington, where he teaches film, literature and cultural theory, with a special focus on Finland. His books include *The Cinema of Aki Kaurismäki: Contrarian Stories* (2013) and *Crime and Fantasy in Scandinavia: Fiction, Film and Social Change* (2008). He co-edited the volumes *Scandinavian Crime Fiction* (2011) and *Transnational Cinema in a Global North: Nordic Cinema in Transition* (2005). He was co-editor of a special issue of the journal *Lähikuva* on Aki Kaurismäki and also served as associate editor of the *Journal of Scandinavian Cinema*.

Eija Niskanen received an MA in critical studies in film and television from UCLA and is currently teaching and researching on the Moomin brand in Japan at University of Helsinki. She has been a programmer for Helsinki International Film Festival since 1989 and is the programming director for Helsinki Cine Aasia Film Festival. Eija also coordinates Finland Film Festival in Japan, as well as working as a freelance film writer and subtitling Japanese films into Finnish. Her interests include East Asian and South East Asian cinema and world animation in general, as well as film festival research.

Lara Perski is a translator and curator of film and video art. She is also an editorial assistant for *Screening the Past* and a co-editor of the Audiovisual Essay website REFRAME. She is based in Düsseldorf, Germany.

Jaakko Seppälä is docent (adjunct professor) in Film and Television Studies, University of Helsinki. His major research interests lie in the field of film style, transnational film history and close textual analysis of meanings. He wrote his doctoral dissertation on the import and reception of silent Hollywood films in Finland. In his work for the Transnational History of Finnish Cinema project, funded by Academy of Finland, he built a method for statistically and qualitatively analysing the style of large bodies of films from a comparative perspective. He is currently exploring Aki Kaurismäki's film style. Seppälä has contributed to anthologies and journals, including *Nordic Genre Film: Small Nation Film Cultures in the Global Marketplace* (2015), *Finnish Cinema: A Transnational Enterprise* (2016) and *Journal of Scandinavian Cinema* and *Projections*.

ACKNOWLEDGEMENTS

This book would not have been possible without the boundless support, advice and companionship of Charlotte Adcock.

Special thanks to Noah Austin, Stella Austin, Guy Austin, Roger Austin, Sue Austin, Margaret Adcock, James Montgomery, Tim Turner, Kristy, Prof G, Prof C and his team, and those who understand the extra symbolism of the cover image. Thanks to Katie Gallof at Bloomsbury for her enthusiasm and support from the start of this project, Erin Duffy and Susan Krogulski, also at Bloomsbury, for advice.

Finally, thanks to Tim Jordan, Frank Krutnik and Matilda Mroz at the University of Sussex; to Kirsi Hatara, Eevi Kareinen and Haije Tulokas at Sputnik Oy for help with illustrations; to Jake Garriock at Curzon/Artificial Eye; and to all the contributors who made this book happen.

INTRODUCTION

Thomas Austin

The cover image for this book, taken from *Mies vailla menneisyyttä* (The Man Without a Past, 2002), captures the arresting moment when the protagonist M (Markku Peltola), having been violently beaten and robbed, then pronounced dead by a doctor, rises from his hospital bed to resume his life but as a homeless amnesiac. By the end of the film, this penniless Lazarus has found a place to live in a marginal but supportive community, a romantic partner and a job as manager of a rock band. Like many of Aki Kaurismäki's films, *The Man Without a Past* is a socially engaged work that complicates realist aesthetics, employing a self-conscious and highly allusive style. It is both a political response to pressing issues of inequality and injustice in neo-liberal Europe and a playful utopian fable. Over the past three decades, this distinct approach, centred on ludic interventions that are simultaneously serious and comic, relayed in a style that combines mimetic and performative modes,[1] referentiality and artifice, realism and anti-realism, has made Kaurismäki a vital auteur in European cinema. Yet his oeuvre, encompassing seventeen feature films, two music documentaries, a television movie and numerous shorts, remains surprisingly under-researched in Anglophone scholarship. This collection aims to redress such neglect, and to interrogate the politics and aesthetics of his compelling body of work, from *Rikos ja rangaistus* (Crime and Punishment) in 1983 to the film which may be his last, 2017's *Toivon Tuolla Puolen* (The Other Side of Hope).[2]

It would be easy to stereotype Kaurismäki's films as drily humorous dramas populated by taciturn underdogs, presented in a predictable style that recycles particular techniques and eschews others.[3] (The former would include a largely static camera, underplayed performance style, ironic tone and a soundtrack composed of early 1960s rock and roll along with Tchaikovsky or Shostakovich.) But this is too simplistic. His output is far from monolithic, and while it evinces important aesthetic and thematic continuities, it also displays a sometimes

Information about Sputnik's business practices provided by Eija Niskanen.

startling range in both of these dimensions. As Jaakko Seppälä's recent research makes clear, 'just because Kaurismäki's oeuvre is recognizably different from that of other filmmakers, does not mean it is stylistically homogeneous.'[4] In addition, Kaurismäki has drawn on a wide range of genres and modes including romance, road movie, film noir and silent melodrama.

Crucial elements of diversity across Kaurismäki's films, along with key continuities, become more evident if one considers his work via the prism of *incongruity*. Discrepancies in narrative content, actor performance and mise en scène provide a source of both humour and political significance, some aspects of which I will adumbrate here. First, his scripts consistently accord attention to unremarkable characters whose insecure labour conditions make them members of neo-liberalism's precariat (shoeshiner, security guard, unemployed hostess, factory worker, unemployed miner, dustman, cashier, etc.). Second, casting decisions confound dominant practice by ensuring that such protagonists are played by actors who are not conventionally good-looking but who are emphatically not comic grotesques played for laughs, as one might expect them to be in much of normative cinema. This comparative incongruity in relation to dominant expectations of scripting and casting is thus a political gesture, one that is considered further in Chapters 1 and 5. Third, incongruity is generative of humour. Sight gags involving objects out of place abound in Kaurismäki, from the payphone on the side of a ramshackle Siberian barn in *Leningrad Cowboys Go America* (1989) to the pineapple carried by Inspector Monet (Jean-Pierre Darroussin) in *Le Havre* (2011). (Kaurismäki's displaced objects are discussed in Chapters 2 and 4.) Other visual jokes are grounded on comic exaggeration or by unexpected revelations of previously unseen space. For example, in *La Vie de Bohème* (1992), Marcel (André Wilms) is drowning his sorrows following a publisher's rejection of his play for being too long when the barman offers to read the manuscript. To the surprise of both the barman and the audience, Marcel heaves an enormous stack of papers on to the bar – '*The Avenger*, a play in 21 acts'. In *Kauas pilvet karkaavat* (Drifting Clouds, 1996), the unemployed Ilona (Kati Outinen) finds work in a downmarket bar. When two customers order food, she walks towards the kitchen, opens the hatch and repeats their order. Only when she enters the kitchen herself and picks up a frying pan does it become apparent that there is no cook and that she is doubling up as both cook and waitress.

Finally, performance style and production design in Kaurismäki's films reject the realist aesthetics commonly associated with socially engaged content as in the work of the Dardenne brothers or Ken Loach, who share thematic preoccupations with Kaurismäki but who are much more concerned with achieving verisimilitude. One of the most obvious instances of this strategy is a laconic and consistently understated performance style which requires that actors refrain from conventionally expressive vocal, facial and bodily gestures and adopt instead a deadpan delivery of dialogue, even when their characters are confronted with stressful, violent and melodramatic situations (analysed further in Chapters 8–10). If incongruity is 'in Wittgensteinian terms [...] a rule that has not been followed',[5] then acting in Kaurismäki's films fails to follow the rules of both naturalistic and expressive performance conventions. Instead, through repetition, it ultimately constitutes a new set of conventions that might be termed Kaurismäkian: 'There is an iron law. I have it understandable to all, in English: "I do not want acting in my movies." The performer should definitely play, but so you cannot tell. He should not wave his hands about or cry.'[6] Undemonstrative performances occur throughout Kaurismäki's films and can be generative of both humour and pathos. For instance, in *The Man Without a Past*, M tries to open a bank account but is interrupted by an armed robber, who apologetically locks M and the cashier in the vault. M deadpans to the cashier in a fatalistic tone, 'It didn't work out then.' 'What?' she asks. 'Opening the account.' Having been arrested by the police, M is rescued by a nameless lawyer, who overwhelms a shell-shocked detective with his precise legal reasoning before presenting M with a cigar. In contrast to M's hangdog demeanour and the curt one-liners he exchanges with the policemen, the lawyer appears both benign and incongruously verbose, albeit in a highly professional manner. (He is played by real-life lawyer and MEP Matti Wuori.) By playing this second tense situation in an emotionless and blank manner, Peltola as M offers the humour of incongruity, while the contrasting profusion of detail in Wuori's vocal performance appears disjunctive in the Kaurismäkian universe. The refusal of naturalism and foregrounding of artifice in actor performance is matched by Kaurismäki's predilection for production design that is rich in anachronistic objects, particularly vehicles, furniture and decor from the mid-twentieth century. These anachronisms in the mise en scène are paralleled by the repeated use of 'dated' music, particularly rock and roll, Finnish tango, and Shostakovich and Tchaikovsky. The political implications of these choices are explored in Chapters 1 and 2.

Over time, the unconventional choices discussed here have been consolidated into a recognizable – but never static – aesthetic, a signature style that provides a 'dominant' from which Kaurismäki occasionally deviates, as in the example of Matti Wuori mentioned earlier. Such aberrations from his own norms enable Kaurismäki to generate impact and surprise from moves that might appear unremarkable in the work of other filmmakers. Some examples of how Kaurismäki figures the interiority of his often tongue-tied characters will serve to elaborate this point. Emotional and psychological depth is largely displaced from dialogue and performance and is instead coded via lighting, mise en scène and music.[7] Kaurismäki notes: 'The music has a similar function to that in a dance hall where people are too shy to talk and leave the songs to make the conversation.'[8] For instance, during a trip to the seaside in *Varjoja paratiisissa* (Shadows in Paradise, 1986), music is deployed along with framing, off-screen space and editing to externalize and amplify the feelings of Nikander (Matti Pellonpää) and Ilona (Kati Outinen). The sequence centres on their cautious mutual desire. Shy, hesitant and uncertain of each other, they book into separate hotel rooms and shake hands goodnight. An eyeline match then connects the two as they look towards their closed bedroom doors; Ilona is listlessly reading a magazine, and Nikander is smoking in bed. The next day, the couple sit on a windy beach with their backs to the camera, looking out to sea and not touching. The radio is playing 'Salattu Suru' performed by Topi Sorsakoski and Agents, a rather mournful cover of The Renegades's 'My Heart Must Do the Crying'. Now shown frontally, Nikander casts a shy sidelong glance and then embraces Ilona, pushing her to ground. The long-awaited kiss happens in off-screen space, implied by a metonymic close-up on Ilona's immobile left hand resting on the sand, still holding a cigarette. Not a word has been said at the beach, in a scene lasting just over half a minute.

In the years since *Shadows in Paradise* Kaurismäki's use of similarly understated and carefully choreographed performances has become so familiar that it can be pared down and used in a highly economic fashion that borders on self-parody. For example, in *Le Havre*, ageing shoeshiner Marcel Marx (André Wilms) arranges for florist Mimi (Mimi Piazza) to reunite with her estranged husband, rock singer Little Bob (Roberto Piazza). When Mimi enters the bar where Little Bob is drowning his sorrows, gently building strings are heard on the soundtrack and a white spotlight suddenly foregrounds them both, while Marcel backs away into shadow. The couple don't touch, merely smile and say each other's names, and the reconciliation scene is complete.

Set against this matrix of familiar techniques, Kaurismäki can construct surprising deviations, perhaps the most striking of which is Valto's daydream in *Pidä huivista kiinni, Tatjana* (Take Care of Your Scarf, Tatiana, 1994). This brief fantasy sequence is particularly egregious in a body of work that circumscribes much dramatic action, often banishing moments of violence to off-screen space and prohibiting characters from laughing, crying and even running.[9] The opening sequence of the film shows three biker couples speeding through an anonymous Finnish town. Each motorcycle is ridden by a man, with a woman riding 'side-saddle' behind in a dress or skirt and headscarf, a 1960s fashion which gives the film its title.[10] Following the title card, the film cuts to a close-up of a sewing machine, and the noise of the motorbikes is replaced by the rhythmic sound of the needle as the camera pulls out to reveal the huge figure of Valto (Mato Valtonen), sat in his mother's kitchen, making clothes. The contrasts with the preceding bikers are many: the freedom and unpredictability of the road versus the familiar confines of a domestic interior; mobile leisure against sedentary, almost static, labour; the differing gendered associations of motorbike and sewing machine; the bikers' heterosexual pairings followed by a grown man who lives with his mother. On the kitchen radio, The Renegades's 'If I had someone to dream of' reiterates Valto's aberrant position outside the logic of heterosexual coupling.

The song is also a subtle indication of the Buñuelian strand that runs throughout Kaurismäki's most oneiric film. Having driven his alcoholic male friend Reino (Matti Pellonpää) and two female Soviet tourists on a taciturn and desultory road trip from the northern countryside to Helsinki to catch the ferry home, Valto returns to Finland alone, since Reino has stayed in Estonia with his new love Tatjana (Outinen). In an unmarked fantasy sequence which only becomes recognizable as such in retrospect, Valto drives his Volga estate, once again laden with the three passengers, through the plate-glass window of a cafe, pulls up and orders a small coffee (Figure 0.1). The television at the counter shows The Renegades performing 'Girls girls girls' live on stage. The grainy footage fills the screen for a minute before the image cuts to Valto looking back from the counter to the now empty car, followed by a relatively rare medium close-up of his impassive face. Perhaps more than any other image in cinema, the close-up of the human face is a surface that conventionally implies intimate access to, and knowledge of, the 'truth' of the human subject. As Mary Ann Doane notes, 'It is barely possible to see a close-up of a face without asking: what is he/she thinking, feeling, suffering? What is happening beyond what I can see?'[11] Valto's blank face gives little away and as the song ends, accompanied by the screams of the audience, he returns to the car in silence. The cafe has been replaced by a small roadside kiosk. The libidinal energy of 'Girls girls girls' parallels the shock of Valto's unexpected action at the wheel, but it also reaffirms his exclusion from a heteronormative economy of desire. Alone, he returns to his mother's house, hangs up his jacket, lets her (dusty but uncomplaining) out of the cupboard in which he had locked her before the trip and sits down to

Figure 0.1 Valto (Mato Valtonen) and friends in *Take Care of Your Scarf, Tatiana* (1994). © and courtesy Sputnik Ltd.

resume his sewing. In a gesture of circularity, the camera tracks in to the needle of the sewing machine, reversing the track out of the first post-credits shot and inviting the questions: Was the entire film, not just the car crash, Valto's daydream? Did the drama take place only in his mind?

****

I have argued that a dynamic of repetition and difference, dominants and deviations, is evident across Kaurismäki's output. However, it is impossible to approach his body of work without also taking into account the media persona that he has cultivated over three decades. As the Finnish newspaper *Helsingin Sanomat* commented in 2008: 'In the course of his thirty year career Kaurismäki has given hundreds of interviews, ranging from Finnair's in-flight magazine to the communist newspaper *Tiedonantaja*. Yet in the opinion of most people, he avoids publicity.'[12] Kaurismäki's paradoxical public identity is not only that of the reluctant interviewee. It also oscillates between gloomy clown and highly competent cinephile. He is happy to perform in self-deprecating deadpan as a morose heavy drinker who hates his own films.[13] This self-presentation exists alongside that of the thoughtful and cultured auteur, as evident in extended discussions with writers such as Peter von Bagh and in some film festival appearances. Kaurismäki's success as a businessman in a highly competitive market is less frequently on show. For instance, Peter von Bagh's *Aki Kaurismäki*, a book of interviews and film analyses published in Finnish in 2006 and translated into German and French the same year, is a vital resource on Kaurismäki's thinking and filmmaking practices but one that downplays economic considerations.[14] Instead, what emerges most clearly from the book is the extent of Kaurismäki's cinephilia (citing, among others, Ozu, Buñuel, Bresson and Sirk), paired with a nonconformist disdain for conventional expectations of how to be a filmmaker in Finland. These attitudes, along with his handling of media and business operations, have enabled him to forge an aesthetically distinct body of work that is grounded in Finnish history, society and culture but also reaches well beyond them, and in the process to achieve the status of an international auteur.

Speaking about the surprise success of his third feature, *Shadows in Paradise*, Kaurismäki tells von Bagh:

> At the time in Finland it was totally unthinkable to make a film about a dustman and a supermarket cashier without guns, or more generally about something equally banal. [...] In the 1980s, filmmakers suffered from a kind of aggrandisement. They thought only of international success, even though the conquest of the world was hardly going to be a resounding triumph. Paradoxically, with its trivial subject matter, *Shadows* was the first Finnish film about which one could speak of a certain amount of international success.[15]

As Andrew Nestingen argues, Kaurismäki's persona and films 'prod us to rethink the fundamental categories and binary oppositions that often structure popular and scholarly discussions of film authorship'.[16] He is an auteur who 'derides cinema as commerce' while embracing 'elements of the same commercial cinema', a bohemian who is also an entrepreneur, operating bars and restaurants as well as film production and distribution companies.[17] Thus, much like auteur cinema itself, Kaurismäki's bohemianism 'occupies a position of symbolic opposition to the mainstream, yet is also historically, institutionally, and economically entangled with it'.[18] Kaurismäki 'must engage in attention-getting action within a media field defined by the economic forces [he] is seeking to critique [via his films]'.[19]

These performances of self can also be approached via Thomas Elsaesser's notion of a 'paradoxical kind of autonomy and agency' that is key to the functioning of auteurs in a globalized marketplace.[20] He notes 'the extraordinary dependency of most of the world's non-Hollywood filmmakers on festivals for validation, recognition and cultural capital', and points to the uncomfortable mix of dependence and claims to independence in twenty-first-century film authorship.[21] Elsaesser proposes Alexander Sokurov as an exemplar of this phenomenon: 'A sign of his own awareness of his dependency on a variety of noncommercial "art cinema" funds and investors is Sokurov's consistent habitus of rebellious insubordination in interviews, "performing" the radical free spirit and independent auteur, both on and off film sets'.[22] Kaurismäki might be suspected of a similar performed non-compliance. Like Sokurov, he has had to do business with international institutions and media companies while avowing his independence. Nevertheless, from the early years of his career, he has maintained a significant degree of autonomy by keeping his production budgets low, retaining financial control and the rights to his films.[23] In this context, Kaurismäki's own interview appearances, by turns pugnacious, self-deprecatory and melancholic, have worked in tandem with his film output to establish and consolidate a recognizable media persona, the auteur as brand.

****

In the early 1980s, Aki Kaurismäki and his older brother Mika established the production company, Villealfa, which co-funded films by both brothers. Kaurismäki set up his own production company, Sputnik, in 1989, while Mika founded Marianna Films. Sputnik's first production was the television film *Likaiset kädet* (1989), Kaurismäki's adaptation of JeanPaul Sartre's play *Les Mains Sales*. Since then, it has co-funded all Kaurismäki's films apart from *I Hired a Contract Killer* (1990), along with a handful of titles by other directors.

Sputnik has repeatedly secured financial support from the Finnish Film Foundation and the European Union Media Programme. The company also distributed the art cinema classics *Seven Samurai* (1954) and *L'Atalante* (1934) in Finland in the 2000s. Accounts for 2016 show revenue of €144,000, down from €621,000 in 2013, most probably reflecting the long gap from the release of *Le Havre* in 2011 to *The Other Side of Hope* in 2017.[24]

In addition to the film-related business interests mentioned earlier, the Kaurismäki brothers co-own the Helsinki entertainment complex Andorra, established in 1993. This houses two bars – Corona, a New York-style bar, and the Soviet-style Kafe Moskva – in addition to Kino Andorra, 'a movie theatre from the good old days', and a small concert/event venue, Dubrovnik.[25] (Kino Andorra does not feature regular film programmes but is rented by different film festivals, used for premieres, seminar events and press screenings.) The complex and the Kaurismäki brothers also owned a film import company Senso Films, established in 1987, which distributed both domestic and foreign art house films in Finland but is no longer in business. Aki Kaurismäki also owns real estate in Karkkila, a small town in Southern Finland, where he resides when in Finland. In addition, he is a partner in the Zetor restaurant, established by Mato Valtonen, leader of the Finnish rock group the Leningrad Cowboys, who appear in several of Kaurismäki's films.

****

The Other Side of Hope premiered at the 2017 Berlin Film Festival as this manuscript was being completed. The film begins with two parallel stories that ultimately converge. Sherwan Haji plays Khaled, a Syrian mechanic who has lost most of his family in the bombing of Aleppo and arrives in Helsinki having stowed away on a coal freighter. Waldemar Wikström (Sakari Kuosmanen) is a shirt salesman who leaves his business and his wife to take over The Golden Pint, a struggling restaurant. The pair meet when Khaled, fleeing deportation, is discovered sleeping behind the restaurant bins by Wikström, who then gives him a job. The political motivation of the film is clear. In Berlin, Kaurismäki joked: '[With *Le Havre*] I wanted to change the world. But my manipulative abilities are not good enough, so I think I have to limit it to change Europe.'[26] Uniquely in his oeuvre, the tone of the film becomes earnest on occasions, especially when Khaled gives an unusually lengthy account of his travails crossing Europe, including losing touch with his sister on the trek.

Kaurismäki was 59 at the time of the film's release and Kuosmanen was a year older.[27] While the restaurant scenes in particular are very funny, the film is often suffused with an autumnal, elegiac tone. The dark skies and wet streets of Helsinki, repeated shots of falling leaves and the institutional grey of three key locations (police station, refugee reception centre and underground car park) reiterate this sense (Figure 0.2). Writing on late style as a distinct aesthetic, Edward Said borrows from Adorno's work on Beethoven to focus on 'intransigence, difficulty, and unresolved contradiction'.[28] In contrast to this recalcitrant, disruptive idiom that Adorno has termed 'devoid of sweetness, bitter and spiny',[29] *The Other Side of Hope* is nearer to a consolidation of Kaurismäki's signature style than a radical, alienated questioning of it. Yet the film is clearly and self-consciously a late and perhaps final work. Adorno warns against relegating late works 'to the outer reaches of art, in the vicinity of document', whereby they are read as traces of the artist's biography or imminent death.[30] Attending to aesthetics can avoid this pitfall and, in the case of *The Other Side of Hope*, reveals a mix of stylistic repetition and innovation alongside foregrounded citations of some of the director's earlier films. The film contains relatively few allusions to other filmmakers but makes several

Figure 0.2 Khaled (Sherwan Haji) in the reception centre in *The Other Side of Hope* (2017). © and courtesy Sputnik Ltd.

references to Kaurismäki's own work.[31] A group of homeless people save Khaled from a night-time attack by a violent racist, much as M is rescued in *The Man Without a Past*. The dog belonging to staff at The Golden Pint is called Koistinen, in a nod to the protagonist of *Laitakaupungin valot* (Lights in the Dusk, 2006). The lorry driver who smuggles Khaled's sister from Lithuania to Finland is called Melartin, after a character in *Shadows in Paradise*. And the ambiguous ending, in which the wounded Khaled sits under a tree awaiting possible rescue and is found by Koistinen the dog, again recalls *Lights in the Dusk* in which the human Koistinen (Janne Hyytiäinen) is gravely injured but is found by the woman who loves him (Maria Heiskanen). At the time of writing, it is impossible to say whether or not *The Other Side of Hope* is to be Kaurismäki's final film. What is certain is that it continues two patterns evident throughout his work: ongoing adjustments and shifts to a style that nevertheless remains recognizable as a signature aesthetic, and a lasting political commitment to stories of the marginalized and excluded.

****

The first part of this book addresses intersections of time and space in Kaurismäki's cinema. Attending to these interfaces necessarily entails a consideration of the imbricating aesthetic and political dimensions of his work. Thomas Austin's chapter examines how the often-noted presence of anachronisms in Kaurismäki's mise en scène, along with multiple allusions to other filmmakers, both from the mid-twentieth century in particular, moves beyond a simplistic nostalgia that recalls a lost past and instead works to reinforce a critique of neo-liberalism's onslaught on social and economic spheres. Austin argues that the double refusal of verisimilitude mobilized by anachronism and allusion operates in tandem with, rather than against, the socially engaged content of films such as *The Man Without a Past, Drifting Clouds* and *Le Havre*, films which query the unattainability of their own narrative outcomes as moments which are politically desirable but currently appear utopian. Analysis of mise en scène is also central to Pietari Kääpä's contribution. Kääpä draws on ecocritical thinking to trace how Kaurismäki interrogates anthropocentric logic. His chapter centres on material objects, the corporeality of the human body, urban spaces and natural landscapes. For Kääpä, Kaurismäki's films are 'contradictory in the sense that they often use elements generated by the superstructures they seek to criticise', but they nevertheless deploy methods of spatial disorientation and displacement to query dominant assumptions about social relations and to rethink the place of humanity in the ecosystem. Lara Perski investigates the interrelationship of on-screen and off-screen spaces in Kaurismäki, including how he uses off-screen space in manifold ways in order to shape comic, melodramatic and fantastical moments. From *Shadows in Paradise* to *Le Havre*, acts of passion, violence and the more or less miraculous repeatedly occur off-screen. Perski argues that the 'volatile, uncertain terrain' of off-screen space facilitates the impossible, whether played for laughs or tears, and sets up a tension with more realistic elements in Kaurismäki's films. Eija Niskanen looks further afield to trace the bidirectional flow of aesthetic influences between Kaurismäki and filmmakers in Japan. Not only does Kaurismäki pay repeated homage to the work of Yasujiro Ozu, but, Niskanen argues, his own films have proved popular with a younger generation of Japanese directors including Nobuhiro Yamashita, Hirobumi Watanabe, Naoko Ogigami and Riichiro Mashima.

Questions of tone and point of view are the focus of the second part. Jaakko Seppälä offers a rare close analysis of Kaurismäki's celebrated but largely taken-for-granted ironic tone, tracing how composition, framing and editing patterns generate comedy and a sense of strangeness, producing disjunctions between characters' and audiences' perspectives. Seppälä locates a mild 'surrealism of everyday life' and what he terms 'ironic minimalism' in the films. This tone accommodates both sincerity and oddity or absurdity and is evident to viewers but rarely noticed by characters. Tonal complexity comes under scrutiny again in the chapter by Panos Kompatsiaris, which considers Kaurismäki's sympathetic representations of working-class characters and associated indictment of the callous attitudes of state and capitalist elites. Paying particular attention to the Finland trilogy (1996–2006), Kompatsiaris explores how the moralizing tendencies of Kaurismäki's class politics are tempered by absurdity and humour 'that subvert any "final" attempt to impose a form of ethical conduct'. He suggests that the films constitute an ambivalent populism in that they adhere to two conflicting positions. Working-class characters' pride in their work, desires for (heterosexual) love and consumerist aspirations are legitimated but also parodied and criticized as the conformist consequences of alienation. The politics of class are also at the heart of Angelos Koutsourakis's examination of the so-called proletarian trilogy (1986–1990). Koutsourakis draws on theories of cultural techniques in order to trace the films' visualization of the classed body at work and leisure, including how 'characters carry the labour conditions of exploitation in their social interactions'. Crucially, Koutsourakis argues, the trilogy 'does not solely show the body as being imprisoned in an alienated world, but also its potential to change'. Finally in this part, Andrew Nestingen asks, 'how do Kaurismäki's films generate [their] intense affective conclusions, and how can we make sense of them?' Drawing on critical approaches to the Hollywood musical from Jane Feuer, Richard Dyer and Amy Herzog, Nestingen plots a different route through Kaurismäki's irony to argue that, like American instances of the genre, his less spectacular films initially polarize reality and fantasy before working to reconcile this duality in redemptive and utopian, yet also ironic, final moments.

Performance is the theme of the book's third part, which begins with two sustained close readings of acting technique. Henry Bacon offers a precise analysis of how *Drifting Clouds* deploys different acting styles and levels of characterization in its 'delicate fusion of toned-down melodrama and farce'. He demonstrates an often-overlooked variety in Kaurismäki's use of scripting and performance, which in *Drifting Clouds* ranges 'all the way from classically realistic to fairly broadly caricatured characters'. Ulrike Hanstein focuses on *Hamlet Liikemaailmassa* (Hamlet Goes Business, 1987), exploring 'the tension between hyperbolic dramatic action, the screen performers' blatant underacting, and ostentatious cinematic mise en scène [and lighting]'. Hanstein analyses how this film-noir-styled adaptation of *Hamlet* displaces expressive functions from actor performance to mise en scène and framing, while also staging an inquiry into 'the intricate relationships between playing, dissimulating, and performing'. Deadpan performance also comes under scrutiny in Michael Lawrence's chapter, which focuses on Kaurismäki's repeated use of both dogs and expressionless humans for comic effect. Lawrence traces links between facial opacity in both human and canine actors and argues that 'because of our belief in the dog's emotional inner life, the dog's face confronts us with the same challenge as the face of a deadpan performer'. Underacting in humans 'obscures the emotions we assume to be there', while the typical inscrutability of Kaurismäki's canine performers both contributes to and complicates 'the comedy that is generated by facial inexpressivity'.

This collection does not aspire to offer a comprehensive survey of Kaurismäki's work across three decades. But it does hope to spur further scholarly engagement with this playful and political filmmaker, especially at a moment when the accelerating pace of capitalism's 'gale of creative destruction'[32] makes his films about the casualties of this maelstrom appear ever more pertinent and necessary.

Notes

1 Lesley Stern, 'Paths That Wind Through the Thicket of Things', *Critical Inquiry* 28, no. 1 (2001): 324.
2 Kaurismäki stated at the 2017 Berlin film festival that he would not make another film. 'Legendary filmmaker Aki Kaurismäki: There will be no more films', yle.fi, online at: http://yle.fi/uutiset/osasto/news/legendary_filmmaker_aki_kaurismaki_there_will_be_no_more_films/94645 04
3 Several of his films are also highly androcentric, notably *Calamari Union*, *Leningrad Cowboys Go America*, *Leningrad Cowboys Meet Moses* and *Pidä huivista kiinni, Tatjana* (Take Care of Your Scarf, Tatiana).
4 Seppälä, 'On the heterogeneity of cinematography in the films of Aki Kaurismäki', *Projections* 9, no. 2 (2015): 36. Seppälä argues that Kaurismäki's film style can be divided into three distinct phases: early films (1983–89), slow films (1993–96) and late films (since 1999). He notes that although Kaurismäki's films 'can be described as slow, his ASLs [average shot lengths] are not even near the extremes of slow cinema' and that he counterbalances long takes with short takes. Kaurismäki deploys 'small and understated' camera movements and tends to use reverse angles at around half the average rate of recent Hollywood. Seppälä, pp. 26, 29, 31.
5 Jeroen Vandaele, 'Humour mechanisms in film comedy: Incongruity and superiority', *Poetics Today* 23, no. 2 (2002): 227, 223.
6 Kaurismäki quoted in Thorsten Stecher, '*Das Weltwoche-Gesprach*: Ich glaube an Baum, nicht an Gott' *Die Weltwoche*, 37, no. 2 (2002): 12, http://www.weltwoche.ch/ausgaben/2002-37/artikel-2002-37-ich-glaubeanba.html, np. See also similar remarks made at the press conference for *The Other Side of Hope*, Berlinale, 14 February 2017. Available at: https://www.berlinale.de/en/im_fokus/videostreaming/videos/06_streaming_long_versions_2017_41341.html?openedFromSearch=true
7 *Juha* (1999), an adaptation of the 1911 Finnish novel in the style of a silent melodrama, retains Kaurismäki's relatively undemonstrative performance style and is heavily reliant on a score by Anssi Tikanmäki. In a film with no recorded speech and very few sound effects, those that are heard become endowed with particular significance, notably in the figuration of character interiority. Thus, when Juha (Sakari Kuosmanen) decides to leave his farm and travel to the city to track down his wife Marja (Outinen) and the smiling villain Shemeikka (André Wilms) who has lured her away and put her in a brothel, his determination is encrypted in two actions which, crucially, can be heard as well as seen: sharpening an axe, signifying intended revenge, and shaving with an electric razor, signifying a trip to the city.
8 Kaurismäki quoted in Peter von Bagh, *Aki Kaurismäki* (Cahiers du Cinema, 2006, trans Anne Colin du Terrail), 189.
9 '"Sex and violence you will never see. [...] For most of my fellow filmmakers sex and violence [is] in the foreground. I care about the other forms of human behaviour." Why do your characters never laugh or cry? "They do not run either."' Stecher, '*Das Weltwoche-Gesprach*'. A very rare exception is Khaled (Sherwan Haji) running to escape the police in *The Other Side of Hope*.
10 See Andrew Nestingen, *The Cinema of Aki Kaurismäki: Contrarian Stories* (New York: Wallflower Press, 2013), my translation, 40.

11 Mary Ann Doane, 'The close-up: Scale and detail in the cinema', *Differences*, 14, no. 3 (2003): 96.

12 Esa Mäkinen, 'Akateemikko Kaurismäen julkikuva on tarkasti luotu', *Helsingin Sanomat*, 22 May 2008, np; quoted in Nestingen, *The Cinema of Aki Kaurismäki*, 79.

13 See for instance, Simon Hattenstone, 'Seven Rounds with Aki Kaurismäki', *The Guardian*, 4 April 2012. Online at: https://www.theguardian.com/film/2012/apr/04/aki-kaurismaki-le-havre-interview

14 Peter von Bagh, *Aki Kaurismäki* (Helsinki: WSOY, 2006); *Kaurismäki über Kaurismäki*, Alexander Verlag Berlin; *Aki Kaurismäki*, Cahiers du Cinema, 2006, trans Anne Colin du Terrail. I have made use of the French version in this book. Von Bagh also discusses the Midnight Sun film festival, founded in 1986 with input from himself and both Kaurismäki brothers.

15 Von Bagh, *Aki Kaurismäki* (my translation), 51–52.

16 Nestingen, *The Cinema of Aki Kaurismäki*, 5. Nestingen argues that four stories recur in the discourses that have shaped Kaurismäki and his cinema: the auteur, the bohemian, the nostalgic and the Finn.

17 Nestingen, *The Cinema of Aki Kaurismäki*, 4–5.

18 Ibid., 7.

19 Ibid., 81. Nestingen notes: 'The central study of Kaurismäki's films in Finnish by Lauri Timonen distances itself from any analysis of the economic dimensions of Kaurismäki's cinema.' He is referring to Timonen, *Aki Kaurismäen Elokuvat* (Helsinki: Otava, 2006).

20 Thomas Elsaesser, 'The Global Author: Control, Creative Constraints and Performative Self-contradiction', in *The Global Auteur: The Politics of Authorship in 21st Century Cinema*, ed. Seung-hoon Jeong and Jeremi Szaniawski (New York: Bloomsbury, 2016), 39.

21 Elsaesser, 25. He also indicts the festival circuit for colluding with cultural tourism and demanding 'a kind of "self-exoticising"' from festival films. Elsaesser, 25. For how the director of the Finnish Film Foundation attempted to promote Kaurismäki's work through a similar logic of marketable alterity, see Nestingen, *The Cinema of Aki Kaurismäki*, 81.

22 Elsaesser, 'The global author', 27–28.

23

I don't use much on materials or supplies, so the cost is significantly less for me than for others. [...] The productions have really been Finnish-German-French cooperation for years. The Germans and French have their funding sources, which they want included in the credits. [...] I maintain one hundred percent control of the films' rights, despite the number of parties involved. They only receive distribution rights. [...] these are relationships based on trust. [...] I make films so cheap that no one takes on a large risk.

Nestingen, *The Cinema of Aki Kaurismäki*, 142.

24 https://www.finder.fi/Elokuvien+levitys+ja+jakelu/Sputnik+Oy/Helsinki/yhteystiedot/345299. The first international sales agent for Kaurismäki's films was World Sales Christa Saredi. When this company closed, Bavaria Film picked up the role. The current distributor is The Match Factory GmbH, which sells regional distribution rights. Under their operation *Ariel* (1988) was screened in fourteen territories outside Finland, while *The Man Without a Past* (2002) was screened

in twenty-one *and Le Havre* (2010) in thirty-four markets, ranging from South America to Romania to South Korea.

25 http://andorra.fi

26 Press conference, Berlin film festival, 14 February 2017. Available at https://www.berlinale.de/en/im_fokus/videostreaming/videos/06_streaming_long_versions_2017_41341.ht ml?openedFromSearch=true. For a further discussion of the politics of *Le Havre* and *The Other Side of Hope*, see Thomas Austin, 'Miserable journeys, symbolic rescues: Refugees and migrants in the cinema of Fortress Europe', in Cinema of Crisis: Film in Contemporary Europe, ed. Thomas Austin and Angelos Koutsourakis (Edinburgh: Edinburgh University Press) forthcoming.

27 Haji was thirty-one.

28 Edward Said, *On Late Style: Music and Literature against the Grain* (London: Bloomsbury, 2007), 7.

29 Theodor W. Adorno, *Essays on Music*, ed. Richard Leppert (University of California Press, 2002), 564, cited in Said, 12.

30 Adorno, *Essays on Music*, 564, cited in Said, 9.

31 However, one of the thugs is played by the Finnish film director Dome Karukoski. Thanks to Jaakko Seppälä on this point.

32 Joseph Alois Schumpeter, *Capitalism, Socialism and Democracy* (Allen and Unwin, 1954), 87.

Part I

TIME AND SPACE

Chapter 1

TEMPORALITY IN KAURISMÄKI: ANACHRONISM, ALLUSION, TABLEAU

Thomas Austin

In Aki Kaurismäki's short film *Dogs Have No Hell* (2002),[1] a small businessman just released from jail has 10 minutes to find the woman he loves and persuade her to take the train to Siberia with him. Initially, it appears that the film may have been made in 'real time' so that a 10-minute running time will match 10 minutes of story time. But this fit can only be achieved by a series of impossible ellipses, allowing the characters to move from scene to scene across Helsinki (prison, workshop, restaurant, station) in a matter of seconds. Rather than frustrating the viewer as a cheat, *Dogs Have No Hell* plays with dominant conventions of film narration to foreground cinema's function as a time machine. In this ludic exercise in temporal compression, Kaurismäki peppers the mise en scène with shots of clock faces, including a huge one on the wall of the jewellers where the couple buy their wedding rings. The film also offers a concise summation of his signature style, including deadpan performances of melodramatic scenarios, predominantly static framing with short track-ins used at key moments, appearances by regular collaborators (Kati Outinen and Markku Peltola) and the diegetic presence of a retro rock band (Marko Haavisto & Poutahaukat).[2] Because of its form, theme and brevity *Dogs Have No Hell* offers a striking instance of Kaurismäki's engagement with the politics of time in the social sphere and his exploration of the representational strategies through which such an engagement might be pursued. Dreams of change, urgency and departure, familiar from the generic clichés of popular cinema, are simultaneously queried and affirmed in the couple's race to catch the train.[3] The tedium and repetition of the quotidian working time which they hope to escape is encoded in the mise en scène of costumes and settings (the uniform of a cook, the space of an underground garage). So too is a complex sense of nostalgia, spatialized in 'outmoded' objects such as clothing (the man's pork pie hat, the woman's bobby socks) and the train itself.[4] Moreover, by holding in tension a self-conscious aesthetic and a generic but nonetheless emotionally engaging narrative, the short attests to its fabrication without sacrificing affect.

What renders the film – and Kaurismäki's work more broadly – both affective and political (indeed, affective *because* political), rather than a series of clever formal experiments, is the classed location of the lead characters. The working-class female protagonist, played as so often in his films by Outinen, is a cook. Peltola's character co-owns a small tyre business, presumably having realized the ambition expressed by several of Kaurismäki's male characters of becoming his own boss. They are here united in the kind of optimistic romantic trajectory that is not usually made available to characters from their class, in scenes typically reserved for normatively 'beautiful' leads in Hollywood and its imitators. Instead, two ordinary-looking working-class protagonists in their forties[5] are dignified and made beautiful in an exchange of looks and granted the filmic attention often reserved for middle-class characters.

When the pair catch sight of each other in the restaurant where the woman works, the use of lighting and the only tracking shots in the film call attention to the moment as both event and representation. The camera moves in to a medium close-up of her and then of him. Each remains silent, expressionless and very nearly static, framed frontally and gazing intently just past the camera, while the band plays a song called 'Thunder and Lightning'.[6] Traditional glamour lighting imparts a movie star glow to her blue eyes, blonde hair and white hairnet (narratively appropriate but incongruous in the romantic rhetoric of the scene).

Side-lit and seated against a wall in a black overcoat and dark grey hat, the man turns his head a little and moves his lower lip very slightly. The *coup de foudre* figured in an emotionally charged exchange of looks is of course a cliché of melodrama and romance, and its status as such is acknowledged here in the knowing tone generated by the dolly shots, lighting and the actors' underplaying. The impact of such distanciation techniques should not be misconstrued, however. Kaurismäki's films are designed to produce an emotional response in tandem with a political one, and the scene is not simply a genre pastiche drained of affect. Instead, it functions to move viewers towards a felt understanding of a transformative moment in the characters' lives, even while it foregrounds its own artifice. The silent look that inaugurates the formation of the heterosexual couple is registered as hackneyed, but it is also portrayed as a gesture of reciprocity suffused with a timid longing and hope. It is as if the everyday world has fallen away into irrelevance, at least temporarily. Concurrent with this, the pointedly ostensive display of film style gestures to a supplementary temporality beyond that of the diegesis: the moment of registration. The familiarity of staging and shooting opens up time further by inviting the recall of countless similar scenes in the history of cinema and in each audience member's particular viewing repertoire. But this temporal aperture is achieved without subverting the emotional drama.

In this chapter, I explore a nexus of issues around temporality, aesthetics, politics and affect in Kaurismäki's oeuvre. I trace three sets of temporal interventions in his films that complicate social realism: first, the presence of anachronisms in the mise en scène; secondly, citations of film history via multiple intertextual references to other filmmakers, popular genres and narratological conventions; and thirdly, the use in some of his more recent feature films of a particular type of tableau or stilled life. This highly charged image briefly halts the flow of narrative progression in a composition which generates political and emotional impact while also emphasizing its own fabrication as a moment of display.

In using these strategies, Kaurismäki defies verisimilitude and thus confounds the familiar binarism that polarizes claims to veracity and an aesthetic play with signification. The two terms, pulling in opposite directions, coexist uneasily in the idea of 'the representation of reality', a notion which Frederic Jameson has called a 'peculiarly unstable concept owing to its simultaneous, yet incompatible, aesthetic and epistemological claims'.[7] In a dialectical move, Kaurismäki stages a productive collision between socio-economic referentiality (bearing witness to poverty, unemployment, homelessness, social exclusion, immigration) and a self-consciously artful, cinephilic and playful address. To borrow Lesley Stern's terminology, his films can be seen as simultaneously quotidian and histrionic, in that they combine both mimetic and performative modes.[8] In the process Kaurismäki refuses the conventional alignment of 'serious' content with realist form, preferring instead a register that repeatedly foregrounds its own construction while retaining a sense of social engagement. Persistent questions of class and history are inseparable from the political and affective dynamics of anachronism, allusion and tableau across this terrain.[9]

Anachronism

Many commentators have noted Kaurismäki's recurrent deployment of 'dated' music, fashions, vehicles and everyday objects from the 1950s and 1960s in particular. In some of his films (*Juha* (1999), *Pidä huivista kiini, Tatjana* (Take Care of Your Scarf, Tatiana, 1994)), their presence is motivated by the historical setting of the narrative,[10] but in others, such as *Mies vailla menneisyyttä* (The Man Without a Past, 2002) and *Le Havre* (2011), they are signalled as anomalous and passé, aligned with characters who are out of touch with contemporary norms. While some such anachronisms – jukeboxes, selected furniture, vintage cars – have been designated as 'classics' via the retro market, this partial recovery of obsolescence is not acknowledged by Kaurismäki, even while his own films participate in a related process by conferring symbolic value upon them. (See, for instance, the jukebox and red sofa which Kaurismäki personally added to the production design of M's converted sea container home in *The Man Without a Past.*) This rehabilitation is accompanied by a simultaneous devaluation, avoidance or expulsion of contemporary objects such as mobile phones, computers and modern architecture.[11] For example, in *Kauas pilvet karkaavat* (Drifting Clouds, 1996), the financial crisis faced by restaurant hostess Ilona and her tram-driver husband Lauri erupts shortly after his purchase of a Sony colour television on easy credit. After they have both been laid off, and the television and sofa have been reclaimed, their luck starts to turn when Ilona makes plans to open a new restaurant, accompanied by rock and roll playing on their unfashionably old, but presumably fully paid-for, record player.

In a Bourdieuian sense, Kaurismäki and his regular production designers Markku Pätilä and Jukka Salmi are in the relatively privileged position of unofficial arbiters in the exercise of taste, imparting a degree of cultural worth to objects that were once discarded or overlooked. (As Bourdieu asserts: 'Nothing is more distinctive, more distinguished, than the capacity to confer aesthetic status on objects that are banal or even "common."')[12] However, the politics of such newly consecrated items becomes further complicated when one examines the class dimensions of their significatory functions. Kaurismäki's anachronisms do not provide the scaffolding for a simple retreat into the past. In his contemporary-set films, they are not dispersed evenly throughout the mise en scène but are commonly distributed according to the classed locations and relations of his characters. For example, in *Varjoja paratiisissa* (Shadows in Paradise, 1986), dustman Nikander (Matti Pellonpää) greases his hair and drives an early 1970s Rover 2000. His rival for cashier Ilona's love manages a clothing store, wears in-vogue baggy trousers and white shoes, and takes her out to a snobbish restaurant. At the film's climax, Nikander rescues Ilona (Outinen) from selling contemporary menswear and takes her on a honeymoon cruise to Estonia. In *Tulitikkutehtaan tyttö* (The Match Factory Girl, 1990), Iiris's melodramatically doomed attempt at cross-class love is in part prefigured by the fashionable forms and objects associated with Aarne, the supercilious middle-class object of her affections: modern dance music at the club where they meet, his modern sports car and his clothing (smart casual checked jacket, beige or grey suits). By contrast, her sympathetic brother, who works as a cook, dyes his hair black, drives a Ford Anglia and has installed a jukebox stocked with rock and roll in his flat. In *Ariel* (1988), unemployed miner Taisto wears a black leather jacket, greased hair, jeans and boots. Contemporary men's fashion is relegated to a bland disguise, worn to fit in after he and his cellmate Mikkonen raid a shop window following their escape from prison. The film makes much of the fetishistic (and commercial) value of Taisto's convertible white Cadillac with its red leather seats and spotless paintwork (Figure 1.1). But Taisto's retention of the huge car while he sleeps in a hostel for the homeless gains its significance in the context of his poverty. The car is an exaggerated marker of both a pride that refuses to abandon dreams for despair and an impracticality that leads to his robbery and unjust imprisonment.[13] This ambiguity is typical of much of Kaurismäki's oeuvre in which rock and roll era stylings and objects are often presented as signs of a precarious and enforced existence on the periphery of contemporary consumer culture but are also recuperated as the trophies of an elective rejection of mainstream society.

Figure 1.1 Taisto (Turo Pajala) in the white Cadillac in *Ariel* (1988). © and courtesy Sputnik Ltd.

These films form what is commonly called the 'proletariat trilogy'. But their lonely subjects are notably lacking in class consciousness, security or solidarity and might be better understood as members of what is now termed 'the precariat'.[14] Kaurismäki offers this definition: 'One step under the proletariat, [people] who are not conscious enough to belong to [the working class]. They go in the union if somebody asks, tells them, but basically they don't even know. So proletariat is the wrong word. Loser is better.'[15] His focus throughout his career on characters from the working classes and below, the kind of people ignored or taken for granted in the social arena, and frequently marginalized or demonized in the representational sphere, offers a persistent reminder of power relations and a repudiation of the norms of dominant cinema:

> I have absolutely no interest in making films about the family problems of the middleclass. Middle-class life just doesn't interest me. Losers do, because I'm a middle-class loser myself. I spent a few years back in the 1970s, you know, when I too was hungry and homeless. [...]
>
> *So your subject matter became the Finnish working class?*
>
> Yes. The people who are hidden, the ugly people, as some critics have called them. But then who is good-looking? I think many Hollywood stars are ugly, horribly ugly... Totally unable to act, these people, *and* totally ugly. So I will stick with my own ugly people. Of whom there are more and more in Finland.[16]

And not just in Finland. In contemporary-set *Le Havre* (2011), Marcel Marx (André Wilms) works as a shoeshiner; his labour thus extends the use value of his customers' footwear rather than complying with the accelerated consumption dictated by fashion. At home, Marcel and his wife Arletty (Outinen) live in respectable poverty, reliant on 1950s/1960s furniture and appliances: old, but not valuable, and largely beyond the legitimation conferred by retro taste. Laura Rascaroli writes:

> Old objects represent them in that they are salvaged remnants of previous epochs, unwanted leftovers, used by people who, by choice or necessity, are extraneous to the logic of consumer society. As such, they are totally devoid of the aura that is normally attached to what is considered retro and vintage. They are not fashionable objects but poor things, though undeniably linked to an oppositional – and somewhat romantic – aesthetics of reusability and sustainability.[17]

Anachronisms in Kaurismäki's films thus often have a doubled sense, as markers of social and economic exclusion remade into a symbolic refusal of contemporary hyper-consumerism. They thereby constitute a rebuttal of the 'intensified consumption' exhorted under the present temporal regime, which Jonathan Crary has termed '24/7'.[18] Crary's 24/7 is 'beyond clock time', a normative 'impossible temporality' that 'disavows its relation to the rhythmic and periodic textures of human life'.[19] He elaborates: 'In relation to labor it renders plausible, even normal, the idea of working without pause, without limits. [...] As an advertising exhortation it decrees the absoluteness of availability and hence the ceaselessness of needs and their incitement, but also their perpetual non-fulfilment.'[20]

Characters such as Nikander and Ilona in *Shadows in Paradise*, Marcel and Arletty in *Le Havre*, or M and Irma in *The Man Without a Past* fail to participate in the fabricated needs, programmed obsolescence and collective amnesia produced under the conditions of neoliberalism.[21] Instead, they embody an intransigent connection to history, to traces of earlier moments which persist as a residue in outmoded material objects and popular cultural forms. In this context, an attachment to older, and slower, ways of consuming or using objects may offer a provisional critique of the present conjuncture – even while such objects and practices, like cinema itself, never fully evade the logics of consumption.

Kaurismäki's dialogue with the past via material culture can be further clarified by reference to C. Nadia Seremetakis's recuperation of nostalgia as a socio-political understanding. When asked in interview 'You're a hopeless nostalgic ... Was everything really so much better in the past?' Kaurismäki replies that it is simply a question of aesthetic values: 'Old cars, old cameras, old radios, old glasses, and old ashtrays are simply more beautiful than new ones.'[22] But, as Seremetakis argues, nostalgia can mobilize a critical notion of identity, location and history grounded in the sensory experience of objects and events:

Nostalghia [the Greek term] [...] is far from trivialising sentimentality. This reduction of the term confines the past and removes it from any transactional and material relation to the present; the past becomes an isolatable and consumable unit of time. Nostalgia, in the American sense, freezes the past in such a manner as to preclude it from any capacity for social transformation in the present, preventing the present from establishing a dynamic perceptual relationship to its history. Whereas the Greek etymology [of the term] evokes the transformative impact of the past as unreconciled historical experience.[23]

Seremetakis writes of the 'sensory displacement' enforced by processes of rationalization and globalization such as those which followed Greece's entry into the European Economic Community (EEC) in 1981. Recalling the gradual replacement of a local Greek peach with imported varieties, she asks: 'Is memory stored in specific everyday items that form the historicity of a culture, items that create and sustain our relationship to the historical as a sensory dimension?'[24] It is in this way that Kaurismäki's nostalgic engagement with the past can be understood. Rather like Seremetekis's lost peach, Kaurismäki recalls the feelings generated by indigenous local and national cultural objects threatened or erased by the forces of globalization. For instance, *Ariel* is dedicated to 'the memory of the real Finland' and the rural scenes of *Tatiana* and *Juha* include footage of old wooden buildings, remnants of previous eras. Kaurismäki comments: 'Starting in the 1960s, under the influence of developers, inept politicians and economists have almost entirely destroyed the Finland that I had become attached to – agrarian Finland, but also the Finland of *Tatiana*, the architecture of its towns and villages. The country has been transformed in a kind of globalisation which has left neither a roof nor a head untouched.'[25] To this extent, his films seem to accord with André Bazin's well-known formulation in which cinema instantiates humanity's 'mummy complex', a preservative obsession seeking 'a defense against the passage of time.'[26] But Kaurismäki complicates the sense memories of filmed objects via their self-conscious mediation, whatever he may suggest in interviews. He asserts the mnemonic function of his loser trilogy as a means of salvaging the past: 'They are all reflections of their time, slices of reality. [...] they'll have an important power of testimony come the time when [...] one studies [...] the image of the 1980s and in particular the image of Helsinki.'[27] Yet these are far from transparent images capturing sites or objects in order to mitigate their loss. Instead, Kaurismäki's anachronisms and allusions contribute to a creative geography in his films. As Henry Bacon has argued: 'Helsinki-milieus in Aki Kaurismäki's films are in a metaphorical relation to the "real" Helsinki: the fictional world in the films both is and is not that city.'[28] Pietari Kääpä notes how Kaurismäki and his production designers seek out liminal sites such as 'the outskirts of the city, harbours, the road, nameless bars'[29] and refashion them as Foucauldian heterotopias, 'counter-sites in which the real sites [...] are simultaneously represented, contested, and inverted.'[30] For instance, the container village in *The Man Without a Past* is located on an undeveloped waterside wasteland in Helsinki, but it was assembled there expressly for the purpose of filming.[31] *Le Havre* was shot in an old quarter of the town about to be demolished, but the site was supplemented and enhanced through the addition of clichéd signifiers of France (a boulangerie, a bar, accordion music), and a strict colour palette (to which I return later).[32]

Furthermore, while television news broadcasts can be deployed as an efficient way to anchor the diegesis in recent history and to register significant events (in *The Match Factory Girl*, the Tiananmen Square massacre;[33] in *Le Havre*, the dismantling of 'the Jungle', a makeshift migrant camp near Calais; in *Drifting Clouds*, the hanging of Nigerian activist Ken Saro-wiwa), the latter bulletin is purposely reassembled rather than relayed as originally screened.[34] Thus, the films encompass two distinct imperatives: as (idiosyncratic) films of record, preserving the profilmic scene at a particular moment (Helsinki in the 1980s, Le Havre around 2010, contemporary television news broadcasts), and also as knowing interventions and fabrications. This recurrent paradox is not a problem in need of resolution but another of the key dialectics that are central to the style and politics of Kaurismäki's work.

Anu Koivunen locates further productive tensions in *The Man Without a Past*'s 'ambivalent affective rhetoric', which 'fuses sentimentality with irony and [class] resentment with melancholia'. The film moves viewers 'between senses of proximity and distance' by both inviting and hindering 'national sentiments and nostalgic pleasures'.[35] She notes the melancholic and nationalist connotations of Annikki Tähti's on-screen performance of her 1950s *schalger* hit 'Muistatko Monrepos'n' ('Do you remember mon repos?'), a song which 'enabled and mobilised [the] mourning of Karelia, the Finnish province that after the Second World War was annexed to the Soviet Union.[36] But, like many other Kaurismäki films, *The Man Without a Past* also celebrates a complex accommodation between Anglo-American cultural exports (music, hairstyles, fashions) and the specifics of the local culture in which they became integrated. The Renegades, whose US-influenced rhythm and blues is heard in *The Man Without a Past*, *The Match Factory Girl*, *Le Havre* and *Tatiana*, exemplify this hybridity. Originally from Birmingham, England, the band recorded and toured extensively in Finland in the 1960s, where they enjoyed their greatest success. (Their single 'Cadillac', which Iiris listens to on her brother's jukebox in *The Match Factory Girl*, reached number two in Finland in 1964.)[37] Born in 1957, Kaurismäki asserts: 'All the Finnish youngsters born in [the] late '50s or early '60s got American and English blues, rhythm and blues and rock 'n' roll from their mother's milk.[38] George Lipsitz has noted: 'For some populations at some times commercialised leisure is history – a repository of collective memory that places immediate experience in the context of change over time.'[39] If popular music can function in this way as a 'memory engine',[40] it does so by mobilizing meanings that are never simply cognitive but are always affective in their resonance and significance. Kaurismäki's use of rock and roll music dating from his own childhood both attests to and extends this process, inflecting tunes like The Renegades's 'Cadillac' and 'Do the Shake' with a new layer of connotations based on their particular deployment in his films.

Rock and roll is not simply heard in the films but is also made visible, figured not just in on-screen performances by The Regals (*Tatiana*), Melrose (*Hamlet liikemaailmassa* (Hamlet Goes Business, 1987), *Lights in the Dusk*), Little Bob (*Le Havre*) or Marko Haavisto & Poutahaukat (*The Man Without a Past, Dogs Have No Hell*), but also via images of associated (and equally dated) musical devices from jukeboxes (*The Match Factory Girl, The Man Without a Past*) to radios (*Shadows, Ariel*) to Valto's in-car record player in *Tatiana*.

Songs thus reach beyond the soundtrack and are materialized in images of the (old) technologies that reproduce them. Moreover, much like the anachronistic objects discussed previously, this music is not distributed evenly but is affiliated with particular characters: the 'loser' protagonists in *Shadows in Paradise, Ariel* and *The Match Factory Girl*; Valto and Reino, the inarticulate but endearing 'stupid Finns' in *Tatiana*; the Leningrad Cowboys; Marcel, his friends and neighbours at Little Bob's 'charity gig' in *Le Havre*.

Perhaps the most overt alignment of rock and roll with the precariat in Kaurismäki's oeuvre occurs in *The Man Without a Past*. Salvation Army worker Irma (Outinen) sleeps in a cheerless hostel. Preparing for bed, she neatly arranges her shoes, stops the draught under the door with a rolled-up mat and stands looking out into the cold night. Then she turns and gazes directly at the camera with a look of loneliness and defiance, an assertion of self that momentarily punctures the diegesis. Irma switches on her aged tape player, and the incongruously cheerful 'Do the Shake' by The Renegades starts up. She precisely folds her dressing gown and then throws it towards the end of bed in a tiny (absurd, unnoticed) gesture of abandon, before lying in bed gazing at the tape player, while the lyrics invite her to join the party ('everybody shaking, dancing in the street now').

Kaurismäki repeatedly deploys music to relay the interiority of his taciturn characters, who rarely find the words to express their feelings. But in this case, Irma's loneliness and yearning for something out of reach is enlarged and articulated to a wider community of invisibles. 'Do the Shake' plays on over a montage comprising static shots of M sitting at the waterside looking at the lights and skyscrapers of modern Helsinki across the bay, then of homeless individuals sleeping rough. As a consequence, The Renegades's song becomes a music of the dispossessed. As Lana Wilson notes, the sequence 'connect[s] Irma to our hero [M] as well as to Finland's homeless population, extending the sympathy we feel toward her to all of the others who come after, and comparing the economic impoverishment of the country to the emotional isolation of one individual'.[41]

In the multifarious ways discussed here, anachronisms serve Kaurismäki's critique of neoliberalism and his celebration of the precarious, quotidian achievement of what Brecht called 'the greatest art of all: *Lebenskunst*, the art of getting through life'.[42] In the following section, I discuss how his use of visual allusions contributes to this political agenda, while also foregrounding, and celebrating, the artifice of cinema.

Allusion

In his work on intertextuality, Mikhail Iampolski argues that quotation within any film 'exposes its textuality'. This 'theatrical' rupturing of textual homogeneity operates as a further emphasis of the materiality of the filmic sign in addition to that immanent in the framing of every image.[43] Intertextuality also creates an accretion of new meanings, a '"piling" of one thing onto another' that Iampolski compares to the multiple significations of a hieroglyphic: 'Intertextuality too superimposes text on text, meaning upon meaning'.[44] I have suggested that there is also an important temporal dimension to intertextuality, which works by opening up supplementary timeframes beyond that of the diegesis. These include the moment of registration, prior film history, the often-recounted formative viewing experiences of Kaurismäki himself[45] and diverse individual repertoires of audience members.[46] Thus, allusions to earlier moments in cinema function much like the anachronisms discussed earlier in that they generate multiple and coexisting temporalities.

Kaurismäki's films (and interviews) abound with citations of other works. Koivunen locates multiple references to Finnish culture in *The Man Without a Past*, including allusions to Hugo Simberg's 1903 painting 'The Wounded Angel',[47] carnivalesque comedies of the 1950s and Edvin Laine's 1945 film *Nokea ju kultaa/Soot and Gold*, 'a film set in a harbour landscape [in which] a man [...] is morally reborn with the help of a female Salvation Army officer'.[48] *La Vie de Bohème* (1992), a loose adaptation of Henri Murger's novel, includes cameo appearances by Jean-Pierre Léaud, Louis Malle and Sam Fuller. In *Juha*, the villain Shemeikka's Corvette sports car is renamed a 'Sierck', after Douglas Sirk's original surname. By Kaurismäki's own account, the film contains more than 100 intertextual gestures.[49] He has described the melodramatic content and vivid yet minimalist style of *The Match Factory Girl* as 'a romance novel, put through a kind of meat grinder with Bresson-Ozu',[50] while *Le Havre* 'attempts to re-create some kind of neorealism in the French style', concluding with 'a perfect Ozu shot'.[51] It is significant that Kaurismäki's allusions are not to screen culture of the moment but to classics of global art cinema and Finnish cinema from the mid-twentieth century. Much like production design and mise en scène, intertextuality in his films devalues or evacuates the contemporary.[52]

In his consideration of cinephilia, Paul Willemen suggests that it 'bonds viewer and film in a particular moment of complicity'.[53] A cinephiliac director's allusions may be double-coded to ensure that not just fellow cinephiles get the reference. Thus, in Godard's *À Bout de Souffle*, Michel (Jean-Paul Belmondo) says 'Bogie' while aping Bogart's mannerism of running his thumb across his mouth in order to 'anchor the cinephiliac dimension'.[54] But at other moments, Godard's allusions remain more or less invisible until he identifies them as such.[55] Kaurismäki also often refrains from double-coding as this comment makes clear:

> Sometimes, I decide to allude in a shot to Rembrandt, Goya, or Vermeer, or to ask Timo Salminen to light it in their style. But that has no special significance, because it is not done to be noticed. [...] My citations of films are of the same order, for example the scene in *Juha* on the bank of the river. It begins via Renoir, moves to Buñuel with the crushed butterfly and ends with *Gertrud* (1964) by Dreyer. To pass the time I play with my memory and engage in an imaginary dialogue with my dead colleagues.[56]

Furthermore, extra-diegetic temporalities are opened up by the dynamic textual and intertextual system of genre, which provides, as Robert Warshow has noted, 'its own field of reference'.[57] There is nothing inherently progressive or reactionary about such a system. But in the case of Kaurismäki, class enables him to stage a 'correction' of certain genres and validates his use of pastiche as a political intervention.[58] I have argued earlier that in the case of *Dogs Have No Hell*, the pastiche of the familiar conventions of romance crucially operates via the working-class identity of the couple. This secures both emotional affect and political impact by resuscitating, for a socially and representationally marginalized class, romantic clichés of personal transformation, and interrogating them at the same time.

Class, as both referent and representation, is the key element that clinches Kaurismäki's social and cultural politics, and which distinguishes his cinephilia from the formal play of early Godard or, more recently, the films of Wes Anderson, which balance distanciation and immersion but to relatively little political purpose.[59] Far from presenting a formal shell of empty mannerisms assembled from the 'lumber room' of past styles,[60] films such as *Drifting Clouds*, *Juha* and *Le Havre* derive political significance from allusion and overt fabrication because they are inhabited by working-class or 'underclass' characters who are validated as worth representing, without reducing them to victim status or elevating them to simplistic icons of heroic labour or 'authentic' folk culture. In the process the films examine class as both cinematically and socially located.

Colour in Kaurismäki is often central to the practice of allusion, and is a significant gesture to filmic textuality, emphatically refusing claims to transparency. His use of colour draws in particular on the political aesthetics of Douglas Sirk and Jean-Luc Godard but has become a distinct element in his mature style. These two key influences each marshal colour to serve a Brechtian distanciation effect but in notably differing ways. Sirk's melodramas exaggerate the expressive functions of colour to the point of anti-illusionism by magnifying and exceeding the conventional motivations of characterization and plot. (For instance, the clichéd symbolism of Cary's red dress in *All That Heaven Allows*, or nymphomaniac Marylee's 'hot pink nightgown'[61] and red sports car in *Written on the Wind*.) The result intensifies the schematic norms of the genre, rather than completely abandoning them.[62] By contrast, Godard's use of non-referential colour is, as Edward Branigan notes, 'nonpsychological, nondramatic, and nonverisimilar'. Subordinated to neither characterization nor realism, colour becomes 'an element of equal significance with other elements [...] capable of connecting to various points in a text and helping to make patterns'.[63] Building on both Sirk and Godard, Kaurismäki's ostensive use of colour in his middle and late career oscillates between the expression of character in 'obvious' and diagrammatic terms, recalling Sirk, and an 'excessive' foregrounding of colour that complicates and contravenes realist mise en scène, recalling Godard.

Colour also functions in more precise allusions such as indirect citations of Ozu's celebrated red kettle in *Drifting Clouds* (a coffee pot), *Lights in the Dusk* (a ketchup bottle) and *The Man Without a Past* (a fire extinguisher). In *Le Havre*, the all-black attire, including hat, of Inspector Monet (Jean-Pierre Darroussin) recalls film noir and the *policiers* of Jean-Pierre Melville, while Julien Allen notes associations with the Western in Marcel's camel-coloured jacket.[64] Kaurismäki, cinematographer Timo Salminen and production designer Wouter Zoon use a largely tricoloured palette for the film, dominated by various shades of blue/grey, against which smaller areas of brilliant red and yellow stand out. He comments: 'Blue-gray is my basic set design color, and that is from Melville, and then I may add some red because a red teapot looks good in Ozu's films.'[65]

In *Drifting Clouds*, like *Le Havre*, colour is granted a degree of autonomy, untethered from its function in the service of verisimilitude. While this liberation never goes as far as Godard's systematic deployment of brilliant, solid colours in films like *Deux ou trois choses que je sais d'elle* (1967), colour is on occasions foregrounded as a conspicuous and anti-illusionist element in the otherwise realist mise en scène. For instance, when Lauri visits his sister at the cinema where she works, red is the dominant colour. The roses that he holds and the decor of the kiosk are saturated reds with quieter white, cream and brown offering points of contrast. And when Ilona supervises work on the new restaurant, she wears blue/green, while the tradesmen's overalls and the walls of the room are varying shades of blue with contrasting smaller objects placed in the centre of the frame such as the workers' red caps, a yellow T-shirt and a green screwdriver.

In its refusal of verisimilitude at such moments, the 'excessive' and allusionist use of colour in *Drifting Clouds* and *Le Havre* asserts the fictionality of each film, a gesture that is also manifest in the self-conscious utopianism which concludes both narratives. Along with *The Man Without a Past*, these films repeatedly bring together realist and formalist elements in the mise en scène: the workers' tools in *Drifting Clouds*' study in blue; the deliberate juxtaposition of brilliant colours (an orange mug, navy-blue ashtray and red fire extinguisher) as M is given a free drink in *The Man Without a Past*; the symmetrical 'A' shape formed by a baguette placed on a green and yellow table in *Le Havre*, an image that is both a metonym for thrift and an avowedly staged glimpse of beauty in the everyday. The duality of these visuals condenses and reiterates the political content of the films. All three offer doubled perspectives on social crises (unemployment, homelessness, poverty, immigration) by combining a political critique of neoliberalism with optimistic outcomes that move beyond both institutionalized escapism and narrow notions of fidelity to the real in order to query the terms of their current unattainability.[66]

Tableau

The final device that I want to consider is Kaurismäki's use of the tableau or stilled life. This image of stasis freighted with particular significance stands out from the flow of narrative events and is comparable to the tableaux in Diderot's theatre, 'during which actors hold their poses and all motion [...] ceases'.[67] But in Kaurismäki, such moments 'out of time' reach beyond the diegesis and temporarily set aside the illusionist conventions of realism to summarize social relations in a move more reminiscent of the Brechtian concept of *gestus*. Roland Barthes characterizes Brecht's *gestus* or social gest as a notable 'pregnant moment', 'a gesture or set of gestures [...] in which a whole social situation can be read'. He asserts: 'Not every gest is social: there is nothing social in the movements a man makes in order to brush off a fly; but if this same man poorly dressed, is struggling against guard dogs, the gest becomes social. [...] [D]istanciation [...] is vital to Brecht because he represents a tableau for the spectator to criticize.'[68]

Kaurismäki has spoken of the importance of Brecht's theories of defamiliarization for his own work with actors:

> I believe that 'acting' should be avoided in films and that actors should avoid identifying themselves too deeply with any role they play. When I was a student, there was a lot of interest in Brecht's theatre, and it's likely that his idea of an epic or dialectical theater, as opposed to a dramatic and illusionist one influenced me. I like Brecht's idea that the actor should regard himself as a narrator who only *quotes* the character he is playing. In this way audiences are provoked to draw intellectual conclusions instead of just becoming emotionally attached to what they see.[69]

This method contributes to the deadpan performances, dry humour and underplayed melodrama evident across many of his films. Conventional acting is negated and made strange so that full dramatic immersion is queried, but, crucially, not at the expense of emotional impact. Instead, audiences are asked to feel themselves both inside and outside the narrative simultaneously.

The technique of the tableau is less prevalent in Kaurismäki's oeuvre but appears in two feature films. A brief instance occurs in the 'Do the Shake' sequence discussed earlier. The montage includes two images of homeless people in static and silent poses, each held for 6 seconds. The first is a frontal shot of an elderly couple sat on the pavement. The man is looking straight at the camera, while the woman sleeps leaning against him. The second shot is of a man lying horizontally across the frame, sleeping next to his crutches on a ground strewn with stones and debris. Both presentational views use *gestus* to foreground their own artifice while retaining an emphasis on the referent, and so confront audiences with their own relations to homelessness as both social fact and image.

A more extended use of the stilled life device appears in *Le Havre*. Armed police, a press photographer and a Red Cross team await as a sea container from Gabon with a human cargo of clandestine immigrants is opened (Figure 1.2). However, when its inhabitants are revealed they are composed in both senses of the word: neatly dressed, silent and almost motionless as they sit in the shadows. The image then cuts to a series of spot-lit medium close-ups: an elderly man, a woman and a young girl, another woman with a baby, a young man, a middle-aged couple, another young man and then a boy of about 12 (later revealed as Idrissa (Blondin MIguel)). All are framed more or

Figure 1.2 Immigrants in the sea container in *Le Havre* (2011). Photographer: Malla Hukkanen. © and courtesy Malla Hukkanen and Sputnik Ltd.

less frontally and looking directly at, or just past, the camera, almost as if posing for photographic portraits. Composition and performance afford the immigrants a quiet dignity and self-possession as they return and refute the 'othering' gazes of the police officers, the photographer and, by implication, the film's viewers. At this moment, the filmic rendition of the inside space of the container confounds verisimilitude not only through mise en scène but also by enlarging this confined space into an impossible, rhetorical one.[70] Kaurismäki has commented:

> I had written that the container with the refugees is filthy, and that some of the immigrants had died. I could not go through with that, and I thought I'd do the complete opposite. Instead, I'd show them wearing their respectable Sunday best – to hell with realism. I'd make them arrive as proud people, instead of having them lie in the container in their own filth, as some of them realistically would have done after two weeks' incarceration.[71]

The political efficacy of the container sequence derives from the dialectical combination within this stilled life of social veracity (the plight of undocumented immigrants) and the blatant impossibility of their figuration here. The gap between the two calls attention to the relative social positioning of (African) migrants and refugees, and the film's (Western) audiences; between the former's experience of deracination and trauma and that of a (presumably) concerned but relatively comfortable viewer whose knowledge and expectations are derived from prior mediations. It also poses the question: what would have to change in the geopolitical order to render these images realistic and hence unremarkable? For Kaurismäki, social engagement and self-conscious fabrication (in both form and content) pivot on the interrogation of such 'impossibilities'.[72]

Le Havre's double plot allows for two happy endings: Idrissa's escape from the police and flight to London, and Arletty's astounding recovery from a terminal condition, presumably cancer. Earlier, when the doctor who has diagnosed her suggests that 'miracles do happen', Arletty's pithy rebuttal of such false hope is a political one: 'not in my neighbourhood'. When the miracle does indeed happen at the end of the film, it is, like the sea container scene and Idrissa's escape, one that is marked by its own implausibility, reiterated in the final image of a cherry tree blossoming out of season (the 'Ozu shot').[73]

These fantastical moments of arrival, escape and recovery both recall and revise Theodor Adorno's statement: 'The loveliest dream bears like a blemish its difference from reality, the awareness that what it offers is mere illusion.'[74] A recognition of the dream as an 'illusion' – replete as it may be with colour, allusion and anachronism – but also of the socio-political conditions that make 'impossible' dreaming necessary at the present moment is a defining characteristic of Kaurismäki's cinema.

Notes

1   Released as part of the portmanteau film, *Ten Minutes Older: Visions of Time.*
2   The group also appears as the Salvation Army band in *Mies vailla menneisyyttä*
     (The Man Without a Past, 2002). An earlier version of the song they play here,
     'Thunder and Lightning', recorded by Haavisto's previous band Badding Rockers,
     is heard in *Kauas pilvet karkaavat* (Drifting Clouds, 1996).
3   Cinema is thus taken to be a temporary respite from the routines of labour even
     while it remains enmeshed in capitalist logics. See also Kaurismäki's short film
     Valimo (The Foundry, 2007) in which workers finish their shift and enjoy watching
     the Lumieres' celebrated *La Sortie d'Usine Lumiere* (1895), a film of employees
     leaving the brothers' factory.
4   The Russian carriages are pulled by a Finnish VR 'blue' model from the 1970s,
     also used in *The Man Without a Past.* On the latter, see Andrew Nestingen, *The*
     *Cinema of Aki Kaurism*äki: *Contrarian Stories* (New York: Columbia University
     Press, 2013), 89. As David R. Shumway suggests, 'It is as untenable to claim
     that nostalgia is always conservative or reactionary as it is to assert that a more
     distanced or critical representation of history is always progressive.' Shumway,
     'Rock 'n' Roll Sound Tracks and the Production of Nostalgia', *Cinema Journal* 38,
     no. 2 (1999): 50. I argue later that Kaurismäki's use of nostalgia contributes to the
     political critique proposed in his films.
5   Outinen was born in 1961; Peltola in 1956.
6   It is notable that in a short film about haste Kaurismäki makes time to showcase
     Poutahaukat's performance on screen as well as on the soundtrack, devoting one
     minute to visual footage of the song. He also plays with pace and music by pairing
     accelerating strings from Tchaikovsky's symphony no 1 in G minor with shots of
     the couple rather sedately riding an ascending escalator.
7   Frederic Jameson, 'The existence of Italy', in *Signatures of the Visible* (New York
     and London: Routledge, 1992), 158. He continues: 'Yet no viable conception
     of realism is possible unless both these demands or claims are honored
     simultaneously, prolonging and preserving – rather than "resolving" – this
     constitutive tension and incommensurability.'
8   Lesley Stern, 'Paths That Wind Through the Thicket of Things', *Critical Inquiry* 28,
     no. 1 (2001): 324. Kaurismäki's films thus offer a particular version of the tension
     which Stern locates in the cinema of Robert Bresson, which 'demonstrates its own
     cinematic performativity at the same time as it draws from the quotidian world of
     things' Stern, 329.
9   As Eugenie Brinkema has recently pointed out, attending to questions of affect has
     often been accompanied by an unhelpful neglect of textual analysis. 'The affective
     turn in film theory perhaps recovered the visceral, but only at the expense of
     [close] reading. […] instrumentalizing […] form to privilege affective experience.'
     Brinkema, *The Forms of the Affects* (Durham: Duke University Press, 2014), 30, 36.
     I hope to avoid falling into the same trap.
10   See Nestingen's discussion of 1960s female clothing and styles for riding pillion
     on motorbikes in *Tatiana. The Cinema of Aki Kaurismäki*, 40. Asked by Peter von
     Bagh when *Juha* is set, Kaurismäki replied that the villain Shemeikka's Corvette is
     a 1967 model, implying that the diegesis is located in the late 1960s or early 1970s.
     Peter von Bagh, *Aki Kaurism*äki (Cahiers du Cinéma et Festival international

du film de Locarno, 2006, trans. Anne Colin du Terrail), my translation, 173. Nevertheless, Juha's kitchen is equipped with a microwave as well as an appropriately dated stove.

11 *Lights in the Dusk* (2006) is an exception, but the protagonist Koistinen's basement flat is nevertheless furnished with 1950s lights, sofa, chair and radio. The police station in *The Other Side of Hope* (2017) is equipped with a laptop and digital camera, but notes are typed up on an old typewriter. Minna Yliruikka contrasts the absence of mobile phones in Kaurismäki's films prior to *Le Havre* with the fact that 'in 1998 more mobile phones were owned per person [in Finland] than anywhere else in the whole world'. Yliruikka, 'The Man Without a Past'. http://touchingcinema.com/the-man-without-a-past/

12 Pierre Bourdieu, *Distinction: A Social Critique of the Judgement of Taste*, trans. Richard Nice (London: Routledge, 1984, 2010), xxviii–xxix.

13 Lauri's 1970s Buick station wagon in *Drifting Clouds* is not fetishized in the same manner but is more straightforwardly a sign of his imprudent attitude to money. *Ariel's* formulaic plot structure of a man from the countryside seeking employment in Helsinki where he becomes a victim of violence and poverty also appears in *The Man Without a Past* and is revised to encompass a woman tricked into prostitution in *Juha*, an adaptation of Juhani Aho's 1911 novel of the same name.

14 However, Francesco Di Bernardo argues: 'Precarity [...] is not any sort of "new" condition, and not the result of unprecedented post-Fordist transformations of labour and production, but rather a symptom of a return to the pre-Fordist and pre-welfare-state labour conditions.' It is therefore 'conceptually misguided to define precarity as a new condition characterising a new social class; precariousness is instead quite simply the condition of the working class under capitalism'. This condition was only temporarily alleviated by post-war social democracy in the West, before the onslaught of neoliberalism. Di Bernardo, 'The Impossibility of Precarity', *Radical Philosophy*, 198 (2016): 9, 14.

15 Interviewed on the French television programme *Cinema, Cinemas*, 1990. Source: https://www.youtube.com/watch?v=d9tp8rAaTsE

16 Bert Cardullo, 'Finnish character: An interview with Aki Kaurismäki', *Film Quarterly*, 59, no. 4 (2006): 8–9.

17 Laura Rascaroli, 'Becoming-minor in a sustainable Europe: The contemporary European art film and Aki Kaurismäki's *Le Havre*', *Screen*, 54, no. 3 (2013): 335.

18 Jonathan Crary, *24/7: Late Capitalism and the Ends of Sleep* (London: Verso, 2012), 39.

19 Ibid., 8, 29, 9.

20 Ibid., 9–10.

21 'The acceleration of novelty production is a disabling of collective memory, and it means that the evaporation of historical knowledge no longer has to be implemented from the top down. The conditions of communication and information access on an everyday level ensure the systematic erasure of the past as part of the fantastic construction of the present.' Crary, *24/7*, 45.

22 Interview with Thorsten Stecher in 2002. He continues: 'My films have never included what mainstream Finnish critics want: no reindeer, no new cars, no computers. The Finnish Tourism Bureau has considered taking legal action against me. Every film I make apparently sets their efforts back a decade.' Thorsten

Stecher, '*Das Weltwoche-Gesprach*: Ich glaube an Baum, nicht an Gott', *Die Weltwoche*, 37, no. 2 (2002): 12, http://www.weltwoche.ch/ausgaben/2002-37/artikel-2002-37-ich-glaube-an-ba.html, cited in Nestingen, *The Cinema of Aki Kaurismäki*, 128.

23 C. Nadia Seremetakis, 'The memory of the senses, part 1: Marks of the transitory', in *The Senses Still*, ed. Seremetakis (Chicago: University of Chicago Press, 1994), 4.

24 Ibid., 3.

25 Von Bagh, *Aki Kaurismäki*, 64. However, as I discuss later, far from being indigenous, much of the music heard in his films and many of the objects that populate them were imported to Finland.

26 André Bazin, *What Is Cinema*, trans. Hugh Gray, vol. 1 (Berkeley: University of California Press, 1967, 2005), 9.

27 Von Bagh, *Aki Kaurismäki*, 64.

28 Bacon, 'Aki Kaurismäki en sijoiltaan olon poetiikka', in *Taju kankaalle. Uutta suomalaista elokuvaa paikantamassa*, ed. Teoksessa Kimmo Ahonen, Janne Rosenqvist, Juha Rosenqvist and P. Valotie (Turku: Kirja-Aurora, 2003), 92, cited in Pietari Kääpä, 'Displaced souls lost in Finland: The Kaurismäkis' films as the cinema of the marginalised', *Wider Screen*, 2006, np, online at http://widerscreen.fi/2006/2/displaced_souls_lost_in_finland.htm Nestingen notes that in *Ariel* Taitso finds a job as a docker at the Sompasaari Harbour, Helsinki, at a moment when it had already become a container port, rendering such labour practices obsolete. Nestingen, *The Cinema of Aki Kaurismäki*, 41.

29 Kääpä, 'Displaced souls lost in Finland', np.

30 Michel Foucault, 'Of Other Spaces', *Diacritics*, 16, no. 1 (1986): 24, cited in Kääpä, 'Displaced souls lost in Finland', np.

31 See Yliruikka, '*The Man Without a Past*', np.

32 'The small neighborhood where the film's main characters live was [...] the only one with curvy streets, everything else has been built in an arrow-straight grid plan. [...] The bulldozers were waiting; we bought the area an extra week of life. As always, the most interesting scenery is destroyed to make room for malls. [...] I use outrageous French clichés – a bread shop and accordion music. [...] but so far the French have so far swallowed it hook, line, and sinker.' Kaurismäki in von Bagh, 'The uncut interview', *Film Comment*, September/October 2011, np, online at: http://www.filmcomment.com/article/aki-kaurismaki/

33 'I used television [in the living room of Iris's family] because I wanted to write the events of Tiananmen Square into the story. The news is thus "immortalised", you could say, in the film, and the crime of that clique of the Chinese ruling class can suddenly appear at a screening no matter where in the world, in 116 years, perhaps.' Von Bagh, *Aki Kaurismäki*, 87.

34 Nestingen points out that Typhoon Angela and the execution of Saro-Wiwa both occurred in November 1995, but a week apart, rather than at the same time, as implied in the *Drifting Clouds* bulletin. Nestingen, *The Cinema of Aki Kaurismäki*, 101.

35 Anu Koivunen, 'Do you remember Monrepos? Melancholia, modernity and working-class masculinity in *The Man Without a Past*', in *Transnational Cinema in a Global North: Nordic Cinema in Transition*, ed. Andrew Nestingen and Trevor G. Nelson (Wayne State University Press, 2005), 138.

36 Ibid., 146.

37 http://www.brumbeat.net/renegade.htm. Key members later relocated to Italy before moving back to Finland to play the nostalgia circuit in the 1990s.

38 Damon Smith, 'Aki Kaurismäki, *Le Havre*', Filmmaker Magazine, 19 October 2011. http://filmmakermaga zine.com/32663-aki-kaurismaki-le-havre/#. VLqBtsZ3b_Q.46. In another interview, with Andrew Nestingen, Kaurismäki uses the term *rautalanka* ('iron string') to describe the music of The Renegades, the most frequently heard rock and roll band in his oeuvre. Nestingen explains that *rautalanka* 'was the first form of rock-blues music associated with youth culture in Finland, gaining a foothold through off-shore broadcasts around 1960'. Nestingen, pp. 143, 152n.

39 George Lipsitz, *Time Passages: Collective Memory and American Popular Culture* (University of Minnesota Press, 1990), 5, cited in Nabeel Zuberi, *Sounds English: Transnational Popular Music* (Chicago: University of Illinois Press, 2001), 4.

40 Zuberi, *Sounds English*, 5.

41 'Iniquity' would be a better word than 'impoverishment' here. Lana Wilson, 'Aki Kaurismäki', *Senses of Cinema* 51 (2009) http://sensesofcinema.com/2009/great-directors/aki-kaurismaki/

42 Bertolt Brecht, cited in Ernst Schumacher, 'The dialectics of Galileo', in *Brecht Sourcebook*, ed. Carol Martin and Henry Bial (London: Routledge, 2000), 111.

43 Mikhail Iampolski, *The Memory of Tiresias: Intertextuality and Film* (Berkeley CA: University of California Press, 1998), 29, 28, 257.

44 Ibid., 27, 28.

45 See, von Bagh inter alia, *Aki Kaurismäki*; Geoffrey Macnab, *Screen Epiphanies: Filmmakers on the Films that Inspired Them* (London: BFI, 2010); Brooke 'Minor Quay', *Sight and Sound*, May (2012), 20.

46 Kaurismäki's repeated casting of the same actors also foregrounds the passage of time. His films offer indices of the ageing of Outinen across nearly 30 years, while the death of his favoured male lead, Pellonpää, is marked in *Drifting Clouds* by a photograph of the actor as a child, and in *The Man Without a Past* by another of him in character as Rodolfo from *La Vie de Bohème*.

47 The painting is shown exhibited in a Helsinki art gallery in *Calamari Union* (1985).

48 Koivunen, 'Do you remember Monrepos?' 139–140. Jarmo Valkola locates in the same film's images of sky and clouds a reference to Teuvo Tulio's 1938 film *The Song of the Secret Flower*. Valkola, *Landscapes of the Mind: Emotion and Style in Aki Kaurismäki's Films* (Lambert Academic Publishing, 2013), 135.

49 Von Bagh, *Aki Kaurismäki*, 177.

50 Ibid., 85. The 'romance novel' relates to Iiris's reading habits in the diegesis and the film's epigraph from Sergeanne Gogol's historical romance *Comtesse Angelique*. In the same interview, Kaurismäki also describes the film as a very loose adaptation of Hannu Salama's 1961 novel *The Usual Story* in which a young working-class woman is abandoned by her lover.

51 Peter von Bagh, 'Aki Kaurismäki: The Uncut Interview' *Film Comment* (September/October 2011), np, online at: http://www.filmcomment.com/article/aki-kaurismaki/

52 *Drifting Clouds* offers a rare, and disparaging, gesture to contemporary screen culture when Ilona and Lauri walk out of a noisy action film which, though unseen, assails its audience with sounds of machine-gun fire and screaming. By

contrast, the cinema foyer is decorated with posters for Bresson's *L'Argent*, Vigo's *L'Atalante* and Jarmusch's *Night on Earth*.

53   Paul Willemen, 'Through the glass darkly: cinephilia reconsidered', in his *Looks and Frictions: Essays in Cultural Studies and Film Theory* (London: BFI, 1994), 241.

54   Ibid., 242. Willemen adds: 'The cinephiliac moment is my preferred description because of its overtones of necrophilia, of relating to something that is dead, past, but alive in memory. [...] you can go back time and again and reconsume it almost ad infinitum. What you are reconsuming is the moment of revelation experienced in an encounter between you and cinema'. Ibid., 227, 237.

55   Iampolski writes about the same film: 'When Patricia looks through the tube of the rolled up [Renoir] poster [at Michel], the film is quoting a scene from Samuel Fuller's *Forty Guns*, in which one of the heroes looks at his enemy through the sights of the rifle. [...] The episode anticipates the hero's tragic death after he is betrayed by Patricia. At the same time, this episode is so organically embedded into the film's narrative [...] that we need Godard's own commentary to recognize the Fuller reference in the heroine's spontaneous behaviour. Without Godard's help this quote would remain indiscernible [...] a buried quote, one that dissolves in mimesis'. *The Memory of Tiresias*, 31–32.

56   Kaurismäki in Von Bagh, *Aki Kaurismäki*, 88–89. *Lights in the Dusk* 'is very influenced by [Edward] Hopper [...] Some months before [filming] I had attentively studied a book on his work, but his influence was so insidious that I did not notice that I had made Hopperesque images until the critic Helena Ylanen asked me that question'.

57   Robert Warshow, 'The Gangster as Tragic Hero', in *The Immediate Experience* (New York: Atheneum, 1971), 127–34, 130.

58   His films can be understood in terms of the positive understanding of pastiche developed by Richard Dyer. In his work 'to rescue pastiche from postmodernism' and the disapproval of scholars who have decried it for vacuity, Dyer argues that, far from precluding affect, the mode can generate intense emotions, along with an understanding of 'the historicity of our feelings'. Pastiche in the neo-noir films of the 1980s and 1990s and Todd Haynes's Sirkian melodrama *Far from Heaven* (2002) does not just move audiences but may also 'enable us to reflect on the fact that how we feel right now is itself framed by the traditions of feeling we inherit, mobilise and hand on'. Dyer, *Pastiche* (London: Routledge 2007), 131, 130, 178.

59   Of course Godard's later films are much more radical in terms of both form and content. His cinephilia persists but serves the political imperatives of a counter cinema.

60   Jameson, 'The existence of Italy', in *Signatures of the Visible*, 59.

61   Barbara Klinger, *Melodrama and Meaning: History, Culture, and the Films of Douglas Sirk* (Bloomington: Indiana University Press, 1994), 47.

62   See Paul Willemen's discussions of the tensions between 'distanciation and implication, between fascination and its critique' in Sirk's films, in 'Distanciation and Douglas Sirk', *Screen* 12, no. 2 (1971), 63–67, and 'Towards an analysis of the Sirkian system', *Screen* 13, no. 3 (1972): 128–143, merged and reprinted with a postscript as 'The Sirkian system' in Willemen, *Looks and Frictions*, 89.

63   Edward Branigan, 'The articulation of colour in a filmic system: *Deux ou trois chose que je sais d'elle*', *Wide Angle* 1, no. 3 (1976): 20–31, revised and reprinted in *Color: The Film Reader*, ed. Angela Dalle Vache and Brian Price (London:

Routledge, 2006), 178. Writing in the 1970s, Branigan suggested that the two predominant ways in which colour in film was interpreted by critics were as 'clues [...] to the psychological states of the characters' or to set 'the mood or tone of a scene'. 'The essence of this method is to shift adjectives and nouns from the narrative and attach them to the appearance of colors.' 'The articulation of colour', 177. These interpretive strategies remain more or less dominant today.

64   Julien Allen 'Paint the town' *Reverse Shot*, 20 August 2012, online at: http://reverseshot.org/archive/entry/1189/le_havre.

65   Von Bagh, 'The uncut interview', np.

66   Fantastical outcomes can also be found at the end of *Shadows in Paradise* and *Ariel*, wherein the protagonists escape poverty and insecurity in Helsinki by sailing to, respectively, Estonia and Mexico. In *Ariel*, the impossibility of this finale is reiterated by a Finnish version of 'Somewhere over the rainbow' playing over the closing credits.

67   Brigitte Peucker, 'Filmic tableau vivant: Vermeer, intermediality and the real', in *Rites of Realism: Essays on Corporeal Cinema*, ed. Ivone Margulies (Durham and London: Duke UP, 2003), 294–295. See also Roland Barthes, 'Diderot, Brecht, Eisenstein', translated by Stephen Heath, in *Image Music Text* (Fontana, 1977).

68   Barthes, 'Diderot, Brecht, Eisenstein', 73–75. See also Joachim Fiebach, 'Brecht: Gestus, Fable, Attitudecum-Stance', *Modern Drama* 42, no. 2 (1999): 207–213. Carl Weber suggests that 'Chaplin's character, the little tramp, seems to have been the first complete achievement of *Gestus* that Brecht observed. In 1926, he wrote about Chaplin: "This artist is a document that is effective with the power of historical events."' Weber, 'Brecht's concept of *Gestus* and the American performance tradition', in Brecht Sourcebook, ed. Martin and Bial, 45, citing Brecht, *Gesammelte Werke* (Frankfurt: Suhrkamp, 1967), vol. 18, 138.

69   Bert Cardullo, 'Finnish Character: An Interview with Aki Kaurismaki', *Film Quarterly*, 59, no. 4 (2006): 7, italics in original.

70   This device recalls Eisenstein's oscillation between the classical delineation of space and spatial expansions and overlaps in *Strike* (1925).

71   Peter von Bagh, 'Aki Kaurismäki: The Uncut Interview', np.

72   This strategy also draws on magic realism, which Ewa Mazierska has located in some of Kaurismäki's earlier films, as 'a testimony of his solidarity with the economically, socially and culturally disadvantaged'. Ewa Mazierska and Laura Rascaroli, *Crossing New Europe: Postmodern Travel and the European Road Movie* (Wallflower Press, 2006), 31, cited in Rascaroli, 'Becoming-minor in a sustainable Europe', 332. Mazierska is referring to the Leningrad Cowboys films.

73   *Le Havre* thus recalls not just Ozu but also the fantastical fate of the homeless at the end of de Sica's *Miracolo a Milano* (Miracle in Milan, 1951). It was released in the Italian market as *Miracolo a Le Havre*.

74   Theodor Adorno, *Minima Moralia: Reflections on a Damaged Life* (London: Verso, 2005), 111, cited in a rather disapproving review by J. Hoberman, 'Dream act: Town rallies to help an immigrant in Utopian Le Havre', *Village Voice*, 2011, online at: http://www.villagevoice.com/2011-10-19/film/dream-act-townralliesto-help-an-immigrant-in-utopian-le-havre/full/

Chapter 2

THREE ECOLOGIES OF KAURISMÄKI

Pietari Kääpä

The cinema of Aki Kaurismäki has met with much appreciation and apprehension in international academic scholarship. On one hand, the films have been interpreted as complex commentaries on Finnish society.[1] Yet, simultaneously, they have been seen as transnational texts capturing the complex patterns of globalization.[2] Others fit them into a lineage of films about European culture[3] while, for some, they form a part of global independent cinema.[4] These perspectives tend to position the films in relation to transnational film studies, whereas others focus more on their style and content. Some of these textual and thematic approaches include the role of intersubjectivity,[5] genre,[6] style[7] and aspects of postmodernity.[8] Clearly, Kaurismäki's 'minimalist' texts open to a rich heritage of meanings and cultural inclinations as befits the director's cineaste roots and the complexities of his political commitments.

The scope in which these films are analysed grows consistently but an area noticeably lacking among all these studies is discussion of their environmental qualities. The study of 'ecocinema' – an approach focusing on humanity's complex relationship with their external environment – is emerging as a considerable and diverse field in contemporary film studies. For example, the works of Kaurismäki's contemporaries such as Jim Jarmusch and Jia Zhangke – auteurs with a substantial influence on global art cinema – have been discussed from an ecocritical angle.[9] Yet, such work has tended to evade Kaurismäki, an omission not entirely surprising considering that the films frequently exclude nature from their representational scope. However, a focus on urbanity does not invalidate them as ecological representations. Monani and Rust make an important point in their study of key patterns in ecocinema as they argue that, literally, all films can be considered from an ecological perspective.[10] This implies that ecocinema not only encompasses those films that deal with environmental issues but also those that tell us of ways in which humanity perceives of its place in the ecosystem. Following this argumentation, it is possible to include films as diverse as urban dramas and environmentalist polemics under the label of ecocinema. The point is that films, as instances of anthropogenic expression, inevitably reveal something about humanity's self-perceptions of its role in the global ecosystem.

To understand the implications of this perspective for analysing Kaurismäki's work, an important distinction has to be made between the concepts of ecology and environment. The latter is predominantly used to refer to natural systems in which humanity plays a part, while ecology as a concept is commonly perceived as an integration of different levels and modes of existence. It focuses on connections and relations that exceed the human. Implicit in this concept is a critical approach to the anthropocentric tenets of cultural production. Ecological approaches emphasize complexity in the production of content as integrated into this process are a range of other elements that hold the power to provide texts with alternative connotations. These include 'the massive and dynamic interrelation of processes and objects, beings and things, patterns and matter' that emerge when we shift our focus outside of strict human subjectivity.[11] A consequence of this shift is an inevitable decentralization of the human as the generator of all relevant meanings.

This chapter will develop an ecological perspective on Kaurismäki's films and suggests that an environmental ethics is a considerable if unexplored factor in the politics of these films. To explore them 'ecologically', I will focus on their sense of being in the world or of their 'Dasein'. I use the concept in its Heideggerian form which focuses on humanity's awareness of the value of the immediate context of their existence. Implicit in this sense of the concept is acknowledgement of the inevitably contingent nature of humanity's involvement with the world, especially in terms of existential questions regarding living within a complex ecosystem, as well as the fragility of that existence. Dasein, taken as a conceptual framework, gestures to the necessity of environmental awareness as generating an ecophilosophical – or ecosophical – mode of enquiry. This is an approach that considers the placement of human subjectivity in the wider ecosystem in ways that do not prioritize this subjectivity. Instead, the focus would be on objects, matter, landscapes, urban spaces, all elements characterized by a human touch but ones also implicated in a whole range of non-anthropogenic relations.

The key to constructing such an ecological perspective lies in undoing the dualistic separation of cultural and non-human environments. Instead of evoking the deep ecology perspective practised by philosophers, such as Arne Naess, which argue for the total immersion of the human in the natural, I focus on Felix Guattari's work on ecosophy[12] and what he calls the three ecologies. These consist of the interacting and interdependent spheres of the mental, social and the environmental or the cognitive, the political and the environmental. For Guattari, these three areas consist of distinct ecologies, of ways of comprehending one's relationships with the external world. The purpose of the conceptualization is to develop ways to overcome the obstacles that block concrete action on contemporary problems such as climate change. To succeed in facilitating transformations in thinking, human awareness of their own role in the environment, the political organization of society and environmental awareness need to come together holistically to generate a shift in perception. Guattari argues that adopting environmentalism is not enough as 'ecology must stop being associated with a small nature loving community. Ecology in my sense questions the whole of subjectivity and capitalist power formations'.[13] For this transformation in perception to happen, environmental awareness must be generated on all three levels in order to create a holistic understanding of global environmental problems.

While the three ecologies could be taken to gesture to a perspective that seems to prioritize homogeneity, Guattari leaves space for heterogeneity and difference by suggesting that to be effective, we must learn to work transversally. In its most practical form, transversality means that we need to consider factors from mental, social and environmental perspectives to construct conditions most conducive for sustainable action. Key here is the need to recognize the specific conditions of each ecology, as well as the rules that govern them. To explain, human subjectivity does not automatically identify with, or agree to, the most productive social welfare or sustainable behaviour. Guattari suggests that this is often the opposite as political concerns override mental awareness of issues such as sustainability, which, in his work, is a particular result of capitalist hegemony on the constitution of normative mental and social ecologies.[14] Instead, it is the 'job' of an ecosophical argument to bind the three ecologies together in ways that lead to productive outcomes while accounting for the diverse requirements embedded in each of the perspectives. In practice, this would take place by ensuring that these transversal connections utilize the particular qualities of each ecology. For cognitive challenges, the focus would be on new ways of thinking and perception. For society, this involves a radical politics that challenges the patterns of normalization hegemonic orders use to maintain dominance. And for an environmental perspective, the emphasis is on highlighting connections that question the normalizing power of capitalist subjectivity.

How do these ideas emerge in films? Ecosophical perspectives facilitate connections that traverse the human–environment dichotomy. They rely on an impetus to see similarities and shared areas between them instead of emphasizing differences and structures of control and domination. For cinema, adopting such an approach would, first of all, require challenging conventional means of representation, including both narrative conventions and semiotic symbolism, that maintain hegemonic structures. Secondly, they would need to rethink politics in ways that pose powerful and transformative alternatives to the ways society is constructed. One of the ways of achieving this would be to refocus attention to the ways films, on both a semiotic and a thematic level, open to different subjectivities, including ones not purely motivated by human intentions. While cinema is an anthropogenic undertaking by its nature, this does not exclude other material elements from playing a considerable role in the construction of narrative significance. Shifting the gaze away from human subjectivity gestures to a more profound non-dichotomized version of reality than is available by focusing only on the sociopolitics of the films, for example. The approach provides the possibility of considering them as an 'alter-tale' where 'the new narrative agents are things, nonhuman organisms, places, and forces, as well as human actors and their words. Together, they anticipate an alternative vision of a future where narratives and discourses have the power to change, re-enchant, and create the world that comes to our attention only in participatory perceptions'.[15] This description provides a new materialist view of narrative agency, where non-human material has an equal level of narrative significance as the human participants.

An ecological perspective as described earlier is especially productive for understanding the narrative and visual world we see in Kaurismäki's films. The world as represented in these films seems consistently out of balance as objects from different time periods intermingle with bodies that seem to be in suspended motion. Bacon has characterized this idiosyncratic worldview as 'displacement poetics'.[16] The use of displacement techniques allows the films to resemble reality while they are also divorced enough from it to enable multiple interpretations. Through this, they avail themselves to critical interpretations that can simultaneously read them as realistic and fantasized versions of that reality. For us, the significance comes from precisely this seeming contradiction between verisimilitude and artistic freedom. By reworking, or displacing, many of the established conventions of representing the world, they fulfil a key prerequisite of a challenge to mental ecology.

The realm of social ecology is addressed through the political content of the films, especially the ways they portray society as a non-conforming and unalterable system. But instead of reinforcing the principles on which this society stands, they provide a displaced version of it that requires that we deconstruct the very principles that support its position of domination. As we will see, the evocation of cognitive challenges and subversive politics also has the potential to lead to a more profound conception of societal sustainability and of an environmental ecology. In exploring how the three ecologies operate in Kaurismäki's films, and how they challenge relations of domination, including that of anthropocentric logic, I will focus on four key areas of 'materiality' that exist outside of pure human subjectivity – these are the objects we see on screen, the role human bodies play, the ways urban environments are chronicled and navigated, and the role of natural landscapes.

Objects

The first area to address when assessing the three ecologies and Kaurismäki's films starts from the role of objects, an area that has met with substantial critical interest. Some of the objects, such as vintage cars, jukeboxes, packaging of consumables and clothes, have been discussed as postmodern performances or as nostalgia that disassociates the diegesis from the present. They act as references to sources as diverse as film history and American and Soviet culture and form a part of the films' transnational levels of connectivity. If we were to observe the placement of such materials in these films, it would be difficult to position them in any clearly delineated time and space. To take an example, *Ariel* starts out at the closure of a mine in Northern Finland. Taisto, the protagonist of the film, decides to seek opportunities in the big cities down south. He discovers a pristine condition Cadillac convertible in the barn of his recently deceased father. The car, a luxury commodity by the standards of a small northern town, is noticeably out of place in the ramshackle barn in which it is housed. To emphasize the discord, the barn collapses as Taisto pulls away in his car. This sets the scene for a humorous, surreal translation of the 'Great Migration' from the countryside to the city, a journey made by many Finns during Finland's tumultuous urbanization between the 1950s and 1970s. As Taisto wraps a scarf around his head to prevent himself from freezing as he cruises down south in the open-top convertible, the cognitive dissonance these scenes evoke provides a challenge to the cohesion of the film's mental ecology – the actions are too out of balance to make sense on a purely narrative level. But seen from the perspective of social ecology with the presence of the Cadillac opening to multiple politicized interpretations – the role of Americanization in social upheaval in Finland being a particular point of reference – the scene's unbalanced qualities start to make more sense. Cultural and historical references combine with Taisto's actions to provoke us to see the scene as something more than simply a comic interlude. They invite us to a diegetic world that defies expectations, a world that exists more as a venue for symbolic critique than conventional reality. The object – in this case, the Cadillac – works in transversal terms to combine provocations to both the mental and the social ecology. It does this through its refusal to fit in with most of the expected referential coordinates for Finnish films at the time or especially those that depict the often painful process of urbanization.

Yet the ideological connotations of such objects, evoking both consumer culture and modernity, are far from certain. Many of these films have been read as anti-capitalist critiques of societal exploitation, which is not surprising, considering their focus on the working and the underclasses.[17] Thus, it is intriguing to note how often objects of capitalist modernity come to the rescue of the protagonists as is the case with the Cadillac. *Mies vailla menneisyyttä* (The Man Without a Past, 2002) illustrates this conflict further through its central storyline focusing on a blossoming romance between a man with no memory and a lonely Salvation Army worker. Displaced in a village for homeless people on the outskirts of the city, the protagonists have built a life for themselves in empty, discarded shipping containers. The containers in their own right are similar transversal objects like the Cadillac in that their reappropriation as homes challenges the cohesiveness of mental and social ecologies of life in a welfare state. I have addressed the out-of-placeness of the containers elsewhere,[18] and they continue to maintain a significant role in the environmental ecology of Kaurismäki's films. For now, I am more interested in the jukebox that sits in the corner of the container and which plays a crucial role in binding the two displaced protagonists together. The object, an example of imported capitalist modernity, is a conflicted vessel for the ideological perspective of the film. It is both a repurposed means to overcome marginalization caused by the hegemonic norms of the surrounding society, but simultaneously, that dominance can only be overcome by the products it produces and upon which its dominance relies. Much like the container, the jukebox does not fit a conventional critique of capitalist consumerism but neither does it provide a clear alternative of a more sustainable life in opposition to the mores of the world outside the village. The argument is accentuated when considering the amount of time the film spends on showing how the marginal community jacks into powerlines for electricity. Again, illegal jacking of power can be seen as a critical action against hegemony, but it also relies on the infrastructure maintained by and enabling the dominant structures. As a consequence, these scenes are curiously impotent as forms of social critique. We will come back to their environmental potential later in the chapter, but for now, the relevance of these objects is to do with their role as displacement signifiers.

Similar scenes are repeated throughout the films. For example, the protagonists of *Pidä huivista kiinni, Tatjana* (Take Care of Your Scarf, Tatjana, 1994), a film set in a curiously timeless world, find their car in need of petrol as they journey to Estonia. Fortunately, they soon come across a gas pump in the middle of nowhere, standing amid a field of grass. Along with other similarly seemingly fantastical displaced but bizarrely appropriate objects, such as a portable LP player and an in-car coffee machine, the gas pump holds a conflicted position within the narrative of the film.

The film has often been interpreted as a nostalgic depiction of political closeness in the Soviet era, an approach which would seem to gesture to a leftist critique of contemporary neo-liberalizing Finland. Yet all of these consumerist objects with largely positive connotations gesture to the West instead of the East, and their complex presence in the narratives challenges both mental and social ecologies – they do not seem to belong within a realistic worldview nor do they conform to any easily agreeable ideological perspective.

One final instance of such a transversal object in *Leningrad Cowboys Go America* (1989) shall suffice to illustrate their ecological potential. The titular band, who, as an intertitle tells us, live somewhere in the tundra, realize that their reclusive geographical location is not best suited to their unique style of rockabilly folk music. Geocultural displacement is already explicit in the name of the band as well as the clothing style combining elements from Eastern and Western iconography. But a challenge to a normally functioning mental ecology is created as the manager of the band simply picks up the phone from a booth located on the side of a barn and arranges a concert across the pond. The phone booth simply should not be there, nor should it function, as we see no electric wires or cable poles to connote that a long distance phone call would be possible. In this signifier of displacement, modernity and tradition combine in ways that break physical laws. Once more, an object acts as the locus of the challenge, and as it is its material qualities that provide its most confrontational aspect, its combination of mental and social ecologies also transverses to an environmental ecology where material objects can hold as much meaning as the actions of human protagonists. The use of these out-of-place objects – including a Cadillac in a small town barn, the jukebox in a rehabilitated container, a gas pump in the middle of nowhere and a phone booth on the side of a barn, as displacement signifiers – contributes to a sense of Dasein out of balance and, thus, opens to a range of radical forms of decentralizing anthropocentric narrative conventions. By providing material objects the power to narrate and guide ideological directions, the films construct the basics of an environmental ecology where the self-assurance of human subjectivity as the only agent with the power to narrate is displaced.

Corporeality

Objects are an initial step in our construction of an ecological understanding of Kaurismäki's films. The presence of the human body in the narrative and the image provides a further evolution of this argument. The exploration here has its roots in the minimalist style of the films, a factor that also foregrounds objects. As critics have often commented, the sets tend to be sparse and there are few movements of the camera. When people are present, they barely move, and if they do, this appears significant without fail. The use of a minimalist style and stillness of movement has led to several interpretations of the reasons for such choices. For some, this indicates an ironic caricature of the Finnish national character, reliant on a set of stereotypical caricatures of a quiet and withdrawn people. For others, the relevance of these elements comes from their role in providing transnational stylistic homages to auteurs such as Bresson and Ozu.

While these perspectives certainly make sense, an ecosophical take starts out from the jarring presence of the human body in the diegesis and, as much as the objects, considers them as tools of contestation. They act as the locus of temporal dislocation, of freezing time to step outside of the hegemonic flows of society. Again, what is at stake here is a transversal flow through mental and social ecologies to arrive at a radical rethinking of the Dasein as a world out of balance. *Tulitikkutehtaan tyttö* (The Match Factory Girl, 1990) provides a dynamic illustration of the ways the corporeal presence of the human body works to fragment the cohesion of a society premised on normative expectations. The film is especially notable for its quiet minimalism, where the lack of movement in and between the images is reflected in the silence of the characters. In a particularly noteworthy scene, Iiris, the protagonist of the film, an exploited factory worker, seeks to elope from the overbearing banality of everyday life by attending a dance. The camera stays focused on her as other women around her are whisked off to dance. The scene is striking in its composition as the lengthy shots force us to witness her humiliation for an uncomfortable duration. A single cut away from her does not alleviate the tension as it reveals other couples dancing to the song 'Onnen maa' (The Land of Happiness). Instead, it only works to create contrast between her alienation and the expected behaviour in such a setting, underscored by the melancholic tango describing a fairy-tale land where dreams come true.

The scene has often been read as critique of social mores and national narratives, showing us a pessimistic view of how individuals are excluded from the fairy-tale promise of the nation. And while such readings are useful, the collision of a mental challenge – an excessive duration and a frozen 'motion picture' – and politics – societal alienation in a welfare state – invites critical introspection. Guattari's ecologies provide a way to see the scene as an instance that materializes societal oppression. With objects, the idea was to provide complex collages of meaning that challenge the political status quo. With bodies, the idea is to materialize this exclusion in ways that merge the mental with the social. As the film practically pauses the narrative for these moments, we are asked to endure marginalization and displacement. Through them, the film makes alienation concrete.

Simultaneously, it emphasizes the extent to which the human body is immersed in the ecology of the frame, a frame where objects and the body exist on an equal material level of signification with the human effectively relegated to just another part of the mise en scène. Through this they again gesture to an ecological comprehension where the human is decentred, no longer the generator of all relevant meaning. But now, what meaning there is to be drawn from the presence of the body suggests a fundamentally dysfunctional sense of society.

Taking our cue from this process of materialization, we shift focus to Guattari's Marxist emphasis on the ability of the three ecologies to undermine or subvert capitalism. For him, this critical view is essential for constructing sustainable perspectives as capitalism relies on processes that make its hegemony appear neutral or even natural. To unravel this dominance, a shock to the mental and social ecologies is required. We see illustrations of this critique in Kaurismäki's work. *The Match Factory Girl* opens with a montage of labour, interspersing scenes of mechanical processes with the tasks of humans on the factory line. The contrast between the dynamic editing of daily work practices contrasts with the stasis of daily life outside the workplace. In what must be seen as a heightened sense of irony, the film seems to suggest that only when working on the assembly line can the labour force feel fulfilled. Outside, they are lost in a world of meaningless connections and distractions.

Popular culture acts as the vessel through which this alienation ultimately takes place. This not only includes songs like 'Onnen maa', promising participation in a utopian welfare society, but also the romantic paperback schlock Iiris consumes on her commutes. They facilitate an all-encompassing comprehensive sense of stagnation that the film captures in its moments of stillness, including another poignant scene where she sits at her brother's home listening to a jukebox. The long shot, both in terms of visual composition and duration, fragments narrative time and cultural cohesion in ways that reorganize the fabric of this dilapidated society. The objects of popular culture such as paperbacks and jukeboxes act as the opium of the common 'man'; yet neither the contemporary nor the retro provide the characters with any sense of connection to allow society to make sense and only serve to sink them into alienation.

A similar set of alienation techniques takes place in *Varjoja paratiisissa* (Shadows in Paradise, 1986). The protagonist of the film, binman Nikander, goes on a spending spree following a breakup. Trying to fill the void in his life, he buys a state-of-the-art home entertainment system. Next, we see him sitting at home with a remote control in hand, surrounded by all the objects on which he has used his meagre savings. The stillness of the scene again challenges our normative expectations as Nikander's ventures into consumerism bring him no joy. The objects and the still human body combine to challenge the dominant ideological mores of Finland of the mid-1980s. This was a society in the midst of a manufactured upswing as foreign investment and stock trading manipulation boosted the economy. Easy access to bank loans, such as the one most likely required by Nikander to purchase the elaborate entertainment equipment, would eventually lead to a recession and bankruptcy for many ordinary people like him. Scepticism over these contemporary developments is communicated via material elements of the images, which find protagonists like Nikander excluded from conventional society and its ideological promises and thus challenge some of the predominant ways the mental and social ecologies of neo-liberalist capitalism operate. The repetition of compressed scenes like this throughout Kaurismäki's films emphasizes that the mental – the expectations spectators may have of the narrative as well as of the society in which they live – collide with the social – such as the Marxist political critiques they propose – in ways that pose penetrating, fundamental questions over the normalization of capitalism as an ecological condition.

Urbanity

If both displaced objects and the human body combine with narrative techniques to facilitate an ecological understanding of life under capitalism, the use of space in these films does this in an even more immersive way. The third area of our analysis will focus on urban landscapes which act as the key setting for the displacement poetics identified by Bacon. For us, they also facilitate a subversion of the ecological holism and of the Dasein described earlier. I have elsewhere suggested that the city provides the films with a universal dimension separated from both conventional time and space.[19] The city seems to be transferable from one context to another as the Helsinki we see in these films is very similar to the London of *I Hired a Contract Killer* (1990), for example.

The ways the films morph the cityscape into idiosyncratic landscapes act as another step towards an environmental ecological perspective. The 'Kaurismäkisinki' (an idiosyncratic variation of Helsinki that can only be found in Kaurismäki's films) is devoid of identifiable landmarks and mostly focuses on side streets that house restaurants and bars that seem to exist outside of conventional history. Here, it is possible to walk into a bar that looks and sounds like it would exist in some fantasized version of the 1950s. Of course, these are yet another challenge to the mental ecology that the films construct. Much like the displaced objects and the human body, time seems to have frozen while any geocultural coordinates are obfuscated. The spaces of the city are thus filled with objects and people who do not seem to belong there. As urban space in different parts of the world shows similar displacement traits, as seen in *I Hired a Contract Killer*, it is clear that 'the working class has no fatherland', as one of the characters in the film suggests.

The abstract adventure film *Calamari Union* (1985) functions as an illustration of the ways these films challenge the mental and social ecologies of neo-liberal capitalism. The film is at its base a capitalist critique of the organization of the city space into zones of deprivation and affluence. It focuses on a group of identically named men, the Franks, who awaken out of the slumber of their subjugated, oppressed existence to seek a way out of the geopolitically coordinated confines of the city. They agree on a path through the city with their journey taking them along a straight route from working-class Kallio to the affluent Eira on the edge of the sea. But the journey proves to be anything but simple. The collective is split up as some of them fall prey to women who seek to subjugate them into conventional family life while others are distracted by fast-food chain restaurants. One of them gets rich on the stock markets but is soon shot to death by a femme fatale. Despite some of the problematic gender politics deployed here that stereotype both men and women, the targets of the critique are clear – this is once more an evocation of the dangers of capitalist society.

Some of the more intriguing instances of what are effectively compressed sketches emanate from moments that suspend belief in geographical verisimilitude. In one particularly striking, and confusing, scene, a Frank shows off his newly accrued wealth and steps into a travel agency in the city centre only to exit at the airport which is nowhere near the original location, perhaps intentionally or otherwise recalling Kuleshov's creative geography. The lack of physical verisimilitude to Helsinki can be interpreted as a complex evocation of the ways that capital shapes the city at will. But for the underclass Franks, the journey of about 45 minutes turns into several days. Only two of the Franks escape on a boat but even this is ultimately blown up. It seems that there is no escape from the confines of the capitalist city. The Frank collective is both fractured and disoriented by the lack of comprehensible coordinates for their journey. Instead of a linear path from Kallio to Eira, the city is revealed as a superstructure with the power to position people of different classes in their place. In the world of the film, an individual is literally subsumed into an environment that has the power to control their every move, bringing to mind the type of capitalist control of urban space critiqued by cultural geographer Mike Davis in his *Ecology of Fear*.[20] Through this the film captures an alternative reality that urges us to rethink the subordination of social space. By refusing to take the city for granted and instead playing up the ridiculous qualities of the Franks' misadventures, the film suggests a cognitive reorientation of space, much like some of the films discussed earlier do with the objects that occupy these spaces. By positioning both objects and space as critical question marks instead of conventional parts of the cinematic world, they gesture to the type of ecological perspective that Guattari discussed – one where film can be a space for a critical anti-capitalist politics to emerge.

Natural Environments

We have now explored the ways in which objects, the human body and the urban environment are portrayed in Kaurismäki's films, suggesting that all three areas challenge the mental and social ecologies of neo-liberal capitalism. In doing so, they form part of a critical perspective that fits in with Guattari's notion of an environmental ecology. This, as we have suggested earlier and as Guattari underlines in his work on the three ecologies, is not only to do with environmentalist argumentation. Thus, adopting such a perspective makes sense as Kaurismäki's films do not work along conventional definitions of environmental film production. As a consequence, it is not that important that the natural landscape is conspicuous with its absence throughout most of the films.

The examples of nature we see are few and far between, but even they contribute to the sense of displacement the films rely on. This especially is the case with early films like *Crime and Punishment* (1983) and *Shadows in Paradise*, both of which feature short scenes where the characters venture briefly outside of the oppressive city to a park and a beach, respectively. The use of nature in these scenes suggests a potential for a romantic interlude, a gesture acknowledging such imaginaries throughout the history of Finnish cinema. But they turn out to be meaningless as once the protagonists return to the city, the familiar sense of oppression and alienation drives the protagonists apart. Even in later films such as *The Man Without a Past* and *Juha*, excursions play out more like cinematic homages to the national romanticism of early film culture or of the studio era in Finland.[21] While nature can be seen as a positive signifier that brings the protagonists together, as ever in the world of these films, even nature is characterized by displacement or a distanced sense of performance. The use of nature tends to be reserved for distraction or a space of transition, but it is never the normal state of being or the goal of the protagonists. The scenes tend to be uneasy or over the top as the human protagonists, grown accustomed to urban dystopias, would only perceive nature as something strange – though this is very different with *Juha* since this film is set in the countryside, regardless of how disassociated even this is from reality. Thus, its role in the films is more effectively described as a form of simulacra as it acts as a point of reference instead of a tangible factor enhancing the narrative or as a reference point to 'real' nature.

As challenges to mental ecology make us question the role of elements we see on screen and provocations of social ecology link this with Marxist politics, the use of nature as a signifier takes us to close proximity with an environmental ecology. In *Ariel*, for example, the natural environment is only visible in the scenes where the protagonist Taisto journeys to Helsinki. He is unprepared for the cold as he is unable to pull the top of the car down, and with only a scarf around his head, he cruises the frozen landscape to the warmer climate down south. Again, the scene is based on comical contrasts and improbable actions with nature providing the crucial displacement signifiers to the scene's mental ecology. For someone who has lived his life in the hostile cold of Inari, Taisto's lack of preparation to meet the demands of the environment is puzzling, to say the least. It simply is not possible to interpret these scenes at face value, that is to say, to interpret them within the framework that would take for granted the constitution of a society that encourages the centralization of peoples in urban centres as a cheap labour force.

While nature is mostly used to consolidate the political critiques of the films, it also acts as a self-reflexive indicator of its own appropriation in anthropogenic narratives. Cultural production has historically used landscape for the construction of a variety of identity politics. These have been especially prolific in evocations of nationhood with the landscape occupying the role of a signifier of authenticity. This sort of appropriation of the natural environment for anthropocentric politics comes unmasked in Kaurismäki's displacement poetics. The suggestion is that if we unravel the appropriation of such elements for the construction of ideologicized narratives, we can undermine the narratives themselves. *Leningrad Cowboys Meet Moses* provides a productive illustration of the ways nature is appropriated as an empty but powerful signifier for ideological domination. In a particularly pertinent scene Vladimir, the manager of the band, now renamed as Moses in a parody of religious fervour, douses a bush with gasoline and sets it on fire. The burning bush acts as a quick joke in this irreverent film, but for us, the subversion of religious dogma is particularly relevant for highlighting the appropriation of nature for ideological purposes. The natural environment has no real meaning in its own right in such views but acts predominantly as a repository of meanings for constructing critical references from politics to ideological preoccupations. By combining challenges to the mental and social ecologies, Kaurismäki's films undo the foundations on which these acts of appropriation rely.

This is, in itself, environmentalist as it reclaims nature from anthropocentric uses. Whether we consider the displaced farmlands or the emptying countryside, the landscape is consistently estranged from its history of representation. It is shown to be a tool designed to wield power in society and to construct dominant patterns of behaviour and thought. Through this, they gesture to an environmental ecology and a more sustainable view of humanity's Dasein and of its very role in the ecosystem.

Constructing a Sustainable Utopia: The Man Without a Past

In contrast to the displacement poetics of many of his earlier films, Kaurismäki's *The Man Without a Past* provides a much more stabilized perspective (Figure 2.1). The politics of the film are, again, premised on temporal dislocations as it can be seen as both a nostalgic evocation of the past and a critique of the present. Nostalgia pervades the film from its warm cinematography to its use of popular music. The critique of the present, on the other hand, emerges from its focus on social alienation and marginalization. The focus of the narrative is

Figure 2.1 Irma (Kati Outinen) and M (Markku Peltola) in *The Man Without a Past* (2002). © and courtesy Sputnik Ltd.

on the failure of the safety mechanisms of the welfare state in its contemporary malformed state. M, the protagonist of the film, loses most of his memory and wakes up on the outskirts of the city. His new home is a village consisting of discarded shipping containers where all types of outcasts have found ways to acclimatize and make this their new habitat. The place seems indifferent to him at first but soon reveals its welcoming side. The village is a utopian version of the egalitarian dream of a society where everyone is welcome and individuals look after each other. Even the authoritarian security guard is revealed to be one of the 'people'. By showing M give up his civic identity, the narrative of the film chronicles the purification of individuals from the societal machinery oppressing them at every turn.

Drawing on the work of Andrew Nestingen, I have discussed the location of the film as a particularly powerful case of environmentalist counter globalization.[22] The containers are the focus of this perspective as these leftovers of global trade are now rusting, completely useless for the original purpose of their construction. The recycling of these objects can be taken to indicate a sense of environmental awareness in themselves. But it is the utopian qualities of life in the village that provide the most productive view of an environmental ecology for this chapter. The displacement on which so many of Kaurismäki's films rely on is now made concrete in the dislocation of the protagonist outside of the city, but this now acts as an indicator of stability, instead of disorientation. This stability, in turn, leads to an alternative sense of sustainability. The challenges to mental ecology are clearly present in the location and constitution of the village as well as the absurdly sunny predilection of its residents. This extends to the social ecology as other narrative strands in the film showcase the ways the neo-liberalist society subjugates and exploits its citizens, including in a previous life, those who have now found a safe haven in the village. The mental and the social combine with the environmentalist connotations of recycled habitats to provide a picture of a sustainable ecology.

This is best illustrated by an early scene in the film. Once M assimilates to life in the village, he begins to build a new persona for himself. A brief montage scene captures his acclimatization to the new pace of life in the village. The focus of the scene involves one of the inhabitants taking a shower. As there is no running water, two boys have to collect the water from the sea and pump it to the shower. The camera moves from this evocation of sustainable resource use to a woman washing clothes with a manual rub and rinse board. Meanwhile, M and another resident enjoy a beer in the idyllic sunlight as another local plays traditional melancholic music on an accordion in the background. The scene moves from one part of this holistic world to another, providing a set of transversal connections that merge it together into a nostalgic and utopian view of harmony. We know this scene is divorced from reality as the evocation of ecological harmony through sustainable consumption practices seems largely unpractical and unrealistic. Yet when we consider this scene alongside the displacement poetics of his other films, we know that the world we are presented with is not to be taken at face value. Instead, it is more appropriate to consider such scenes on the level of symbolic critiques of the contemporary social order, though in comparison to most of his other films; this time we are actually presented with an alternative to the social predicament. What we see in this scene is a realization of the principles of Guattari's combination of the three ecologies for a more sustainable worldview. It may not be practical but as a means to guide our thinking towards sustainability, it works very effectively. While one could argue that what takes place in the film is a case of environmentalist idealism, which Guattari warns against, this is another one of Kaurismäki's displaced suggestive perspectives, where it is the thought process that matters, not the practicalities of an action.

Conclusion

I have used the three ecologies as a framework to rethink some of the readings associated with Kaurismäki's films and work towards an ecological understanding of their content. The films are often interpreted as politically committed texts, and their relationship with capitalism is well documented. But capitalism is also detrimental to the environment, making it necessary to interrogate the films' commitment to sustainability. Kaurismäki's films are well known for their focus on urban environments, which provides a (superficial) obstacle to understanding them from an environmentalist perspective. As any film text will tell us something about humanity's relationship with the environment, the evocation of such obstacles is merely an instance of taking the anthropocentric foundations of such arguments for granted. Yet gesturing only to certain elements of the films – the use of nature, capitalist critique – without any real systematic means of analysis would also be counterproductive. A much more rigorous method of analysis is necessary to understand the environmental potential of these complex films.

Guattari's work on the three ecologies provides such an intellectual method. As we have argued earlier, in his evocation of the three ecologies, Guattari was addressing problems he had identified in environmentalist critique and activity. The first level of complication comes from the ineffectiveness of environmentalist rhetoric as environmentalists, politicians, regulators and the public are rarely in agreement about best practice for sustainability. Another problem is that when humanity considers its environmental role, it often does not fully take into account its own immersion in the ecosystem it exploits. Thus, it is necessary to radicalize human cognition of its Dasein and combine this with political movements and environmental argumentation to attain a more complex view that emphasizes that humanity relies as much on the environment as it considers it a resource base. The mental, the social and the environmental ecologies comprise the three ecologies, which I suggest present a way into Kaurismäki's ecocinema.

These ecologies function transversally with elements from one influencing the other in the creation of an environmental consciousness. In this chapter, I have focused on four areas in which such transversal influences occur most visibly. These are composed of objects, the human body, the space of the city and the role of landscape. Objects provide the first challenge to the mental ecology, conceptualized here as the normative hegemonic means through which society, including its art, is organized. The films are replete with objects that stand out from the diegesis and challenge our perspectives on cultural and historical norms. They create a sense of disorientation on historicity and temporality and question the world we witness, suggesting that there is something fundamentally wrong with the world we take for granted. Corporeality comes next as many of the protagonists are captured in stasis at key moments of the films. Still imagery and the unmoving body fragment temporal expectations and again challenge our expectations of societal norms. Whether these be focused on spaces of national inclusivity or on the potential of consumerism for self-realization, the lack of movement in these key moments ensures that they communicate only emptiness. The promises of a neo-liberalist society are revealed to be superfluous as these challenges to mental ecology flow to social ecology, facilitating the formation of an anti-capitalist and, therefore, an environmentalist perspective.

The city is seen as a space designed to optimize economic efficiency and marginalization of undesired classes, a notion complemented by the depiction of cityspaces in much of contemporaneous Finnish film culture. Kaurismäki's films unravel this politicized coordination by focusing on depictions of spatial disorientation. The refusal to navigate the city in the expected ways comes through in the narrative shortcuts films such as *Calamari Union* take. But ultimately, this is shown to be futile as the hegemonic organization undermines the rebellious attitudes of our socialist rebels. Yet this pessimism is part of the rhetoric of the film. Kaurismäki's films are contradictory in the sense that they often use elements generated by the superstructures they seek to criticize. Nature is one such element which is often appropriated for a range of anthropocentric purposes, such as the act of narrating the nation and of using it as a symbol for progress and development. The films use all four areas not as to vindicate any ideological connotations these materials – the objects or the spaces – conventionally have but to argue that we should not just accept the state of society but struggle to find new alternative ways for rethinking its constitution. These films offer us anarchic perspectives on societal and political mores that urge us to consider a new radical politics. In addition to being about nation, gender, transnationalism and genre, as well as a host of other areas of analysis, they also provide a way of rethinking the role of the human in the ecosystem.

Notes

1   Anu Koivunen, 'Do You Remember Monrépos? Melancholia, Modernity and Working-Class Masculinity', in *Nordic Constellations*, ed. C. Claire Thomson (Norwich: Norvik Press, 2006); Peter von Bagh, *Aki Kaurismäki* (Helsinki: WSOY, 2007).

2   Andrew Nestingen, ed., *Aki Kaurismäki: Aesthetics and Contexts* (Ontario: Alphasia Books, 2004); Pietari Kääpä, *The National and Beyond: The Globalisation of National Cinema in the Films of Aki and Mika Kaurismäki* (Oxford: Peter Lang, 2010).

3   Sanna Peden, 'Crossing Over: On Becoming European in Aki Kaurismäki's Cinema', in *Frontiers of Screen History: Imagining European Borders in Cinema, 1945-2010*, ed. R. Merivirta, K. Ahonen, H. Mulari and R. Mähkä (Bristol: Intellect, 2013).

4   Jochen Werner, *Aki Kaurismäki* (Mainz: Bender Theo Verlag, 2005).

5   Tarja Laine, *Shame and Desire: Emotion, Intersubjectivity, Cinema* (Oxford: Peter Lang, 2007).

6   Ewa Mazierska and Laura Rascaroli, *Crossing New Europe: Postmodern Travel and the European Road Movie* (London: Wallflower Press, 2005).

7   Jaakko Seppälä, 'On the Heterogeneity of Cinematography in the Films of Aki Kaurismäki', *Projections* 9, no. 2 (2015): 20-39.

8   Roger Connah, *K/K: A Couple of Finns and Some Donald Ducks* (Helsinki: VAPK-Publishing, 1991).

9   Tommy Gustasson and Pietari Kääpä, ed., *Transnational Ecocinema: Film Culture in an Age of Ecological Depravation* (Bristol: Intellect, 2013); Sheldon Lu and Jiayan Mi, ed., *Chinese Ecocinema* (Hong Kong: Hong Kong University Press, 2011).

10 Salma Monani, Stephen Rust and Sean Cubitt, ed., *Ecocinema: A Reader* (London: Routledge, 2012).

11 Matthew Fuller, *Media Ecologies: Material Energies in Art and Technoculture* (Cambridge: The MIT Press, 2005), 2.

12 Feliz Guattari, *The Three Ecologies* (London: The Athlone Press, 2000).

13 Guattari, *The Three Ecologies*, 35.

14 Ibid. 34.

15 Serenella Iovino and Serpil Opperman, 'Material Ecocriticism, Materiality, Agency and Models of Narrativity', *Ecozone*, 3, no. 1 (2012): 88.

16 Henry Bacon, 'Aki Kaurismäen sijoiltaan olon poetiikka', in *Taju kankaalle - uutta suomalaista elokuvaa paikantamassa*, ed. Kimmo Ahonen, Janne Rosenqvist, Juha Rosenqvist and Päivi Valotie (Keuruu: Otava, 2003).

17 Andrew Nestingen, 'Leaving Home: Global Circulation and Aki Kaurismäki's Ariel', in *In Search of Aki Kaurismäki*, ed. Andrew Nestingen (Ontario: Aspasia books, 2004), 96-115.

18 Pietari Kääpä, *Ecology and Contemporary Nordic Cinema* (London: Bloomsbury, 2014).

19 Kääpä, *The National and Beyond: The Globalisation of Finnish Cinema*.

20 Mike Davis, *The Ecology of Fear* (New York: Metropolitan Books, 1998).

21 Sakari Toiviainen, *Uusi suomalainen elokuva* (Helsinki: SES, 1975).

22 Kääpä, *Ecology and Contemporary Nordic Cinema*.

Chapter 3

BEYOND THE EDGES OF THE FRAME: THE INVISIBLE IN AKI KAURISMÄKI'S FILMS

Lara Perski

'All films are a small region of light in a continent of the not seen.'
Tom Suttcliffe[1]

Aki Kaurismäki's *Varjoja paratiisissa* (Shadows in Paradise, 1986) opens with a shot of a nondescript grey wall. Its blandness is punctuated only by a vertical line that divides it and the screen in half, and by an outline of a door. Although the latter hints at a space behind it, it is the currently impenetrable surface which we have no choice but to focus on and that dominates the screen and our attention. The shot, flat and facile, is held for 15 seconds, with only the camera's slight shaking indicating it is indeed a moving image and not a photograph that we are seeing, and nothing but remote sounds of chirping birds to suggest a presence of any living beings within walking distance.

Then, just as the film title is superimposed upon this most unremarkable of shots, the frame is split in two as the 'wall' suddenly comes alive and slides apart, revealing itself to be a garage gate. The musical score, unhurried and melancholic, sets in, and workers in blue uniform walk from the right off-screen space towards and through the now-open gate to start a new workday. The diagonal trajectory of their movement aligns with the now visible lights on the garage ceiling and is directed towards an invisible vanishing point (it lies somewhere behind the garage), reinforcing the impression of depth and openness. The gates glide further and further apart until they disappear beyond the edges of the frame, as if stressing its finitude, as well as the fact that the workers are not a sudden apparition: they have been right outside the frame all the time, just as the spacious garage has always been hiding behind the closed gates.

The image that just seconds ago appeared shallow and uninviting – a literal dead end – has been transformed, and when the reverse shot shows the workers walk towards and past the camera to the unseen depths of the garage and, finally, the following shot brings the entire structure into view, this transformation is consummated and celebrated.

Here, the film establishes itself as a work where spaces are revealed and concealed and the visible and the invisible are engaged in a meaningful dialogue. This opening, apart from setting the tone (calm and melancholic) and the pace (slow and measured) becomes a self-reflexive meditation on cinema as 'an art of absence, of partial views, an art that hides more than it shows'.[2] There is an entire world lying beyond the edges of the frame, hidden but biding its time to make an on-screen comeback. It is reawakened every time a character looks off-screen, or mentions something the audience cannot see, or whenever we hear a sound coming from the 'off'. The constant tension between what is shown and what is hidden is ingrained in the very fabric of cinema, but not every director is capable of making this tension truly expressive or even noticeable.

Kaurismäki's films are teeming with silences and omissions. Key narrative events often happen off-screen. The inscrutable faces of his characters are thin veneers of snow that cover deep crevasses of emotion. They are often seen gazing at nothing in particular or at least at something Kaurismäki's camera will not reveal in a handy reverse shot. And most of them dream of a happier 'Elsewhere', of some grandiose escape from their current lives, and so his films will often end with a departure, and we watch 'the bike, the boat, the train – all disappear in the horizon'.[3]

Kaurismäki's filmmaking style itself is frequently opaque, mostly characterized by 'minimalism, asceticism, laconicism, [and] ellipticism',[4] although occasional melodramatic elements will still find their way onto the screen here and there, breaking the pattern and rendering generalized summaries inadequate. To fully understand his filmmaking style, we must therefore question his choices, pause at the ellipses and survey the off-screen alongside the on-screen.

Empty Frames, Indifferent Moods

Over a century of cinematic convention had – not without exception – bolstered the very logical and generally 'self-fulfilling belief – that something held in the centre of our field of vision must have significance'.[5] Now and again, individual directors have explored and exploited this belief to disrupt the way we watch films. There is Antonioni in whose films 'unresolved absences'[6] and a 'frequent lack of anthropocentric images and gazes brings about an unnerving affectivity for the viewer'.[7] There is Michael Haneke, who will likewise leave the frame uninhabited and create 'suspense by simultaneously foregrounding off-screen space and withholding information about it'.[8] Then there is Aki Kaurismäki in whose films empty frames and unpeopled images are a commonplace yet meaningful reoccurrence. Neither unnerving nor suspenseful, they punctuate his filmography in a semi-regular rhythm, often opening or closing a scene (as in the example given earlier), casting a shadow of melancholy onto his cinematic worlds and attesting to the narrative potency of absence.

Deserted roads and vacant rooms pervade Kaurismäki's films, which are riddled with static exterior shots that are completely marginal in character and devoid of any action, save for one or two desperate souls that populate his films passing through them. Formally, these shots are, of course, reminiscent of the 'pillow' or 'curtain' shots that permeate the films of Ozu Yasujirō. In Ozu's films, these serve as a transition device and carry a complex narrative function, not to mention a plethora of interpretations they may encourage.[9] Kaurismäki, while borrowing from or referencing the Japanese filmmaker, puts his own twist on what might have been a purely transitional element by explicitly tying it to his characters.[10] Especially in his earlier films, drab walls or grey deserted streets will usually serve as a background for the characters' traversal across the screen, filling the film world with apparent dead ends, making it seem narrow and claustrophobic, adding to the feeling of the Antonionian 'confinement, hopelessness, and pure existential dread'[11] that Kaurismäki's films often convey. In *Lights in the Dusk* (2006), such transitory shots are paired with the overhead camera angle, 'transform[ing] the character into geometry, actor into pattern'[12] and evoking the character's helplessness in the face of his destiny.

The static camera and its refusal to follow the characters' movement also contribute to the sense of the world's indifference towards the human beings who inhabit it. After all, his films are filled with characters who are ignored by their fellow society members. There is a brief musical montage in *Ariel* (1988) during which Turo Pajala's character wanders from employment offices to a restaurant's kitchen to a construction site to factory, looking for work. Notable here are not only the repeated rejections he receives but how many of the characters he comes across completely fail to notice him. In *Tulitikkutehtaan tyttö* (The Match Factory Girl, 1990), which tells the story of one young woman's 'ostracisation, exploitation, and ultimate fall',[13] this same indifference is directed towards the film's protagonist and becomes one of the film's central motifs (Figure 3.1).

Figure 3.1 Iiris (Kati Outinen) in *The Match Factory Girl* (1990). © and courtesy Sputnik Ltd.

The girl, Iiris (Kati Outinen), leads a life of dreariness and isolation, and part of the tragedy of the film lies in the fact that her struggle goes unnoticed by the world at large, and the unremarkableness of her existence is shared, highlighted and heightened by the camera's unequivocal disinterest in its subject. It often ignores her, letting her slide out of sight into the off-screen. Many a time, we see her enter the frame from one side and walk through it only to disappear off-screen again, while the camera lingers, often longer than a few seconds, on the empty space left behind. As the camera dwells upon the vacant and unmovable image, satisfying its 'urge for concretion',[14] the already graspable presence of the static and unchanging space makes the girl's absence more acutely felt. She becomes a character who disappears out of sight and into nothingness without the world (or the film) noticing or caring.

The film highlights the invisibility of her suffering when a cataclysm which unfolds halfway around the world finds its way into an ordinary living room. At home, as Iiris's parents watch TV during dinner, the camera watches with them forcing us to do the same, and we see a long extract from a newscast relaying the events of the Tiananmen Square Protest. The heavy familiarity of the iconic image of an unidentified man standing in front of a column of tanks exposes the visibility of some tragedies and the obscurity of others. Linking Iiris's anguish with the fate of the protesters, the film seems to contemplate its own relevance.

The film's willingness to disregard Iiris's presence and to replace it with absence is particularly evident during a dance she attends. The tango that plays at the dance can be already heard as a sound bridge while she is hopefully putting on her make-up and before a cut transports us to the event. A long shot shows a singer and a band on stage with a sea of dancing couples below, and the camera remains with the celebrating crowd whose movement distracts us from the fact that the girl is nowhere to be seen. A full minute later, the film returns to its protagonist, who is now shown sitting near a wall accompanied by four other women. But not for long: one by one they are approached by cavaliers who take them by the arm and lead them away, towards the right off-screen, all of them briefly passing in front of the girl, once more hiding her from view. As they disappear off-screen, their shadows are thrown onto the wall behind her, taunting her, making her rejection both by her peers and by the camera complete. Over the next 35 seconds, the camera stays with her as she, seemingly on the verge of tears, watches the togetherness of others in complete solitude.

The tango, indifferent to her pain, continues, and so does the scene. The camera leaves Iiris behind once more and returns to the singer, this time coming closer. Then, once again, a wider shot dwells on the dancing crowd. As the couples waltz, moving in and out of frame, the tragedy of her isolation is both foregrounded and ironized. When we, at long last, return to her, still at the same place, she is finishing a small bottle of juice. As she leans over to place the empty bottle on the floor, the camera tilts down, showing a sizeable collection of juice bottles, all empty. The empty bottles become the last shot of the scene, held until the screen goes dark as the tango ends.

Here the camera's dwelling on the bottles becomes a placid but nonetheless explicit statement on the period of time Iiris has spent in the club, ignored by all, including (for some of the time) the camera. It is a declaration of tragedy made in a tone so faint it might go unnoticed – a common attribute of Kaurismäki's films. But even less noticeable, although no less meaningful, is the camera's willingness to follow her gesture.[15] Static for most of the film,[16] here the camera moves to reveal something that a cut could just as easily have brought into view. This decision to avoid a cut matches the absence of a cut in the musical score: the music has not been tampered with, meaning that Iiris has been off-screen for the duration of one song. And if it is true that 'to shift the frame via camera movement […] is to impose an order of perception on objects which exist in a continuous time and space',[17] the camera's tilt stipulates that the many juices were drunk *before* the camera cut to Iiris, while she was off-screen, during the *single song* which is *still* playing. It is as if the girl's banishment to the off-screen has created a different, unique timeline for her, making her separation from the dancing crowd absolute, contesting her presence at the event, robbing her of her physicality, blurring her very being.

Often compared to Robert Bresson's *Mouchette* (1967) *The Match Factory Girl* also bears undeniable resemblance to Chantal Akerman's *Jeanne Dielman, 23, quai du commerce, 1080 Bruxelles* (1975), another stark minimalist film about a woman who leads an isolated life, which also culminates in murder and which, too, focuses on the banal and the quotidian while (mostly) omitting the sensational. Here as well, the camera often lingers in the empty rooms of the protagonist's apartment prior to her entering them or after she has exited, making her 'a ghost even in her own domestic realm. Her visual absence in these moments represents quite literally the invisibility of her plight: a life lived in the shadows, a fate suffered just around a corner, conveniently out of view for the rest of society'.[18]

Similarities aside, the plight of the two women ends in different outcomes: the controversial murder in the end of *Jeanne Dielman* is both an 'act of liberation'[19] and a strong break from the rest of the film. A brutal moment in the film of the mundane, it is 'a gesture which annihilates order',[20] so powerful that 'although downplayed dramatically, the scene effects a switch from the literal to the fictive, and intimates the absolute necessity of drama – of a fictional, narrativized closure'.[21]

Iiris, on the other hand, exacts her revenge on the world in a far less dramatic way. While she does poison her parents, her former lover and a stranger who had the bad fortune to meet her in a bar, the impact of their deaths is muffled by the fact that they are never shown. The final scenes of the film are surprisingly, almost uncomfortably, upbeat. The ultimate shot shows her at work. She looks tired and unhappy but the lush, melancholic song that plays over the scene is 'sufficiently excessive to discharge the pathos Iiris has generated over the course of the film, the humour absorbing the pity the viewer may feel towards [Iiris]'.[22] Then, two men in coats walk in, show her what we can only assume is a police badge and take her away, leaving the frame empty once more. An entire minute passes before the end credits finally start to roll. The insistent lingering on the empty room becomes a taunting withholding of a resolution. As Iiris disappears off-screen one last time, her fate remains unclear and her tragedy has been turned into a farce. In his stern 1993 review of the film, Jonathan Rosenbaum remarked that this 'ending invalidates most of what precedes it' as the heroine's 'plight is treated not so much as pathetic or tragic as hilarious. [...] It's an extreme and "satisfying" melodramatic finale deliberately inspiring camp laughter, not belief'.[23] I would argue that by keeping the closing events of the film under wraps, Kaurismäki suppresses true 'satisfaction' and 'melodrama', muting any particular response the ending might provoke. In a final cruel turn of events, Iiris' insurgence seems to have had no impact on the film.

Comedy and Tragedy: Ariel, Lights in the Dusk

Kaurismäki's formal repertoire seems to be informed by a relatively small variety of distinct stylistic choices, but the outcomes of these choices will vary from film to film. This applies to his tendency to relay important narrative events off-screen. The decision not to show can be mischievous and comical, a conscious suspension of audience's expectations, or poignant and eloquent, a revelatory concealment.

In *Ariel*, the decision to move a major narrative event off-screen results in comedy. Towards the end of the film, Taisto Kasurinen (Turo Pajala) and his former prison cellmate – now partner in crime Mikkonen (Matti Pellonpää) – find themselves robbing a bank in order to join the ranks of Kaurismäki characters who manage to flee Finland on board a ship. The entire hold-up takes place within a single 45-second-long shot and happens off-screen. It starts with the camera waiting in front of the bank, watching their car arrive and screech to a halt and accommodating its movement with a small pan. As the newly made robbers scurry into the bank, clumsily dropping their gun in the process and abandoning the cool composure we saw them display a moment ago, the camera follows them to the entrance and then inexplicably stays there while they go inside. Instead of the heist, we are left to watch the reflection of the deserted street in the glass facade of the bank.[24] Fifteen seconds later, Taisto and Mikkonen re-emerge, one after another, and run back towards the car, this time dropping some of the money – proof of their success. The camera, again, tracks their jog back to the car, returning to its original position from where it – now completely stationary – watches them struggle with the transmission and waits for them to drive out of the frame and away.

It is not only the disobedience of the cinematic convention, which of course would have prioritized and shown the bank heist, it is also the decisiveness with which the camera first follows the characters, only to be left behind and to omit the highlight as well as the purpose of their visit to the bank that makes the camera itself visible. The omittance of what might have been an equally comical hold-up becomes comedic in itself, a tongue-in-cheek comment on the incompetence of the characters and a (quintessentially Kaurismäkian) self-deprecating joke by the film itself: When it comes to bank heists, it pretends to be just as clueless as the robbers and gleefully misses the entire affair.

Lights in the Dusk has two scenes in which the camera behaves in a similar manner, leaving out what purports to be their most significant parts. The first scene occurs towards the beginning of the film, when the protagonist, night watchman Kostinen (Janne Hyytiäinen), spots a dog that is chained outside a bar and goes inside to have a talk with its owners, who had left it there for a week. A kid sitting outside the bar warns him that 'they are quite big', but Kostinen heads in anyway. Once inside, the camera tracks him walk up to the counter where he inquires to whom the dog belongs – once again matching the decisiveness of his movement. Placed in front of him, this time around it does not follow him but instead prefigures his movement. After a brief look at the thugs and a shot of whisky, he walks up to them, joining them in the long medium shot, and starts talking. Once he confronts them, the camera moves to show a close-up of his face. A reverse shot shows one of the thugs, who suggests they discuss it outside. The camera stays at Kostinen's eye level, and although thug does not quite loom over it, there is a sense of a crescendo that matches the escalation of the conversation. But Kaurismäki does not allow us to see the culmination of this exchange: Another medium shot shows the entire company – Kostinen and the three thugs – leave the table and disappear through the side corridor that we can only presume leads to a back alley. The camera stays inside in grim expectation. We are left with a shot of their temporarily empty table, their beers waiting for the return of their owners and the small swing door they had to pass through swaying back and forth until it comes to a full stop. Twenty-five seconds later, they come back, one of them extinguishes a cigarette we never saw him light, and they grin and return to their beers. A separate shot shows Kostinen emerging from the side alley outside the bar, beaten up, as we knew he would be. And herein – in this knowledge, in the fact that the off-screen does not *truly* conceal anything from us but rather simply allows us to avert our eyes – lies the true tragedy of the film.

By omitting the actual violence in favour of silent resignation, Kaurismäki paints a grim portrait of a world in which decency is a weakness to be exploited. Showing the beating would have emphasized the violence itself, the pain and misery of defeat. Leaving the camera inside the bar, instead of having it follow the characters, and the nonchalance with which it is done, confronts us with the fact that we do not need to see Kostinen be beaten up to know it happened. This knowledge aligns us with his character, who likewise knows how this walk outside would end, and conjures the sense of inevitability that echoes through the film – including the aforementioned overhead shots of characters passing through the frame and leaving it empty. This is reinforced by a very similar scene – another off-screen beating – that takes place towards the end of the film as Kostinen attempts to confront the criminal who framed him, attacking him with a knife. As he begins to approach his would-be victim, the camera is once again in front of him, backing away as he walks right towards it – another frontal tracking shot. But his attack is unsuccessful; he is immediately overpowered and thrown into a car by the man's security guards who are given the command to beat him up. A long shot then shows the car drive off into the left off-screen, while the villain and his female accomplice slowly walk off in the opposite direction, draining the frame of life. Cut to a dark road outside the city port. The car drives up to the camera and Kostinen's unconscious, or as one might briefly assume, dead, body is thrown on the ground. The empty frame becomes a signifier of a cold society that dooms the helpless, pointing to a spiral of violence that mostly goes unnoticed and unacknowledged.

Hidden Melodrama, Invisible Kisses

For all their cynicism, many of Aki Kaurismäki's films are 'derivative of and a commentary to the classical melodrama'.[25] This might seem like an odd match considering that 'melodrama [...] aimed to carry its audience over the top, with heightened situations and excessive passions, [and] offered a corresponding licence to explore the possibilities of a flamboyant visual rhetoric'[26] while Kaurismäki mostly favours understatement and stylistic and narrative economy. Yet he often manages to reconcile the two, finding ways to revise the melodramatic tradition by filtering the excess through means of his own.

Throughout *Shadows in Paradise*, its two protagonists, supermarket cashier Ilona (Kati Outinen) and garbage collector Nikander (Matti Pellonpää), find themselves, time and again, united and separated. What in a more melodramatic film could be described as a turbulent relationship is here treated with measured restraint, which may hide the film's incontestable deep underlying romanticism that is most evident in the way Kaurismäki stages their first – and hidden – kiss.

Blue sky and yellow sand briefly fill the frame before the camera pans downwards to reveal Ilona and Nikander sitting on the sand facing a calm sea, a cordless radio, which appears to be the source of the music that is playing, beside them. A reverse shot shows us their faces, which betray signs of worry, but its strict compositional unity implies a completeness usually found in a film's (happy) ending, and in its openness and brightness this shot is radically divorced from the scenes that have preceded it. It is, therefore, not surprising that it is here that Nikander leans over to kiss Ilona. As they fall on the ground together, the camera moves closer but just as their lips touch a cut intrudes and hides their embrace, replacing it with a shot of Ilona's hand instead. A close-up shows her wrist (the unfinished cigarette still between her fingers) drop – coolly and indifferently – on the sand and remain there in a relaxed near-equilibrium, only an occasional delicate quiver reminding the audience of the now invisible kiss just left of the screen.

In many Hollywood melodramas, the idea of love and its often delayed but highly anticipated consummation – the romantic kiss – borders on the sublime in its 'limitlessness [...] with a super-added thought of its totality'.[27] Aesthetically, this manifests itself by the unmistakably melodramatic mode of representation that is most apparent in the way many classic Hollywood kisses are often presented as climatic events, almost inevitably accompanied by an emotional close-up that reinforces intimacy just as it invites voyeurism and the 'soundtrack music swelling to the crescendo'.[28] These instances of stylistic excess transform the kiss from an ordinary event into a spectacular one, marking the kiss 'as "special," particularly meaningful and worthy of aesthetic appreciation, critical attention, and emotional involvement'.[29] As such, they are also moments of heightened self-reflexivity that puncture the otherwise 'serenely intact'[30] narrative structure and elevate the kiss to another reality: one that is closer to the pro-filmic but paradoxically also slips deeper into utopian fantasy.

Romance is thus associated with and represented by a distancing or partial withdrawal from reality (which is not to say that characters necessarily succumb to the illusion, although that remains a possibility and an existential threat). An apotheosis of such romantic displacement is surely the camera's circling movement around the kissing couple often found in Alfred Hitchcock's films.[31] Veiling the tightly embraced lovers in privacy, which it simultaneously intrudes upon, the camera glides around them, severing them from the outside world (sometimes literally, as in *Vertigo* (Alfred Hitchcock, 1958, USA)). Their kiss exists in a small and intimate world of their own, occupied by no one else, other than the camera, which grants the spectator access to witness and to testify to its intimacy.

One would be hard-pressed to find a circling camera within the laconic deadpan of Kaurismäki's cinema. The moment that comes closest is the kiss in *Calamari Union*, where after catching a kiss between two characters up close, the camera, in a separate shot, tilts upwards and loses itself as it starts spinning ever faster. Yet there are other, more subdued ways for Kaurismäki to conceive of a couple's unity as a temporary escape from reality: by forgoing the pathos of a close-up which would appropriate the private moment[32] and moving it off-screen.

Unseen, Ilona and Nikander's first kiss remains private, hidden from the ever-watchful eye of the camera and the voyeuristic spectator. The unequalled impenetrability that the off-screen provides endues this romantic exchange with ambiguity and mystery as its nature is unknown to the audience. And, because the off-screen is not a physical place that can be described in terms of time and space, it raises the kiss towards the level of the metaphysical without, however, quite achieving its dimension as Ilona's hand anchors it in the physical. She binds the kiss to the visible, not letting it slip into what otherwise might have been 'a more radical Elsewhere, outside homogenous space and time'.[33]

As the camera, banned from the intimacy of the embrace, lingers and fixates on Ilona's hand, its presence becomes a vexation. Notably, she does not let go of the cigarette to put her arm around Nikander, leaving the frame empty once more and completing the idyll, perhaps ending the film. Instead, her hand simply lays there, silently announcing her submissive passivity as opposed to active involvement. Its on-screen presence is also Ilona's partial absence from their shared off-screen. Her wrist and the coarse sand underneath it are solidified by the motionless camera and together with the cigarette – an everyday quotidian object – uncloak the ordinariness of the shot and call forth its banality. Ilona's unmanicured fingers, the fingernails somewhat longer than appropriate (and slightly dirtier) – a reminder of her working-class standing and the harsh financial reality that has brought the characters together again and that awaits outside the romantic retreat – become a bearer of hopelessness and dead ends that will precede the final happy ending and dampen the otherwise hopeful tone of the scene, robbing it of its climax. The hand and the cigarette – linear and pointing away from the newly found closeness – puncturing, if not bursting, the utopian bubble, throw a shadow onto the paradise. Without dispelling the romanticism of the scene, the shot contextualizes the invisible embrace and grounds it in reality, bringing it – quite literally – down to earth.

We encounter a similar shot, albeit one that carries a very different meaning, and another off-screen kiss in *La vie de Bohème*, Kaurismäki's most boldly sentimental film. Towards the end of the film, the star-crossed lovers Matti Pellonpää's Rodolfo and Evelyne Didi's Mimi are enjoying a short trip to the countryside. Amid the peace and quiet that bring to mind the idyll of Jean Renoir's *Partie de campagne* (1936), Rodolfo falls asleep against a tree trunk and Mimi sits next to him playfully tickling his face with a wild flower. He opens his eyes, smiles at her and playfully pulls her over, throws her on the ground and then kisses her. They kiss for a few moments before the film cuts away to a shot of Mimi's hand, the flower still between her fingers. She lowers her wrist onto the ground, slowly, elegantly – a gentle and choreographed movement. Her fingers hold onto the flower until her hand touches the ground, which is when they relax and let go. The camera lingers on this shot ever so briefly before cutting to two swans peacefully gliding over undisturbed water surface. A few seconds later, the screen fades to black, Tschaikovsky's Serenade for Strings Op. 48 that has been playing over the scene subsidies as well, ending the sequence.

The bittersweetness of the image that supersedes the couple's kiss epitomizes their relationship. Romantic and tender, it testifies both to their love and its ephemerality. The frailty of the flower, the thinness of its stem, the delicacy of the hand gesture – so different from Ilona's innate, careless hand movement – foreshadow the fragility of the couple's happiness. If the shot of Ilona's hand was creating tension, the image of Mimi's arm serves to further romanticize the sequence.

Moving an event off-screen and editing around it allows Kaurismäki to both dramatize and characterize it. It becomes a significant event that signifies beyond itself. Instead of being diminished, the moment becomes more meaningful. It uproots the characters from the iron grasp of the film's physical reality and its particularities, The photographic nature of film grounds the medium in the visible and, therefore, the physical. Thus 'movies are fixed in that specific collection of human beings with which movies have been made – in their utterly specific rhythms of voice and gesture and posture, and in those particular streets and carriages and chambers against and within which those specific beings had their being'.[34] The off-screen, however, is free from such physical constraints. Cutting away transforms the particular into indefinite, figurativism into abstraction, prose into poetry.

Off-screen Deaths and Magical Resurrections

These qualities of the off-screen make it an ideal refuge for matters that are private, and there is, perhaps, no matter as private as death, as 'one's death is already one's own. It belongs to nobody else: not even to a killer'.[35] And no death is more private than one by one's own hand, which is why suicides that sometimes quietly shake Kaurismäki's films are always hidden from our impertinent gaze. Other characters may react to these tragedies (in *Ariel* or *The Man Without a Past*) with calm composure and remain unfazed, but their hiddenness constitutes a rueful gesture on behalf of the film itself, awarding these characters the dignity that had been missing from their lives – an extradiegetic sign of compassion.

Occasionally – as in *Juha* or *The Match Factory Girl* – Kaurismäki will opt to keep the violence and death completely hidden, but oftentimes a clever montage will edit around the brutality itself, avoiding the spectacle, and, much like with the two kissing scenes discussed earlier, another image will take its place. In *Ariel*, the fatal stabbing of Matti Pellonpää's character is not shown; instead it is his hand reaching for a stack of banknotes that occupies the screen. In slow motion, we see it pick the money from the floor and then suddenly let go of it, the fingers stretching out and extending, as if convulsing from the invisible pain. In a film that is arguably about an 'all-powerful capitalist system crushing [its] diminutive citizen',[36] this interrupted motion comes to not only stand for the violence happening off-screen but also to symbolize a release from the oppressive system of capitalism, conjoining the two.

In *Crime and Punishment*, the moment of the titular crime eludes the camera. Following a series of dramatic close-ups – first of the victim's face, then of the murderer Rahikainen (Markku Toikka) and then of the gun as it is being fired – we see the former's face distorted by pain as he begins to sink to the floor, slowly sliding out of the frame. A separate shot shows his arm as he tries, in vain, to hold onto the desk for balance, knocking over a flower vase which hits the floor in the next shot and shatters, the flowers spilling. Cut to a longer shot that shows the shooter lower the gun, turn down the volume of the music that is coming from the radio and then pause, looking over the completely motionless body of the now dead man, slowly walking over and crouching next to it. The body itself is clearly visible but the man's face remains concealed even as Rahikainen reaches out to touch the large blood stain that has spread across the dead man's chest. Doubling the fall of the victim (and the moral fall of the protagonist), the shattered vase comes to mirror the shattering of a life and represent the senselessness of the murder: a pointless act of destruction that even if premeditated is akin to an irreversible accident, a terrible mishap, the consequences of which are too far reaching to foresee.

This way of staging the overrepresented and yet 'unrepresentable, unknowable, and invisible event of death'[37] is the most acutely Bressonian element of Kaurismäki's style. In Robert Bresson's *Diary of a Country Priest*,

> the viewer likewise does not see the death of the priest. The dropping of his diary and then his pencil, and his effort to regain them, substitute for facing the event head-on. [His death is conceived as his incapacity to reach for his diary notebook; thus, the film characterizes death not in terms of its suddenness or its finality but in terms of the priest being unable to continue with the routine things.[38]

Klevan maintains that the diary's cogent presence throughout the film and the weight it had been afforded by the narrative allow it to compensate for the absence of a more direct or melodramatic presentation of the priest's death and still convey a resonant sense of loss.

> The film has earned the right for the dropping of his diary to stand in for his death, and the mundane rustle of papers as they slide against the ground here represents the full weight of life. This would be a less successful moment, trite almost, had the diary not been so fully and meticulously integrated into both the voice-over narration and the narrative more generally.[39]

Aki Kaurismäki's films seldom display this level of consistency and rarely does an object accumulate the level of significance of the priest's diary. The objects – or rather the images of the objects – that stand in for the images of death and violence are more akin to accidental symbols, briefly meaningful only by virtue of the moment they are implicated in, but meaningful nonetheless. Ironically, this lack of consistency is perhaps the most persistent element of Kaurismäki's style and part of what makes up that 'certain twistedness'[40] responsible for Henry Bacon's terming of the director's style as one of 'poetics of displacement'.[41]

And Kaurismäki's use of off-screen space facilitates inconsistencies, tonal and narrative, which find their way into even his less ironic works. *Le Havre* (2011) is one of his most earnest and coherent films, and the theme of hiddenness, of concealment can be traced throughout it. This is first introduced in the startling opening scene that takes place at the train station, a setting that can be identified as much by the overhead announcements and train whistles that come from the off-screen as it is by the sign that says 'Le Havre'. Underneath the sign, two shoeshiners stand still as crowds rush by without taking notice of them. A separate shot makes the passers-by invisible instead, as Kaurismäki shows their briskly moving shadows fall across the currently unused shoeshining tools (bringing to mind the similarly constructed shots in *The Match Factory Girl* and *Lights in the Dusk*). Then a mysterious man with a briefcase chained to his arm has his shoes polished and is promptly gunned down by other mysterious men in broad daylight but away from our curious eyes. We hear the sound of screeching tyres, the shots being fired, a woman screams, but what we are seeing are the sombre faces of Marcel Marx (André Wilms) and his colleague Chang (Quoc Dung Nguyen). A sudden and mysterious event that happens entirely off-screen and is never again mentioned by any of the characters, it dissolves into the fabric of the film.

The film's two main plotlines likewise concern themselves with concealment. The first centres on Marcel's efforts to help a young Congalese refugee Idrissa (Blondin Miguel) evade the police and escape to London. The other plotline revolves around his wife Arletty's (Kati Outinen) discovery that she is terminally ill and her attempts to hide the severity of the situation from Marcel. Kaurismäki, however, lets us in on her secret, and we see her holding an X-ray – a diagnostic tool that reveals hidden ailments – and surrounded by her doctors who spell out her eviscerating diagnosis: nothing can be done. This storyline is, therefore, geared towards her imminent death, which would come as a devastating shock to Marcel but which we come to warily anticipate.

This taciturn yet real awareness of approaching tragedy is awoken each time we see Arletty in the hospital and is never stronger than during Marcel's final visit. He walks up the hospital staircase (another shot that begins and ends with an empty space) and into her room, to discover that she is not there. Her absence is conspicuous: the empty bed, the bundle with her yellow festive dress she had asked him to bring by earlier still unopened – a separate shot brings it forward in a grim reminder – become harbingers of the terrible news we know he is about to receive and are brought into view before he enters the room, the smile on his face disappearing at the sight of them. As a nurse arrives to retrieve him, Marcel solemnly places the yellow roses on her bed and vacates the room and the frame. The sight of a man laying down flowers on his wife's bed is an elegiac one, bringing to mind a grave visitation, and it is an unspoken – but strong and resounding – suggestion that Arletty had indeed passed away while Marcel and the viewer were preoccupied with the other plotline.

In the next shot, the anticipatory camera waits for Marcel and the nurse further down the hallway, and they walk towards it and she then turns back while he walks past it, towards his fate. The hopeful musical score swells up in an apparent contradiction to what we are seeing on screen as the camera looks up to Marcel's stern face and moves with him in another fateful frontal tracking shot, but it quietens down as he comes face to face with Arletty's doctors. Their words – 'I'm sorry. I don't know what happened' – seemingly confirm our suspicions which he now shares: having previously told him her sickness was not serious, surely their apologies now must mean her condition has deteriorated. But then Marcel slowly turns his head and the music swells up again as a reverse shot reveals a smiling Arletty, wearing her yellow dress. The camera zooms in on her – a celebratory movement that wishes to alleviate any disbelief that it really is her, even as it adds to the irreality of the moment – and for a few seconds, they simply look at each other in mutual appreciation, and then she says she is cured.

It is, we now learn, not her death that had happened off-screen but her miraculous recovery. This ending is decidedly Capraesque in its 'knowledge, if less than conscious, of the discrepancy between the complex nature of [the] film's recurring antitheses and the evasive facility of their reconciliation'.[42] Here, the 'facile reconciliation' of Arletty's magical resurrection is enabled by Kaurismäki's habit of moving crucial events off-screen, where they remain vague and anonymous allowing the film to dive into fantasy and wish fulfilment that is more bittersweet than camp or ironic. A volatile uncertain 'terrain created partly by the audience's imagination and partly by camera-actors-director'[43] rather than a perennial stable entity, the off-screen encourages inconsistencies. It is controlled and summoned by sound, character movements and shot composition, and it is extinguished by the visible upon the director's command. It is not subject to the same laws of physics as a realistically conceived on-screen space; instead it is clouded with unknowness and ambiguity (which is why not-showing in cinema is often associated with an expression of ineffability). In other words, off-screen everything is possible.

There is a similar magical resurrection in *The Man Without a Past* (2002). Although equally startling, it is even more incredible as this time the character's death is confirmed by other characters as well as communicated by the film's framing which insistently hides his face, marking the on-screen events as serious (as well as perhaps evoking a burial custom). The protagonist is beaten up and left for dead by thugs who mockingly place his welding helmet – a representation of his identity that he will lose track of as a result of this attack – on his face. Then, as he stumbles into a public bathroom and collapses onto the floor where he is discovered by a janitor who calls the authorities, proclaiming 'there is a dead man', the frame obscures his face. Finally, the hospital doctors wrap his entire person in bandages – implying the janitor must have spoken too soon – and then as his electrocardiogram (ECG) flatlines call the time of his death, cover his lifeless body with a sheet. This is when the protagonist who will be henceforth referred to as 'M' suddenly sits up and frees himself from the ECG cables – a healed man.

The abruptness of this turn of events and M's decisiveness – the impossible, cartoonish straightening of his broken nose – make the scene seem comical and absurd. 'The happy endings of comedy are often ironic endings, frankly contrived and intended to evoke a smile of disbelief',[44] but here it is the beginning of the film that is so openly, dizzyingly preposterous. Is it that the straightforward implication is that we are seeing a fantasy, a sudden turn for the better that can only occur within the magical bounds of a silver movie screen, making the film a grave indictment of the reality we live in? And would this interpretation contradict the humanism of the rest of the film? Or is it simply a typically Kaurismäkian attempt to subvert filmic convention? Perhaps a dissection of the way we ingest information we are presented with? This reversal brings to light the limitations of the camera when it comes to capturing the truth, especially when the truth is complex and incomprehensible.

***

What to make of a director who makes films set within the most prosaic of settings and whose characters are simple people dealing with everyday problems and yet in whose films the ambiguous off-screen infringes on the visible and implicates the camera in its deceits? The persistent convergence of the off-screen and narrative space seems like an unlikely match for a filmmaker whose films are generally treated as sociopolitical commentaries. The ellipses in his films can be telling and silences can speak volumes, but they also can remain secretive, imposing the ambiguity of the off-screen onto the on-screen images. The camera in Kaurismäki's films lies as much as the off-screen does, undermining the perhaps most basic condition of classical film narration, the fact that 'the existence of an intelligible course of fictional events in film depends at several levels upon our being able to take what is shown on the screen as a reliable indicator of what has and has not transpired within the story'.[45]

For all the formal similarities his films bear to those made by Bresson, one must acknowledge that Kaurismäki's sensibility is radically different. Whereas Bresson's cinema insists 'on the irrefutability of what he is presenting. Nothing happens by chance; there are no alternatives, no fantasy',[46] Kaurismäki remains as much of a prankster behind the camera as he is in front of it, 'consistently [sabotaging] every proposal for existence of specific meaning or intent behind their work'.[47] His cinematography comes to reflect the deadpan non-sequitur humour while remaining concisely meaningful. This constitutes the phenomenon that is Kaurismäki's cinema and is perhaps the reason his controversial and contradictory interview statements invariably find their way into the critical writing about his films – usually accompanied by an admission that he is a contrarian and a trickster whose words are to be taken with a grain of salt.

Focusing on the off-screen space in Kaurismäki's cinema helps highlight his inventiveness and shows that most labels currently attached to his oeuvre are incapable of accurately conveying the complexity and paradoxicality of his style. Criticism of his films needs to reflect both his obvious urge to experiment with cinematic convention as well as his indebtedness to a range of revered filmmakers and the anomalous results of this amalgamation. Incontestable, however, is the fact that the intricacy with which he negotiates the on-screen and the off-screen, the visible and the invisible, the hidden, the implied and the revealed shows him to be a master of the 'intimate metamorphosis' that is cinema.[48]

Notes

1   Tom Sutcliffe, *Watching* (London: Faber and Faber, 2000), 106.

2   Gilberto Perez, *The Material Ghost: Films and Their Medium* (Baltimore: Johns Hopkins University Press,1998), 387.

3   Tytti Soila, 'The Landscape of Memories in the Films of the Kaurismäki Bros', *Film International*, 1, no. 3 (2003): 14.

4   Sakari Toiviainen, 'The Kaurismäki Phenomenon', *Journal of Finnish Studies*, 8, no. 2 (2004): 25.

5   Sutcliffe, *Watching*, 135.

6   Perez, *The Material Ghost*, 387.

7   Hamish Ford, 'Antonioni's *L'Avventura* and Deleuze's Time-Image', *Senses of Cinema*, 28 October 2003, www.sensesofcinema.com/2003/feature-articles/l_avventura_deleuze/ (accessed 11 January 2017).

8   Libby Saxton, 'Secrets and Revelations: Off-Screen Space in Michael Haneke's *Caché* (2005)', *Studies in French Cinema*, 7, no. 1 (2007): 11.

9   Cf. Edward Branigan, 'The Space of Equinox Flower', in *Close Viewings: An Anthology of New Film Criticism*, ed. Peter Lehman (Tallahassee, Gainsville: Florida State University Press, 1990), 75–77; Andrew Klevan, *Disclosure of the Everyday: Undramatic Achievement in Narrative Film* (Trowbridge, Wilts: Flicks Books, 2000), 143–145; et.al.

10 Pure transitional shots that feature open spaces or natural landscapes do indeed sometimes appear in Kaurismäki's film (e.g. *Juha, La Vie de Bohème, Lights in the Dusk, Le Havre*), but these are more scarce and unconnected to the characters.

11 Marc Saint-Cyr, 'Aki Kaurismäki and the Art of Getting By', *Cineaction*, no. 92 (2014): 20.

12 Robert B. Ray, *The ABCs of Classic Hollywood* (Oxford: Oxford University Press USA, 2008), 56.

13 Andrew Nestingen, *The Cinema of Aki Kaurismäki: Contrarian Stories* (London and New York: Wallflower Press, 2013), 44.

14 Siegfried Kracauer, *Theory of Film: The Redemption of Physical Reality* (Princeton: Princeton University Press, 1997), 297.

15 This interpretation owes much to Victor Perkins's discussion of a similar decision in favour of a camera movement in *All I Desire* (Douglas Sirk, 1953, USA) (Victor F. Perkins, 'Where Is the World? The Horizon of Events in Movie Fiction', in *Style and Meaning: Studies in the Detailed Analysis of Film*, ed. John Gibbs and Douglas Pye (Manchester: Manchester University Press, 2005), 30–31).

16 Jaakko Seppälä had pointed out that Kaurismäki's camera moves more often than it is generally assumed, there being 'a noteworthy discrepancy between the fact and impression'. Jaakko Seppälä, 'On the Heterogeneity of Cinematography in the Films of Aki Kaurismäki', *Projections*, 9, no. 2 (2015): 29. I would argue that the impression of immobility – especially one that is shared by so many viewers – is perhaps as important and that the misapprehension itself arises from the 'twisted' nature of Kaurismäki's filmmaking style I will address later in the text.

17 Victor F. Perkins, 'Moments of Choice', *Rogue*, no. 9 (2006), www.rouge.com.au/9/moments_choice.html (accessed 8 March 2017).

18 filmscalpel, 'Sound Unseen: The Acousmatic Jeanne Dielman', www.filmscalpel.com/sound-unseen/ (accessed 12 March 2017).

19 Jayne Loader, 'Jeanne Dielman. Death in Installments', *Jump Cut*, 16 (1977), www.ejumpcut.org/archive/onlinessays/JC16folder/JeanneDielman.html (accessed 12 March 2017).

20 Brenda Longfellow, 'Love Letters to the Mother: The Works of Chantal Akerman', *Canadian Journal of Political and Social Theory*, 13, 1–2 (1989): 84.

21 Ivone Margulies, *Nothing Happens: Chantal Akerman's Hyperrealist Everyday* (Durham: Duke University Press, 1996), 5.

22 Nestingen, *The Cinema of Aki Kaurismäki: Contrarian Stories*, 44.

23 Rosenbaum's view on the film seems to have changed over the years, and while posting his original review on his site, he remarked: 'I may have underrated this movie' (Jonathan Rosenbaum, 'Wallflower's Revenge', *Chicago Reader*, 19 February 1993, www.jonathanrosenbaum.net/1993/02/wallflower-s-revenge/ (accessed 12 March 2017)).

24 This scene could also be a reference to *Gun Crazy* (1950, Joseph H. Lewis), a film noir that similarly features an off-screen bank robbery. In that film, however, the camera is highly motivated to stay outside the bank as it accompanies Peggy Cummins's character who is forced to 'deal' with a potential saboteur in the face of a policeman.

25 Soila, 'The Landscape of Memories in the Films of the Kaurismäki Bros', 10.

26 Perkins, 'Moments of Choice'.

27 Immanuel Kant, *Critique of Judgement* (Oxford: Oxford University Press, 2007), 75.

28 Thomas Patrick Doherty, *Hollywood's Censor: Joseph I. Breen & the Production Code Administration* (New York: Columbia University Press, 2007), 100.

29 Sidney Gottlieb, 'Hitchcock and the Art of the Kiss: A Preliminary Survey', in *Framing Hitchcock: Selected Essays from the Hitchcock Annual*, ed. Sidney Gottlieb and Christopher Brookhouse (Detroit: Wayne State University Press, 2002), 134.

30 George Toles, *A House Made of Light: Essays on the Art of Film* (Detroit: Wayne State University Press, 2001), 172.

31 A brief and by no mean extensive list of examples: *I Confess* (Alfred Hitchcock, 1953, USA), *Marnie* (Alfred Hitchcock, 1964, USA), *Notorious* (Alfred Hitchcock, 1946, USA) and *Strangers on a Train* (Alfred Hitchcock, 1951, USA).

32 Cp. Charles Affron, *Cinema and Sentiment* (Chicago: University of Chicago Press, 1982), 61.
33 Gilles Deleuze, *Cinema 1: The Movement-Image* (Habberjam: University of Minnesota Press, 1986), 17.
34 Stanley Cavell, *The World Viewed: Reflections on the Ontology of Film* (Cambridge, London: Harvard University Press, 1979), 68–69.
35 John Berger, *And our Faces, my Heart, Brief as Photos* (London: Bloomsbury, 2005), 33.
36 Nestingen, *The Cinema of Aki Kaurismäki: Contrarian Stories*, 106.
37 Catherine Russell, *Narrative Mortality: Death, Closure and New Wave Cinemas* (Minneapolis and London: University of Minnesota Press, 1995), 18.
38 Klevan, *Disclosure of the Everyday*, 85.
39 Ibid.
40 Seppälä, 'On the Heterogeneity of Cinematography in the Films of Aki Kaurismäki', 22.
41 Henry Bacon, *The Fascination of Film Violence* (Basingstoke: Palgrave Macmillan, 2015), 170.
42 William S. Pechter, *Twenty-Four Times a Second: Films and Film-Makers* (New York, Evanston, London: Harper & Row, 1971), 128.
43 Manny Farber, 'Introduction to Negative Space', in *Farber on Film: The Complete Film Writings of Manny Farber*, ed. Robert Polito (New York: Library of America, 2009), 696.
44 Perez, *The Material Ghost*, 12.
45 George Wilson, *Narration in Light: Studies in Cinematic Point of View* (Oxford: Oxford University Press, 1989), 39.
46 Susan Sontag, *Against Interpretation* (London: Vintage, 1991), 194.
47 Soila, 'The Landscape of Memories in the Films of the Kaurismäki Bros', 4.
48 Adrian Martin, 'Intimate Metamorphosis: Film & Architectural Space', *Architectural Review Asia-Pacific*, no. 128 (2013), www.australiandesignreview.com/features/28050-intimate-metamorphosis-filmarchitectural-space (accessed 12 March 2017).

Chapter 4

KAURISMÄKI AND JAPAN

Eija Niskanen

Japan has provided one of the most significant overseas markets for Kaurismäki's films, and has also been the source of mutual influence between him and Japanese filmmakers. Kaurismäki has a keen love for the cinema of Yasujiro Ozu, to whom many Japanese also compare his work. 'If I go to a lonely island, the only film I would take with me is *Tokyo Monogatari*,' he has said.[1] The late Peter von Bagh, film scholar, Midnight Sun Film Festival artistic director and a close friend of Kaurismäki, wrote in his book on Kaurismäki's cinema, how, when introducing films for the Finnish Film Archive screenings, he would always see a lanky young man sitting in the front row - the young Aki. Ozu and other Japanese directors such as Kurosawa and Mizoguchi were frequently screened during that time, not only at the film archive, but at the Diana theatre, which Kaurismäki also frequented.[2] Diana was owned by Aito Mäkinen, an importer of Japanese films to Finland.

Influences from Ozu's cinema, including what David Bordwell has defined as the 'parametric style in cinema', can certainly be traced in Kaurismäki's découpage.[3] According to Bordwell, in parametric narration, 'the self-referring aspects of stylistic patterning could create an independent level of the text'.[4] This is achieved 'by creating a narrow and strongly individual bunch of parametric qualities and then repeating them regularly across the film'.[5] Bordwell gives Ozu as an example of a filmmaker utilizing parametric repetition with slight variation, and the same could be said about Kaurismäki's oeuvre. The non-naturalistic acting style of Ozu's films, with formal poses, eternal smiles on the faces of the actors and eye lines slightly passing the camera, works in favour of creating a seemingly very Japanese performance, often seen in the eyes of foreigners as exemplifying Japanese restrained aesthetics, but departing from the more realistic acting employed by Ozu's contemporaries. This formal performance style has in Kaurismäki's films morphed into his working-class protagonists' literary utterances using perfect grammar and their restrained manner of communicating and holding one's space in interaction, especially when a man and woman are becoming romantically entangled. This style, typical to Kaurismäki's contemporaries Jim Jarmusch and Hal Hartley, is also related to the French new wave acting style, especially Godard, including how Godard's actors address the camera. This non-naturalistic performance forms a diametrical opposite to the Method Acting style, which spread in post-war American cinema. Ozu, who is often seen as the 'most Japanese of Japanese directors' is actually not depicting Japanese people in a realistic way. The slight smile and awkward repetition of everyday expressions relating to Japanese small talk exaggerated ad infinitum are echoed in Kaurismäki character's stagy and formal sitting positions, the formal use of correct literary Finnish and frequent references to classical literature in dialogue.

Similarly, the regular cast of actors and the repetition of similar sets and situations from film to film resemble the oeuvre of Ozu, whose films seem to follow on from each other, with Chishu Ryu frequently playing the father and Setsuko Hara often cast as the daughter. Common scenes in Kaurismäki, similar from film to film, include characters enjoying meals or drinks in homes and restaurants, live music gigs and card games. The prevalence of these moments makes the films appear to be almost continuing the same story, just as Ozu's films seem to be an ongoing domestic drama. Kaurismäki also employs frequent shots of Helsinki trams, just like Ozu used shots of Tokyo's trains. The Finnish director uses an ensemble of actors, with Markku Peltola and Sakari Kuosmanen following Matti Pellonpää as recurrent male leads, and Kati Outinen, Maria Järvenhelmi and Kirsi Tykkyläinen in female roles. Newcomers, like Sherwan Haji in *The Other Side of Hope*, adapt to Kaurismäki's acting style. 'I had seen Kaurismäki's films already in the Syrian Art Academy, where a teacher was showing his films, so I knew how you act in his films,' explains Haji.[6] Haji's adoption of the deadpan Kaurismäki style can be seen in the scene where he is forgotten in the restaurant restroom, as Wikström and his staff have been trying to get through a health authority check by hiding Khaled (Haji) and the dog Koistinen there. When released, Khaled explains with a deadpan face how during their long hideout he taught Arabic to the dog, which also converted to Islam.

Furthermore, Kaurismäki's gentle humour, arising from characters' situations, comes close to Ozu's moments of 'nonsense humor'.[7] Both directors' films raise a complex, bittersweet feeling of nostalgia and use pillow shots of unpopulated space as a narrative punctuation at the end and beginning of scenes. In Ozu's films, these include shots of traditional Japanese homes, narrow street views of residential areas and night shots of bar exteriors in Tokyo. Kaurismäki likes to shoot Helsinki streets and harbour at night, along with details of his stylized interior sets. Both Ozu and Kaurismäki have employed a modernist, parametric style in their filmmaking:

Ozu's 360-degree space, low camera angle and empty shots of spaces are famous. Kaurismäki employs similarly recognizable stylistic features, ranging from mostly static camera and simple set design, emphasizing past decades of Finnish working-class interior style, often realized together with head set designer Markku Pätilä. In Ozu's late colour movies, Ozu emphasized his favourite colour, red, by being careful to have one red object in each frame. Kaurismäki emphasizes colour design and selects a limited, but clear colour scheme for each film. In post-production, the colours red and yellow are brought to the surface.[8]

Kaurismäki's films also have several direct references to Japan or to things Japanese, mostly involving music and food. In *The Man Without Past*, the protagonist M (Markku Peltola) finally finds out who he is and that he is married. He says goodbye to Irma (Kati Outinen), with whom he has just started a love affair, and travels north by train to meet his wife. Luckily things turn out well: his wife has found a new man and is willing to get a divorce. Relieved, M travels back south and to Irma. In the train's restaurant car, the waiter brings him a sake *tokkuri*, and M enjoys his sake and a sushi meal. At the same time, 'Hawaii no yoru (A night in Hawaii)' by the Japanese rock and roll group Crazy Ken Band starts playing on the soundtrack – one of the rare occasions when Kaurismäki, who through the rest of the film uses diegetic concert scenes, uses non-diegetic music (or perhaps it is playing through the train's loudspeakers?). In reality, Finnish Railways does not serve sake and sushi on their trains. Hence, by having M enjoy a Japanese meal with the gentle promise of a night in Hawaii, sung in Japanese, Kaurismäki steps into the mind of M, underscoring the relief and happiness of M now that he is able to travel back to Irma as a free single man.[9]

In *The Other Side of Hope*, the sushi motif is foregrounded even more clearly. Early on in the film, a clothes retailer, played by Kati Outinen, buys shirts from the travelling salesman Wikström (Kuosmanen). Wikström is about to leave his job and offers his stock to a character played by Outinen, who refuses, as she is also planning to close shop and to move to Mexico 'to dance hula hula and drink sake'. Later in the film, Wikström has bought a restaurant, but business is slow. An employee suggests adding sushi to the menu, as he has heard it to be fashionable. The restaurant's name is changed from The Golden Pint to Imperial Sushi, and the staff create sushi for a full room of Japanese customers from Finnish canned salted mackerel with full spoonfuls of wasabi on top (Figure 4.1). They are dressed in cheap and clichéd Japanese outfits, including the Syrian refugee Khaled, who has by now been employed by Wikström. The sushi restaurant proves to be disastrous. Here the sushi motif is played for comic effort. It is noteworthy that although Japanese culture, misinterpreted by Wikström and his staff, is brought out in a humorous light, another foreign culture, that of Syria, is treated in serious tones, with the sad music played by Khaled at the refugee centre, underlining the seriousness of his situation.

Kaurismäki's Influence in Japan

A counterflow of influence can be traced in Kaurismäki's impact on Japanese independent filmmakers such as Nobuhiro Yamashita. 'My generation of Japanese filmmakers sure got influenced by Kaurismäki,' says Yamashita, born in 1976, about two decades later than Kaurismäki. One reason could be the mutual liking of Finns and Japanese, who see in each other's long silences, shyness and humble behaviour, punctuated by drinking buddy camaraderie, something familiar. These are the types of characters that Kaurismäki likes to depict.

Figure 4.1 The staff of The Golden Pint try going Japanese in *The Other Side of Hope* (2017). Photographer: Malla Hukkanen. © and courtesy Malla Hukkanen and Sputnik Ltd.

Kaurismäki's sympathetic underdogs are similar to some of Japanese independent filmmakers' characters. For example, Yamashita's *Ramblers* (*Riarizumu no yado*, 2003) features two seemingly aimless wanderers in the Japanese countryside, encountering eccentric characters and situations, in a toned-down humour. 'I was told when I started making films that they resemble Kaurismäki's films. I think people saw my regular actor from that time, Hiroshi Yamamoto, who acts in a very straight-faced style, resembling typical Kaurismäki acting style,' says Yamashita.[10]

Another Japanese indie director who calls himself a fan of Kaurismäki is Hirobumi Watanabe (born 1982). When Watanabe's first feature, *And the Mud Ship Sails On* (*Soshite Dorobune wa Yuku*, 2014), was screened at Helsinki Cine Aasia festival, Watanabe was delighted to find out that his film was showing in the Kaurismäki brothers' Andorra film theatre. Watanabe's films have eccentric rural characters, who have a hard time confirming to the social norms. They are underdogs, unemployed or in low status jobs that require no official training. They are thus similar to Kaurismäki's characters, who often work in jobs that Kaurismäki himself used to do before launching full time in filmmaking (restaurant work, construction, etc.) or what his father's occupation was (travelling salesman). Watanabe himself has worked both as a farm helper, like the protagonist of *Seven Days* (2015), and as a municipal pool assistant, like the main character in *Poolsideman* (2016). Watanabe's silent protagonists, surviving day to day in surrealistically repeating situations, form a weird, black humour which could be called Kaurismäkian.

Influences can also be traced in Naoko Ogigami's films. Bufo production company head Mark Lwoff, who co-produced *The Other Side of Hope*, worked as an assistant director for Ogigami's film *Kamome Diner* (*Kamome shokudo*, 2006), shot on location in Helsinki. One of the Finnish actors appearing in the film is Markku Peltola, the lead actor in *The Man Without a Past*. In Ogigami's films, the silent, eccentric outsiders are female characters, who tend their *onigiri* (Japanese rice ball) restaurants as carefully as Kaurismäki's restaurant owners run their small enterprises.

A complicated nostalgia for past decades is another theme pleasing to Japanese audiences. During this millennium, a phenomenon labelled as 'Showa nostalgia' has become visible. Showa era, meaning the time of Emperor Hirohito's rule (1926–89), is detectable in films, TV dramas, anime, design patterns, theme restaurants, coffee shops and such. The most popular times for reference are those around the 1960s (Showa 30s), which accord with Kaurismäki's love of the early 1960s, even though the exact details of mise en scène may be very different.

Masato Hojo from Eurospace, Kaurismäki films' distributor in Japan, argues that the resemblance to Ozu is a key factor in his popularity in Japan: 'Kaurismäki and Ozu do not overtly show emotions, but under the cool surface there is a warm heart', says Hojo.[11] He considers that Kaurismäki's films are 'adult fairytales', not strictly realistic depictions of humans or society, but stylized little worlds. Finnish and Japanese people have a somewhat similar sense of humour, claims Hojo. Also silences and shyness connect these two nations: 'Finnish and Japanese men don't talk when they are interested in a woman. That is totally opposite to French people, who talk a lot.' He suggests that the silent female characters of Kaurismäki resemble 'typical' ideas of Japanese women. Hojo also thinks that Kaurismäki makes films that appeal to both cinephiles and ordinary people, as they are not hard to understand. Kaurismäki's quirky cinematic style has proved to be so popular in Japan that a Japanese fashion label, Earth Music & Ecology, ran a series of advertisements which were shot in Finland on typical Kaurismäki locations (and one in a bar owned by the Kaurismäki brothers), featuring the famous Japanese actress Aoi Miyazaki surrounded by Finnish characters who very much look like Kaurismäki film regulars.

Perhaps the oddest filmic homage to Kaurismäki in Japan is by Riichiro Mashima in his mockumentary *Ski Jumping Pairs* (2003). In this fake documentary, a Hokkaido-based professor invents a new winter Olympic sport: ski jumping in pairs with two jumpers on the same skis. In the first international competition for this new sport, several national pairs gather in Hokkaido to compete, including Finland's representatives, the brothers Aki and Mika Kaurismäki. The jumping sequences and the unrealistically sporty-looking Kaurismäki brothers on skis are executed in flash animation.

The mutual love of Kaurismäki for Japan and Japanese filmmakers and cinephiles for Kaurismäki has flourished for decades. Kaurismäki has crafted his films with the same dedication to cinema and its inheritance as Japanese people do with their traditional crafts. His silent melodrama *Juha* was premiered in Japan as a *benshi* performance, with the famous female *benshi* Midori Sawato performing all the character voices and giving extra explanations about locations such as 'Helsinki Railway station'. Kaurismäki sat in the audience and went on stage after the film to thank the performer with a kiss on her hand. The performance was a combination of homage to the first filmed version of *Juha*, during the silent era, and the *benshi* tradition of Japanese cinematic history. Kaurismäki has grown to be a cult figure in Japan with film fans following him and the actors and the musicians who appear in his films. But in the end, it is the taciturn characters in his films, and the audiences in cinemas, Finnish or Japanese, who find a connection over the projections on screen.

Notes

1   Asahi Shinbun interview https://www.youtube.com/watch?v=PdX0Tyt7I4Q. Sodankylä, Midnight Sun Film Festival, 2014. Kaurismäki also says that Japanese culture and aesthetics, with its harmony in even small details, fascinate him.
2   Peter von Bagh, *Aki Kaurismäki*, 2006, pp. 6, 8. In von Bagh's interview, Kaurismäki tells how as a young man arriving in Helsinki he would deliver newspapers during the early mornings and then have a strict programme of film viewings at the film archive theatre and other venues. He claims to have known his film viewing schedule months ahead. Ibid., p. 18.
3   David Bordwell, *Narration in the Fiction Film* (Madison, WI: University of Wisconsin Press, 1985), 274–310.
4   Ibid., p. 277.
5   Ibid., p. 286.
6   Sherwan Haji, at *The Other Side of Hope* press event, Andorra film theatre, Helsinki.
7   David Bordwell, *Ozu and the Poetics of Cinema* (Ann Arbor, MI: Michigan Publishing, University of Michigan Library, 1988) 18, 54, 68, 151, 154–5, 348.
8   Von Bagh, *Aki Kaurismäki*, p. 184.
9   Kaurismäki's interest in Japanese music led him to produce in 2012 a CD of Finnish songs sung in Japanese by Toshitake Shinohara.
10 Eija Niskanen, Interview with Nobuhiro Yamashita. Udine Far East Film Festival, April 28, 2017.
11 Eija Niskanen, Interview with Masato Hojo, Eurospace office, Shibuya, Tokyo, March, 2017.

Part II

TONE AND POINT OF VIEW

Chapter 5

THE CAMERA'S IRONIC POINT OF VIEW: NOTES ON STRANGE AND COMIC ELEMENTS IN THE FILMS OF AKI KAURISMÄKI

Jaakko Seppälä

Aki Kaurismäki is known for making melancholic films that discuss pressing social issues from poverty to loneliness; yet paradoxically his films have a reputation for being funny. It is known that 'many have walked out of his films uncertain whether they have seen a comedy at all'. As Andrew Nestingen argues, the cinema of Kaurismäki is characterized by contradictions.[1] Even the filmmaker proclaims: 'Never take what I say seriously. Irony is my style.'[2] When it comes to Kaurismäki's public performances, this is a matter of fact. He often speaks in self-deprecatory and contradictory terms with the intention of making fun of the questions he is being asked. And in Kaurismäki's feature-length fictional films, things are frequently said and shown as if in inverted commas, no matter how serious they are. This is a characteristic of postmodern artworks,[3] a category into which Kaurismäki's seemingly classical films can be productively placed.[4] Because Kaurismäki's 'irony works against the possibility of empathy',[5] it can be difficult for the audience to assess whether the filmmaker is being sincere or simply tongue-in-cheek. But irony and empathy are not mutually exclusive; rather, in Kaurismäki's films, they habitually coexist. There has been a consensus among critics ever since the early 1980s that Kaurismäki's films are ironic,[6] but the ways in which irony manifests itself in his systematic and significant use of cinematic devices and how these are aimed at eliciting thoughts and emotions in the audience have not been explored in detail. The current critical understanding of his cinema is partial at best.

An illuminating example of saying and showing things as if in inverted commas is the sequence in *Hamlet liikemaailmassa* (Hamlet Goes Business, 1987) in which the titular character talks about his miserable life to his chauffeur. 'Do you know what I do first thing in the morning?' 'I don't care,' the chauffeur replies. 'I throw up. That's how bad I feel.'

Even though the dialogue is absurd, it is delivered in literary Finnish with a serious voice, devoid of emotion, slang intonation and contemporary phrasings. In the real world, while all Finns hardly speak in the same way, to be sure, almost nobody speaks like this. There is a quality of strangeness to the dialogue that is aimed at making it amusing. But looking at the serious faces of the characters, they do not find any humour in Hamlet's comment. The discrepancy between the spoken words and bodily language only adds to the strangely comic nature of the conversation. The sequence is typical for Kaurismäki: for the characters, there is nothing amusing in their actions and discussions, but the audience can find them humorous. As Sanna Maskulin argues, Kaurismäki's dialogue is self-conscious, even artificial, and often challenges the continuity of fictional reality.[7] The same can be said of his mise en scène. Hence, I do not fully agree with Pietari Kääpä who suggests that the world of Kaurismäki's films is conveyed to the audience as the protagonists view it.[8] The matter is more complicated than that because Kaurismäki plays on a disjunction between character and audience point of view: the audience can see and hear things as strange or comic, but the characters usually cannot – this is dramatic irony.

Focusing on Kaurismäki's collaborations with his praised cinematographer Timo Salminen,[9] I examine how the camera guides the audience to respond to the diegetic world and its characters, regardless of whether that response is actually experienced. My anthropomorphic concept of the camera's character refers to the audience's possible experience of a camera as a human-like entity that has a personality. The examination will add a new layer to my argument that the camera offers the audience a minimalist point of view that resembles the way in which Kaurismäki's protagonists view the world and directs the audience to experience the films in a certain way. The point of view can be metaphorically described as 'that of a socially excluded, sympathetic stranger who observes people and their gestures with keen interest and would like to engage with them, but is unable to make his presence known'.[10] Here my argument is that the camera provides the audience with a double perspective that allows viewers to see the dramatic world from a point of view that is close to that of the characters and from a point of view that clearly surpasses that of the characters. According to Claire Colebrook, 'irony tends towards the multiplication of viewpoints and incoherence'.[11] Following her idea, I argue that the latter perspective is the camera's ironic point of view, the function of which is to indicate that the represented events should not be taken too seriously. This point of view creates aesthetic distance. The two points of view are partly overlapping and partly competing with each other, which explains why the audience experiences are often contradictory.

I will begin my analysis of the camera's ironic point of view by briefly discussing the concept of irony, after which I will explore in detail some of Kaurismäki's ironic camera techniques. Then I will closely analyse the camera's role in the surreal and quirky sequences of his feature-length fictional films, indicating how cinematography correlates with other cinematic devices to create irony.

Making Sense of Cinematographic Irony

The difficulty involved in analysing irony in film lies partly in that throughout its history, the concept has been used in various ways.[12] When it comes to analysing films that are experienced as ironic, one cannot define irony as saying one thing and meaning the opposite, as that explains very little. According to Linda Hutcheon, 'in visual art [...] it is possible to think of irony [...] as a process of communication that entails two or more meanings played off, one against the other'.[13] In cinema, such playful communication processes can encompass visual and auditory elements. The sequence in *Hamlet Goes Business* is ironic because the titular character looks and sounds totally honest when he says that he throws up first thing in the morning, even though nothing else in the film supports his absurd claim. There is a discrepancy between the spoken words and the way things are in the story world: the character is speaking the truth, but the mise en scène indicates that this cannot be the truth. Because one cannot say that Hamlet is saying something and meaning something else, it would be a mistake to conclude that Hamlet is being ironic. But then again, if this is irony and it is not Hamlet who is being ironic, who is? I argue that it is Kaurismäki himself. He is telling the profound story of William Shakespeare's classic play, but at the same time, he undermines the seriousness of its treatment with the ridiculous comment. 'Because it has a fundamentally expressive purpose, irony often conveys no factual information,' Gregory Currie argues.[14] This is absolutely true when it comes to the sequence, as the comment could be removed from the film without violating the story in any way.

I define the concept of irony rather loosely, as a playful juxtaposition of cinematic elements that function as, to borrow the words of Currie, 'an expression of the film-maker's ironic attitude to the project'.[15] When it comes to Kaurismäki's representations of his characters and their affairs, he seems to take them more seriously than he actually does: the strange and comic elements are an expression of his ironic attitude. According to Nestingen, Kaurismäki 'uses the image ironically, always saying something slightly different than he means'.[16] Anu Koivunen agrees with him in that Kaurismäki's 'irony requires a shared understanding of a text's different levels, of what it says and what it means'.[17] There is some truth in these claims, but the important thing to notice is that it is often impossible to say what Kaurismäki means. His irony has a lot in common with romantic irony where 'what is said is both meant and not meant'[18] at the same time. Hamlet speaks the truth, but the audience is guided to think that he cannot be speaking the truth. As the example illustrates, Kaurismäki's irony does not necessarily solve contradictions; on the contrary: it typically intensifies them, which is productive and engaging in his aesthetic discourse.

Currie makes an analytically illuminating distinction between representations of irony and ironic representations.[19] The difference is that a shot can be of an ironic situation or it can be ironic in nature. When it comes to analysing cinematography, I think these categories form a continuum. Even ironic situations of a simple kind need to be shot in a way that prompts the audience to notice the irony. Thus, the camera always participates in the creation of visual irony. An example from the other end of the continuum would be a shot that makes a neutral situation seem ironic due to a cinematographic technique. In short, cinematography cannot be analysed without closely looking at mise en scène as well. This kind of irony has a lot in common with visual comedy, especially with what Noël Carroll has termed the 'sight gag': 'a form of visual humor in which amusement is generated by the play of alternative interpretations projected by the image or image series'.[20]

Irony divides the audience into those who get it and those who do not. Viewers can also interpret ironies where none are intended. So how can one recognize irony? Wayne C. Booth is of the opinion that 'anyone who can develop a pattern of expectations, and then recognize that it has been falsely suggested and then violated, can recognise irony'.[21] Colebrook makes a similar point by claiming that 'a word is being used ironically when it seems out of place or unconventional'[22] in its context and violates assumed norms and values. I think these arguments are true of camera techniques as well. But as Hutcheon reminds one, 'nothing is an irony signal in and of itself'.[23] Following Colebrook's rule of thumb, I will begin my analysis of visual irony in Kaurismäki's feature-length fictional films by exploring those camera techniques that seem out of place, unconventional or just strange in their contexts but participate in a process of communication where meanings are played off, one against the other. Because these are deviations from cinematic conventions that Kaurismäki typically follows, it is reasonable to suppose they are intentional. On the continuum, these techniques tend to be at the end of the representational ironies.

Ironic Camera Techniques

When compared to Kaurismäki's minimalist camera techniques,[24] his ironic camera techniques are a more heterogeneous group. Some of the techniques have been used only once while others have been used repeatedly but in modified forms. The techniques that I have chosen for detailed analysis include cuts from close views to large views, ironically open closed framings, cropped views of characters and anticipatory camera movements. The list is not exhaustive. All ironic camera techniques add comedy and strangeness to the films, always indicating that the filmmaker is being tongue-in-cheek.

It is the convention of mainstream filmmakers to open a scene with an establishing shot that shows all the important areas of the space from which they then cut to closer views of the space. This tactic is analytical editing. It makes sure the audience knows where everything is located in the scene's space even at times when only parts of the space are shown. Kaurismäki occasionally reverses the order by cutting from a smaller opening view to a larger view to create a strange or comic contrast. A good example is found in *Tulitikkutehtaan tyttö* (The Match Factory Girl, 1989), which tells the story of Iris Rukka, who at one point of the story moves to her brother's apartment after their stepfather has thrown her out. In a relatively flat, long take, the camera follows Iris in a long medium shot as she walks to her brother's jukebox, turns it on and then walks back to a corner of the room where she sits down and begins to smoke a cigarette in her loneliness. When she has sat for as long as 47 seconds, Kaurismäki shows the apartment properly for the first time by cutting from the long medium shot to a long shot. Contrary to what the evoked schemas have guided the audience to expect, the room is dominated by a full-size pool table that fills the vast majority of the space. Next to the massive green table and colourful balls that lie on it lonesome Iris looks pale and out of place, even ridiculous. It is as if the camera was bored and decided to amuse itself by creating a sight gag. The sequence is an instance of visual irony where emotional sincerity is mixed with a distanced way of looking at it, which dampens the sympathetic effect by making the moment both melancholic and humorous.

Kaurismäki makes 'closed films'[25] in that 'the frame of the screen totally defines the world inside as a picture frame does'.[26] But at times, Kaurismäki's closed frames are ironically open, which makes the closed nature of his cinema strangely funny. An illuminating example is found in *Hamlet Goes Business*. When Hamlet and Ophelia are strolling in Helsinki at night, they stop by a shop window. The characters look at items on display in a long take that is shot from where the window is supposed to be. 'See anything you'd fancy there?' Hamlet, who tries to seduce Ophelia, asks. 'No. I want ice cream,' she replies. Hamlet exits the frame to the right for 12 seconds, but the camera stays in its place and keeps rolling. During the seconds Hamlet is away, the audience can hear his footsteps receding and then closing in. He returns to Ophelia and hands her an ice cream in a cone: 'There you go.' The shot is strange and comic because the audience is unexpectedly guided to think that there is an ice cream stand somewhere beyond the fixed frame, even though nothing in the frame suggests that there is. The punchline is that Hamlet can reach the stand, buy the ice cream and return to Ophelia in approximately 10 seconds, which is of course impossible in the real world. In a sense, the ice cream stand is there and is not there at the same time. The function of the ironically open closed frame is to evoke mirth by indicating that the off-screen space of the film is even more artificial than the closed screen space.

An attention-grabbing variation of the ironically open closed frame is found in *Calamari Union* (1985). The film ends with a sequence in which two characters (both named Frank, just as most major characters in this films) leave Helsinki in their attempt to reach Estonia by a small rowing boat. As they are on their way, the camera unexpectedly turns its gaze away from the Franks and shows only water when an explosion is heard on the soundtrack. The irony lies in that when something crucial happens in the diegesis, the camera decides not to show it. Here it is playing its tricks on the audience. It is difficult to figure out what happens in the off-screen space because there is nothing in the film on which interpretations can be grounded. This is atypical for Kaurismäki. In a sense, the boat is blown to pieces and is not blown to pieces. In the context of the explosion, the camera movement is a strange and disorienting joke. Whereas Hamlet departs from the frame in the example mentioned earlier, here it is the frame that departs from the Franks. In both cases, the ironically open closed framings heighten the artificial nature of the closed films.

Kaurismäki occasionally crops parts of his characters off the screen, which is another way in which he uses framing in the service of visual irony. When Henry Boulanger has lost his job in the drab office of Her Majesty's Waterworks in *I Hired a Contract Killer* (1990), the camera shows the static character sitting next to his desk, but the framing is unconventional: Boulanger's head is cropped out of the image. The job has been his whole life. By cropping Boulanger's head off the screen, the camera makes an exaggerated statement that he has just been executed as if by a guillotine. The camera makes a humorous comment by juxtaposing his actual dismissal with an idea of execution. It is obvious that Boulanger feels bad, but instead of representing his situation and emotions with dignity and sincerity, the camera makes an amusing statement on his condition. In short, the cropping has a motivation in the drama of the film, but visually the device is so powerful that it guides the audience to experience it as ironically overstated.

Kaurismäki's camera, which moves more often than critics have realized,[27] can uncannily know what is about to happen before it actually happens – hence, it can be called anticipatory. The audience can become aware of this by looking at how the camera moves. One example of this is found in *Laitakaupungin valot* (Lights in the Dusk, 2006). Before the femme fatale of the film, Mirja, seduces the lonely security guard Koistinen in a bar, she orders herself a cup of coffee. The audience first sees Mirja in a long shot as she walks towards the camera. The shot is carefully framed when it comes to the representation of the bar, but untypically for Kaurismäki, there is a lot of headroom above Mirja while her feet are partly cropped. As she reaches the counter, the camera pans to the left, tilting up a bit. It has to tilt because the man behind the counter is so very tall that his head would not have been visible in the original framing, even though there was a lot of headroom waiting for him. The climax of the shot in which the characters stand facing one another is amusing as it juxtaposes the extremely tall bartender and medium-height Mirja for comic effect that does not serve the story in any way. This is the moment that the camera had planned to reach. Had Kaurismäki not had that extra headroom in the opening of the shot, the camera would have had to tilt a lot more, which would have called attention to the camera movement at the expense of the tongue-in-cheek composition.

In the examples mentioned earlier, the camera enables the audience to see the world in a way in which the characters cannot see it. To state the obvious, because the characters are not aware of the camera, they cannot feel insulted when the camera decides to play its tricks on them. While the ironic camera techniques are perceptually powerful and add to the strange comedy of the films, they do not advance the audience's understanding of the plots or characters. The techniques are aimed to call attention to themselves and/or the effects they create; they are designed to elicit pleasant artefact emotions,[28] as Ed S. Tan would put it. Considering that Kaurismäki's ironic camera techniques retain a perceptual interest beyond their narrative functions, they are, to use Kristin Thompson's concept, instances of excess.[29] Thus, Kääpä is absolutely right in stating that the films 'combine minimalism and excess'.[30] The function of this excess is to alert the audience to various forms of humour of the films.[31] I argue that Kaurismäki's excess of this kind is ironic in nature, as he uses it to express his playful attitude to the events. In what follows, I will scrutinize the many surreal and quirky sequences of Kaurismäki's films that are best understood as manifestations of his ironic attitude. On the continuum, these are closer to the end of representations of irony, but there are exceptions.

The Surrealism of Everyday Life

'I am a surrealist of the 1980s',[32] Kaurismäki once remarked. He admires the surreal cinema of Luis Buñuel, but little is known about the latter as an influence. Henry Bacon comes close to discussing the role of surrealism in Kaurismäki's cinema in his analysis of the filmmaker's style as the poetics of displacement, as his cinema makes no claim to conventional realism.[33] According to Bacon, Kaurismäki's films are characterized by elements such as restrained acting and absurd dialogue that together create a sense of everyday life that is distinguished by weirdness. As Mary Ann Caws has put it, 'Surrealism is above all about discovering the terrains of the extraordinary in the midst of the ordinary, quotidian world.'[34] Kaurismäki is a surrealist in the sense that he aims to evoke a sense of strangeness by juxtaposing ordinary and peculiar elements in a context that is straightforward and understandable. Angela Dalle Vacche argues that 'the celebration of displacement and unexpected analogies' was at the heart of the surrealist movement that aimed to 'shock, jolt, and twist'.[35] Typically in the art works of the movement, the contrasted elements were so far removed from one another that their appearance together was irrational. Because of the various juxtapositions, the world of Kaurismäki's films is simultaneously real and surreal, at times even magical. The influence of Buñuel is evident in the disorienting aspects of Kaurismäki's films. After all, Buñuel is celebrated for having 'advocated new realism in cinema, a new and unconventional way of seeing the everyday world that was both socially critical and marvellous and irrational'.[36] This is exactly what Kaurismäki does when he relies on 'bizzare designs and juxtapositions'[37] that can seem out of place in his socially critical films. While Buñuel 'sought to tap the unconscious mind' with 'startling juxtapositions' and stories that 'follow the inexplicable logic of a dream',[38] Kaurismäki's surrealism is not this radical. The world of his films appears only borderline surreal. Kaurismäki's vein of surrealism is best understood as the surrealism of everyday life. This is my concept for a very mild form of surrealism that manifests itself in peculiar cinematic elements that lack a narrative or realistic motivation and can thus disorient the audience. I will start by looking at the mildest forms of Kaurismäki's surrealism and move from there towards more striking instances.

An illuminating example of the surrealism of everyday life is found in *Le Havre*. After inspector Henri Monet has had a conversation with the greengrocer, he spontaneously buys a pineapple. The pineapple is an everyday item, but in this sequence, it seems to contrive a strange atmosphere, which emanates from deep inside. One reason for this is that there was no way for the audience to know that Monet would buy the fruit because it is not related to his work, which has motivated his actions so far. Furthermore, the pineapple stands out in the full shot because it is contrasted with Monet's all-black clothes. Hence the fruit looks out of place and humorous in his hands. Kaurismäki opens the next scene, in which Monet enters a local bar, with a camera movement that follows the pineapple in an extreme close-up. The fruit is the important detail, the camera implies. He sits down and puts the pineapple on an empty table while everyone in the bar stares at him and his purchase. 'Is it for me?' the owner of the place, who comes to talk with Monet, asks. 'No.' The pineapple is not seen again, and the question why he bought it does not get answered. The fruit is an enigma, a mysterious element that Kaurismäki plays off against the comprehensibility of the world of the film: its function is to puzzle the audience.

Typically, everything within the world of a closed film has its place in the plot of the film,[39] but the pineapple has no narrative function whatsoever. 'I didn't write the character very well, and the pineapple just happened to be there,'[40] Kaurismäki explains. 'Then I remembered *Nazarín* [Buñuel, 1959] – in the last scene he's [the titular character] walking with the pineapple in Calanda.' Kaurismäki does not say what it was that impressed him in this sequence, but in an earlier interview, the filmmaker mentioned he admires Buñuel's skills in bringing objects to life.[41] In the Calanda sequence, Buñuel has done just that.[42]

Thus, *Le Havre's* pineapple sequence can be understood as Kaurismäki's tribute to Buñuel whose films display 'cluttered landscapes composed of a heteroclite collection of "random" objects (whose illogical juxtapositions recall the fundamental principles of Surrealism)'.[43]

The pineapple sequence is a good example of how representations of irony often get fused with representational irony. According to what is known as Hitchcock's rule, 'The size of an object in the frame should be directly related to its importance at that moment'.[44] The close framing and the camera movement guide the audience to pay particular attention to the fruit. Were these techniques not used, the audience might not think twice about the pineapple's function in the narrative, and thus it might not disorient. The joke is that the camera techniques make the fruit seem like an important element in the narrative even though it is not. The sequence is an instance of visual irony in which the sense of disorientation arises from the juxtaposition of the profilmic elements and camera techniques in the context of the story. An orange has a similar function in *The Match Factory Girl*.[45]

The world of Kaurismäki's films is strange, but its surreal elements rarely get attention from his characters. As Felicity Gee puts it, 'neither magic realism nor Surrealism questions the believability of marvellous events, they are part of the reality'.[46] An early example of this is found in *Rikos ja rangaistus* (Crime and Punishment, 1983). The protagonist of the film, murderer Antti Rahikainen, is planning to escape the police who are after him by taking a ferry with his friend to Sweden. When Rahikainen arrives by car to pick up the friend, he is shown sitting on a red children's tricycle. Its presence is not emphasized in any way: it is a small, strange detail in the extreme long shot for the audience to spot. As the sequence takes place in a forlorn harbour, the tricycle looks out of place. Questions that the sequence can evoke in the audience – why the friend is sitting on the tricycle that is too small for him and why it is in the harbour in the first place – do not puzzle the characters in the least. The tricycle is an example of a barely noticeable surreal element that the characters are not interested in, but the audience can find perplexing. Like the pineapple, the tricycle is a visual joke that has no function in the narrative. It is as if the camera is interested in situations it finds amusing, but the characters see differently.

Some of Kaurismäki's films contain juxtapositions that are significantly more surreal, for instance, *Leningrad Cowboys Go America* (1989) and *Juha* (1999). The first-mentioned begins with a sequence in which a useless band plays its music to (what the credits identify as) Siberian Svengali in a ramshackle barn 'somewhere in tundra … in no man's land', as an intertitle informs the audience. When the band's manager is told to take his group to America, he makes a long-distance phone call. The camera shows him in a medium close-up talking on a payphone. In the previous shot, the musicians were watching their manager and listening to his call from a window in the barn, but the location of the telephone was not made explicit. The following shot is a long shot in which the manager hangs up. The audience can now see that the payphone is fastened to the wall of the barn. It is as if the camera wanted to create tension before revealing where the phone is located. The juxtaposition of the ramshackle building and the payphone is absurd, and not least because the barn is not connected to telephone lines. Even though the payphone has a narrative function, it calls attention to itself and appears displaced because its presence on the wall is anything but realistically motivated. Whereas Buñuel's surreal juxtapositions are sexually loaded and dreamlike, those of Kaurismäki are better described as comic or simply strange.

Another disjointed juxtaposition is found in the sequence in *Juha* in which the titular character tries to fix a broken sports car with the biggest imaginable spanner. In a full shot, he uses the spanner on the engine, lifts the tool to adjust it a bit and continues the work. The full shot enables the audience to see both the huge tool and the fancy car at the same time. The shot is outright absurd because there is no way someone could fix an engine of a sports car with such an unpractical tool, and yet that is precisely what Juha is doing. It is as if the camera is quietly smiling at him. Both this sequence and the one in *Leningrad Cowboys Go America* recall silent slapstick comedies that relied on bizarre juxtaposition.

Buñuel's surrealist masterpiece *L'Age d'Or* (1930) is a film Kaurismäki loves.[47] He has not tried to replicate its radically disjointed structure and dreamlike atmosphere in his own films, except in certain sequences in his most surreal works *Calamari Union* and *Take Care of Your Scarf, Tatjana* (1993). The moments I will now analyse are departures from Kaurismäki's style (and therefore from the camera's character), but they are worth discussing in this context. In the sequence in *Calamari Union* that is set on an airport, one of the sixteen men named Frank on their odyssey from Kallio to Eira blames a woman for destroying her own life by working as a secretary. After the woman has unexpectedly shot Frank, she walks towards the camera with the purpose of leaving the crime scene. This shot is followed by a shot in which she opens a door and comes to a quiet street in Helsinki. This is an instance of continuity editing where two locations that simply cannot be located next to one another are connected: the airport and the quiet street in Helsinki.

The most surreal shot in Kaurismäki's cinema is found in *Take Care of Your Scarf, Tatjana*. In it, Valtto drives his black station wagon Volga through a window into a lonely cafeteria. Because the camera is waiting for the car inside the cafeteria, as if uncannily anticipating what is about to happen, the full shot is not only strange but also dreamlike. As the previous shot showed Valtto deep in his thoughts on a ferry from Estonia to Finland, the audience is guided to think that he is dreaming. But to complicate the matter, the cafeteria sequence ends abruptly with an extreme long shot in which Valtto is leaning on a kiosk somewhere in Finland. Critics have offered different interpretations of the sequence,[48] but it is difficult to license these to any significant degree by what one can reasonably hypothesize are the filmmaker's intentions, as the sequence is underdetermined. This is a characteristic of surrealism: 'even less than in other artistic and literary movements will one reading suffice'.[49]

Kaurismäki's more sombre melodramas contain some magical and dreamy sequences, but they are not even nearly as obtrusive as the ones just analysed. For example, when a garbage collector dies of a heart attack in *Varjoja paratiisissa* (Shadows in Paradise, 1986), the audience is shown a black dog running across a forsaken landscape. There is little to suggest what the dog represents, but it can be seen as standing for the freed soul of the garbage collector. This particular juxtaposition is better described as poignant than funny. Its likely influence is Buñuel's *Los Olvidados* (1950) in which Jaibo, the leader of a juvenile gang, dies and in a magical sequence seems to metamorphose into dog form.

The Quirky Touch

Kaurismäki's films are often compared to those of his friend Jim Jarmusch. When asked why their films are alike, the latter joked: 'I steal all my ideas from Kaurismäki so that is what explains it.'[50] The cinema of Jarmusch is also characterized by irony. He says: 'I don't think my characters are flippantly ironic in their attitudes, but their stories – their gestures – are very ironic.'[51] Critics and reviewers call Jarmusch's films quirky. 'Man, is it the only adjective they know? [...] It's like every time I make a goddamn movie, the word "quirky" is hauled out,'[52] he complains. The aesthetics of quirky have attracted critical attention recently. According to Geoff King, quirkiness is 'a matter of slightly unusual juxtapositions, combinations or variations, either of characters/objects, events or in various aspects of audio-visual form.'[53] Thus, what is quirky is often ironic in the sense that I use the concept here – a process of communication where meanings are played off, one against the other.

The word 'quirky' has been used occasionally in discussions on Kaurismäki's films,[54] but it is more closely associated with postmodern American independent films such as *Rushmore* (1998), *Punch-Drunk Love* (2002) and *Juno* (2007). When it comes to quirky aesthetics, the similarities between these works and those of Kaurismäki are remarkable, as I demonstrate later. Considering that Kaurismäki has influenced Jarmusch[55] (and the other way around, no doubt) and that the latter has influenced a whole generation of American independent filmmakers,[56] it might even be that Kaurismäki has played some role in the development of quirky aesthetics, which I understand as a domesticated postmodern form of modernist innovation. In the place of actual innovation, which is impossible since it has all been done already, the quirkiness of filmmaker and characters comes to be a key topos in the films. Here I analyse *Mies vailla menneisyyttä* (The Man Without a Past, 2002) as an example of the quirkiness in Kaurismäki's cinema.[57] In its quirkiness, it is fairly representative of Kaurismäki's oeuvre, but some of his films (*The Other Side of Hope*, 2017) are significantly quirkier than others (*Crime and Punishment*).

James MacDowell argues that 'the quirky is closely related to the comedic'.[58] He sees as a unique feature of quirky films the combination of three comedic modes: slapstick, pathetic yet poignant and deadpan. I have discussed Kaurismäki's use of surreal juxtapositions that are reminiscent of silent slapstick films, but I now want to add that his films contain moments of physical comedy without realistic consequences, too. When badly beaten M, the protagonist of *The Man Without a Past*, lies in a hospital bed, he is swathed in bandages like the titular characters in *The Mummy* (1932) and *The Invisible Man* (1933). After being pronounced dead, he gets up looking like an undead and sees his face in a mirror (Figure 5.1). The camera anticipates what is about to happen and guides attention to his nose by showing it in the middle of the frame: the nose is big and crooked because of the beating. M straightens it with his bare hands, and the audience can hear a violent bone-crushing

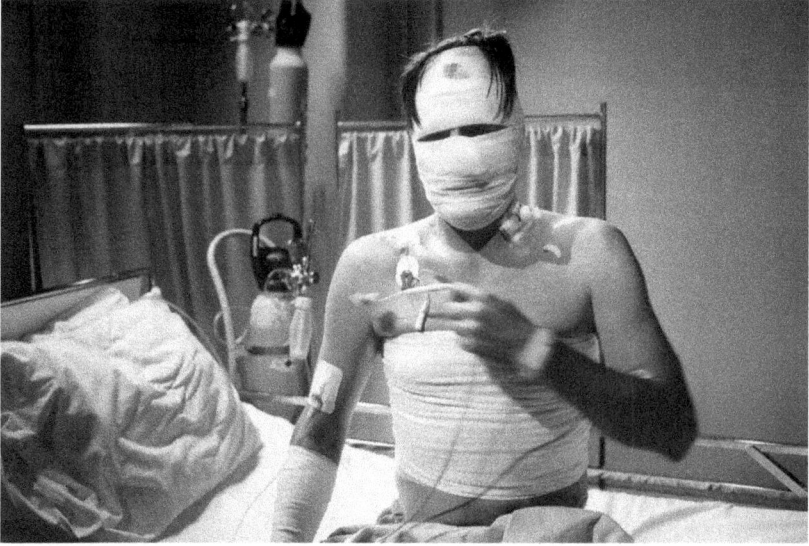

Figure 5.1 M (Markku Peltola) rises from his hospital bed in *The Man Without a Past* (2002). Photographer: Malla Hukkanen. © and courtesy Sputnik Ltd.

sound. Now that the nose is fixed, delicate music adds an ironic contrast by rising to a crescendo as if promising a new, better future for M. Unlike in this incongruous sequence (that recalls moments when slapstick comedians fix their postures after a beating), in real life, the operation would be painful and would end badly.

Kaurismäki's characters and the situations in which the camera finds them are often pathetic yet poignant. After being told that he needs to pull himself together, M, who has become a member of a community of the underprivileged living in abandoned sea containers, wants to get his clothes washed. He asks for help from a friend of his but learns that the friend does not have any credit and therefore no washing machine. 'But my neighbour has one, because he's wealthy,' the friend says and nods towards the off-screen space on the left. Together with the conversation the nod evokes expectations about the washing machine. Contrary to what widely shared schemas guide the audience to expect, the washing machine, which is now shown in a long medium shot as M uses it, is an antiquated, hand-operated model. Thus, the juxtaposition of these two shots creates an ironic effect. The audience is guided to see the washing machine as the characters see it, as a luxury item. Yet, in comparison to real-world standards, it is a piece of junk from a bygone era. Here the characters are situated as simultaneously pathetic and poignant as a result of which the audience can feel pity for the characters, as they do not have anything better than the rusty old machine but also envy them. Indeed, ironically enough, the characters are content with what they have.[59] To put it differently, in this era of plenty, it is possible to envy the characters for being happy with so little.

The camera repeatedly contributes to Kaurismäki's signature understated style of deadpan comedy. When the coarse security guard Anttila, from whom M has rented a container, comes to collect rent, he has his 'killer dog' with him. As Anttila steps inside the makeshift home, the first thing the camera shows is the mutt at his feet in a medium shot. It puts the emphasis on the dog, raising expectations about its role in the sequence. This is the first time when the audience sees the mutt properly, the role of which, Anttila has guaranteed, is to bite M's nose off if he does not pay his rent in time. Contradicting Anttila's threats, the dog appears to be friendly. The joke is that Anttila believes he has bought himself a beast and acts accordingly. 'Looks cosy. Perhaps I should raise the rent,' he remarks to M. 'That's what I wanted to talk about. I can't pay until Friday.' Now the audience is shown a medium close-up of Anttila's static and serious face: he shifts his gaze down at his feet where the mutt is. In the following shot, the animal is shown in a close view as Anttila drops the lead to the floor: 'Attack!' The mutt merely lowers her head as if submitting in front of M. 'You were lucky. Usually people end up dead,' Anttila says calmly. He is probably disappointed with the dog's reaction, but he keeps his emotions inside. In this sequence, Kaurismäki's understated style of deadpan comedy is played to the point of absurdity, as the camera juxtaposes Anttila's fierce face and his violent expectations with the relaxed dog, making fun of the character.

Artificiality and simplified, childlike purity are two other characteristics that MacDowell relates to the aesthetics of quirky.[60] Many of Kaurismäki's protagonists are simple and childlike. Irma, the Salvation Army worker who falls in love with M, even calls him 'the child of sorrow'. Kaurismäki's films have an artificial look because he often relies on two-dimensional pictorial organization. This is eye-catching because in mainstream cinema the appearance of three-dimensionality is the norm. It is the pull of apparent three-dimensionality that makes the two-dimensionality of the screen so powerful aesthetically in film.[61] In two-dimensional pictorial organization, the outlines of characters and objects dictate how they are staged for the camera. Ideally, they should not hide things behind one another. A good example of such flat tableau shot in *The Man Without a Past* is the one in which the friend is dressed in a suit as he comes to meet M who is sitting in front of a container. As the shot begins, the camera follows the friend's movement from the opening of the container to the yard, but when the men meet, the camera stops, stays locked and shows them straight on from chest level in a long medium shot. The composition, in which M is on the left and the friend on the right with some random items around them, closely follows the rule of thirds. As depth cues are missing, it looks particularly flat: the characters are in the foreground and the container right behind them blocks the view. As everything is evenly distributed, the shot feels carefully balanced. It evokes a sense of uniformity to heighten that the men are equal even though M is like a child who is dependent on the hospitality of his friend's family.

Everything that is needed to understand the meaning of the shot is present in the centripetal composition, and thus it does not guide the audience to think about the off-screen space. To use the words of MacDowell, shots like this are excessively neat because they are characterized by 'extraordinary formality'.[62] Such two-dimensional formality is reminiscent of Jean-Luc Godard's films of the 1960s and paintings in the pop art style, but looking at the postures of the characters and the light blue, red and green colours that dominate the shot, the paintings of Edward Hopper can come to mind. This shot and others like it encourage the audience, to borrow the words of MacDowell again, 'to notice that they have been constructed especially for the camera (and for precisely *this angle*)'.[63] It is as if the camera reminds the audience of the artificiality of the perspective it offers. Such artificiality is not only amusing on its own right but also functional as it makes it easy for the audience to adjust to the ironic playfulness of Kaurismäki's films by heightening the fact that the world on the screen is nothing but make-believe even though it can feel poignant.

Ironic Minimalism

The most distinctive characteristic of quirky is 'a tone that exists on a knife-edge of judgement and empathy, detachment and engagement, irony and sincerity',[64] MacDowell concludes. Because of the camera's dual point of view, the exact same thing can be said about Kaurismäki's cinema. When watching his films, Roger Connah argues, 'one cannot quite laugh […] nor break down tragically'.[65] In accordance with the ideals of romantic irony, the filmmaker is sincere and tongue-in-cheek at the same time: thus, his films do not appear sentimental. The camera's minimalist point of view is the sincere point of view, the purpose of which is to evoke feelings of sympathy, empathy and understanding towards the characters. It is the dominant point of view in the films. The camera's ironic point of view is partly overlapping and competing with it, offering both ironic representations and representations of irony. This point of view is typically detached from the characters and aims to make fun of them and/or their situations, but it can also make a point about something by comparing it to something else. Because both points of view direct 'the audience to look at the characters and their situations as if from the outside',[66] they work well in concert.

'Irony is the resistance to a single fixed point of view',[67] as Colebrook claims. Stylistically, it is also a matter of excess, because there is nothing in the stories that would have obliged Kaurismäki to use it. The balance between sincerity and irony, engagement and detachment, empathy and judgement varies from one film to another, but both the camera's minimalist and the ironic points of view are present in all of them. Thus, there is always a 'co-presence of proximity and distance', as Koivunen has put it.[68] I therefore specify my metaphorical description of the camera's character: the socially excluded, sympathetic stranger who observes people and their gestures with keen interest and would like to engage with them but is unable to make his presence known has a strange sense of humour. Because of the dual point of view, the audience can experience Kaurismäki's films as melancholic or funny or melancholic and funny at the same time. Questions like 'why is Kaurismäki ironic' and 'what are the sources and genealogy of his irony' are left to be answered in detail in future studies.

The style of Kaurismäki's cinema as a whole is best understood as *ironic minimalism*. With this, I seek to take into account the complex internal dynamics and contradictions of the films which motivate one to think about them in relation to the cinematic styles of the past: the concept points towards the modernist and postmodern aspects of the seemingly classical films and in so doing emphasizes their intertextual and transnational character. The concept does not imply that the films are stylistically alike, only that the analysed tensions are present in all of them – some of Kaurismäki's films are more ironic, whereas others are more minimalist. Bacon's concept of poetics of displacement should be understood as a salient aspect of ironic minimalism. Even though the aspect of strangeness is a noticeable element in the films, it is only one among many others. The concept of ironic minimalism is broad enough to encompass the stylistic differences among the films yet accurate enough to provide a powerful tool for understanding and analysing their aesthetics in the context of world film history.

Notes

1   Andrew Nestingen, *The Cinema of Aki Kaurismäki: Contrarian Stories* (New York: Columbia University Press, 2013), *passim*.

2   Thomas Linares, 'The "Lost" but Never Defeated Heroes of Aki Kaurismäki', in *Aki Kaurismäki*, ed. Elena Christopoulou (Athens: 53rd Thessaloniki International Film Festival, 2012), 62.

3   Linda Hutcheon, *The Politics of Postmodern* (London and New York: Routledge, 2002), 2.

4   Henry Bacon and Jaakko Seppälä, 'Two Modes of Transnational Filmmaking', in *Finnish Cinema: A Transnational Enterprise*, ed. Henry Bacon (London: Palgrave Macmillan, 2016), 217–218.

5   Sanna Kivimäki, 'Working-class Girls in a Welfare State: Finnishness, Social Class and Gender in Aki Kaurismäki's Workers' Trilogy (1986–1990)', *Journal of Scandinavian Cinema*, 2, no. 1 (2012): 83.

6   Anu Koivunen, 'Do You Remember Monrépos? Melancholia, Modernity and Working-Class Masculinity in *The Man Without a Past*', in *Northern Constellations: New Readings in Nordic Cinema*, ed. C. Claire Thompson (Norwich: Norvik Press, 2006), 143.

7   Sanna Maskulin, '"Kinkkua, anna minä" – "Ham, let me" – kaurismäkeläisen dialogin erityispiirteitä', *Lähikuva*, 4 (1999): 35–36.

8   Pietari Kääpä, *The National and Beyond: The Globalisation of Finnish Cinema in the Films of Aki and Mika Kaurismäki* (Oxford: Peter Lang, 2010), 74, 112, 118 and 122.

9   Jaakko Seppälä, 'On the Heterogeneity of Cinematography in the Films of Aki Kaurismäki', *Projections*, 9, no. 2 (2015): 20–21.
10 Jaakko Seppälä, 'Doing a Lot with Little: The Camera's Minimalist Point of View in the Films of Aki Kaurismäki', *Journal of Scandinavian Cinema*, 6, no. 1 (2016): 19.
11 Claire Colebrook, *Irony* (London and New York: Routledge, 2004), 44.
12 Ibid., *passim*.
13 Linda Hutcheon, *Irony's Edge: The Theory and Politics of Irony* (London and New York: Routledge, 2005), 105.
14 Gregory Currie, *Narratives & Narrators: A Philosophy of Stories* (Oxford: Oxford University Press, 2010), 154.
15 Ibid., 170.
16 Andrew Nestingen, 'Aki Kaurismäki's Crossroads: National Cinema and the Road Movie', in *Transnational Cinema in a Global North: Nordic Cinema in Transition*, ed. Andrew Nestingen and Trevor G. Elkington (Detroit: Wayne State University Press, 2005), 190.
17 Koivunen, 'Do You Remember Monrépos? Melancholia, Modernity and Working-class Masculinity in *The Man Without a Past*', 144.
18 Colebrook, *Irony*, 58.
19 Currie, *Narratives & Narrators*, 149.
20 Nöel Carrol, 'Notes on the Sight Gag', in *Comedy/Cinema/Theory*, ed. Andrew Horton (Berkeley, LA and London: University of California Press, 1991), 26.
21 Wayne C. Booth, *A Rhetoric of Irony* (Chicago and London: University of Chicago Press, 1975), 226–227.
22 Colebrook, *Irony*, 16.
23 Hutcheon, *Irony's Edge*, 159.
24 Seppälä, 'Doing a Lot with Little', 9–18.
25 Seppälä, 'Doing a Lot with Little', 13–15.
26 Leo Braudy, *The World in a Frame: What We See in Films* (Chicago and London: The University of Chicago Press, 2002), 48.
27 Seppälä, 'On the Heterogeneity of Cinematography in the Films of Aki Kaurismäki', 28.
28 Ed S. Tan, *Emotion and the Structure of Narrative Film: Film as an Emotion Machine* (New York and London: Routledge, 2011), 65.
29 Kristin Thompson, 'The Concept of Cinematic Excess', in *Narrative, Apparatus, Ideology: A Film Theory Reader*, ed. Philip Rosen (New York: Columbia University Press, 1986), *passim*.
30 Kääpä, *The National and Beyond*, 155.
31 Nestingen, *The Cinema of Aki Kaurismäki*, 58.
32 Christine Haas, 'Sanoitteko Kaurismäki?', *La Strada* No. 4 (1988).
33 Henry Bacon, 'Aki Kaurismäen sijoiltaan olon poetiikka', in *Taju kankaalle: Uutta suomalaista elokuvaa paikantamassa*, ed. Kimmo Ahonen, Juha Rosenqvist, Janne Rosenqvist and Päivi Valotie (Turku: Kirja-Aurora, 2003), 89–97.
34 Mary Ann Caws, *Surrealism* (London: Phaidon Press Limited, 2004), 24.
35 Angela Dalle Vacche, 'Surrealism in Art and Film: Face and Time', in *Global Art Cinema: New Theories and Histories*, ed. Galt Rosalind and Karl Schoonover (Oxford: University of Oxford Press, 2010), 181–197.

36 Felicity Gee, 'Surrealist Legacies: The Influence of Luis Buñuel's "irrationality" on Hiroshi Teshigahara's "documentary fantasy"', in *A Companion to Luis* Buñuel, ed. Rob Stone and Julián Daniel Gutiérrez-Albilla (Malden et al.: Wiley-Blackwell, 2013), 572.

37 Roger Connah, *K/K A Couple of Finns and Some Donald Ducks* (Helsinki: VAPK, 1991), 399.

38 Kristin Thompson and David Bordwell, *Film History: An Introduction* (Boston et al.: McGraw-Hill, 2010), 163.

39 Braudy, *The World in a Frame*, 46.

40 Michael Brooke, 'Minor Quay', *Sight & Sound*, 22, no. 5 (2012): 20.

41 Mikko Piela, 'En ole löytänyt vielä omaa tyyliäni', *KU-Viikkolehti*, 24 December 1983.

42 Gilberto Perez, 'The Priest and the Pineapple. Buñuel's *Nazarin*', *La Furia Umana*.

43 Wendy Everett, 'Through a Fractal Lens: New Perspectives on the Narratives of Luis Buñuel', in *A Companion to Luis* Buñuel, ed. Rob Stone and Julián Daniel Gutiérrez-Albilla (Malden et al.: Wiley-Blackwell, 2013), 523.

44 Gustavo Mercado, *The Filmmaker's Eye: Learning (and Breaking) the Rules of Cinematic Composition* (Amsterdam et al.: Focal Press, 2001), 7.

45 Henry Bacon and Jaakko Seppälä, 'Two Modes of Transnational Filmmaking', 218–219.

46 Gee, 'Surrealist Legacies', 577.

47 Peter von Bagh, *Aki Kaurismäki* (Helsinki: WSOY, 2012), 206.

48 Sanna Peden, 'Crossing Over: On Becoming European in Aki Kaurismäki's Cinema', in *Frontiers of Screen History: Imagining European Borders in Cinema, 1945–2010*, ed. Raita Merivirta, Kimmo Ahonen, Heta Mulari and Rami Mähkä (Bristol: Intellect, 2013), 128–129; Tzvetomila Pauly, 'Take Care of Your Scar(f), Lilya! De-stigmatizing the Image of the Post-Soviet Other in Nordic Cinema', *Baltic Screen Media Review*, 2 (2015): 52.

49 Caws, *Surrealism*, 28.

50 Anonymous, 'Kaurismäen Arielille kiitosta New York Timesissä', *Uusi Suomi*, 26 September 1989.

51 Juan Antonio Suárez, *Jim Jarmusch* (Urbana and Chicago: University of Illinois Press, 2007), 160.

52 Sean O'Hagan, 'Wandering Star', *The Guardian*, 2 October (2005).

53 Geoff King, *Indie 2.0: Change and Continuity in Contemporary American Indie Film* (London and New York: I. B. Tauris, 2014), 26.

54 David Stratton, 'Leningrad Cowboys Meet Moses', *Variety*, 21–27 February 1994; Nestingen, 'Aki Kaurismäki's Crossroads', 285; Kääpä, *The National and Beyond*, 1.

55 Pietari Kääpä, *The Cinema of Mika Kaurismäki: Transvergent Cinescapes, Emergent Identities* (Bristol: Intellect, 2011), 168.

56 Suárez, *Jim Jarmusch*, 2.

57 Elle Rees has studied the film in similar terms but with a different emphasis and in less detail. Elle Rees, 'The Nordic "Quirky Feel-Good"', in *Nordic Genre Film: Small Nation Film Cultures in the Global Marketplace*, ed. Tommy Gustafsson and Pietari Kääpä (Edinburgh: Edinburgh University Press, 2015), 155–156.

58 James MacDowell, 'Notes on Quirky', *Movie: A Journal of Film Criticism*, 1, no. 1 (2010): 3.

59 Koivunen, 'Do You Remember Monrépos?' 139.

60 MacDowell, 'Notes on Quirky', 4–10.
61 Bence Naney, 'Two-Dimensional Versus Three-Dimensional Pictorial Organization in Film', a Presentation in the The Society for Cognitive Studies of the Moving Image 2015 conference (London: 18 June 2015).
62 MacDowell, 'Notes on Quirky', 5.
63 Ibid., 6.
64 Ibid., 13.
65 Connah, K/K, 262.
66 Seppälä, 'Doing a Lot with Little', 11.
67 Colebrook, *Irony*, 80.
68 Koivunen, 'Do You Remember Monrépos?' 144.

Chapter 6

DREAMERS AND OTHER SENTIMENTAL FOOLS: MONEY, SOLIDARITY AND AMBIVALENT POPULISM IN THE FILMS OF AKI KAURISMÄKI

Panos Kompatsiaris

Introduction

A persistent representation in Aki Kaurismäki's cinema renders the members of the working class as longing for an 'ordinary' life, a life involving secure employment, conventional love and a middle-class lifestyle. Rather than pursuing a rationally calculated career, goal-oriented plans or competitive positioning in the marketplace, however, Kaurismäki's heroes inhabit an emotional tonality marked by the opposite values; humility, compassion, solidarity and an underdog eccentricity. The customary modalities of subaltern bonding sketch here a working-class culture that does not rely on reasoning and careful planning but flourishes on the spontaneity, solidarity, counter-intuitiveness, musicality and poetic inspiration of the characters' lives and wandering. The culture of this urban working class is at once permeated by a sense of distrust against authorities as well as a dignified moral code of pride and self-sacrifice. Against this improvising subalternity, pushed to the margins by capitalist realities and its own idiosyncratic reclusiveness stand the figures of power. Kaurismäki customarily sketches archetypical authority figures, such as the capitalist, the boss, the banker and the bureaucrat, as ruthless, cold and dehumanized, perversely sadistic and pushing the formulas of the law to their suffocating extremes. These figures lack any sense of flexibility and compassion and most often work to annul the 'ordinary' working-class desire.

The antithesis between the spontaneity and benignity of the working class versus the ruthlessness of the agents of the capital and the state provides a starting point of exploration in this chapter. In drawing a line between the dominated and the dominant, Kaurismäki crafts a peculiar populist articulation in which the excluded, as both victims and heroes,[1] express positive social values, while the dominant, the state and the capital, perform a callous logic of power and discipline. Even though this narrative is often reshaped by the general ironic mood that overshadows his films and the extensive use of laconic aesthetics, it regularly provides a pattern through which the labour-capital relation can be read. Yet, as we shall see, this populist articulation is further complicated as the working-class attempts over and again to overcome its subaltern position not by overturning social hierarchies but either by integrating itself into a petit bourgeois universe by means of 'alienated' practices (consumption, romantic love, work stability) or by emotional and unplanned outbursts against injustice. The exploited then primarily actualize a personalized and improvised ethos of doing, a 'punk ethos',[2] that may involve moments of spectacular negation against power but treats with indifference the prospect of transgressing capital and social alienation through organized political formations and strategic planning. Indeed, the privileging of practices of spectacular negation rather than calculated sobriety is to be found in Kaurismäki's own, often half-ironic, words. 'For mankind', as he puts it in a recent interview, 'I can't see any way out, except terrorism. We kill the 1% [...] The 1% who have put us in the position where humanity has no value. The rich. And the politicians who are the puppies of the rich.'[3] This formulation hails a common 'we', a collective that ought to act together against the elites, and structures the prospect of capital transgression in terms of victimhood and heroism. The voluntaristic act of terrorism then signals a modality of resistance that can possibly suspend class differences.

This working-class relationality, its affects and sensibilities, as well as Kaurismäki's crafting of a variation of left-wing populism,[4] can be productively seen in relation to contemporary debates around class composition, class positioning and possible 'effective' modes of resistance in the context of a rising authoritarian, right-wing populism in the United States and Europe.[5] Kaurismäki's combination of a destructive punk ethos and latent moralizing[6] stands in tension with the idea of resistance as affirmation of modern progress, whether conceived as a mode of organization that relies on technologization and the application of reason, for example, digital communism,[7] accelerationism[8] or resistance as networked connectivity.[9] In terms of his cinematic aesthetics, we find an equal denouncement of modernity and progress. Drawing on the tradition of Nordic rural melodrama, Kaurismäki advances an anachronistic filmic style in which a sense of melancholy, despair and a blatant nostalgia for the past prevails.[10] The idealization of the past life, in which human relationships were supposed to be purer and more 'real', is followed by the gesture, both aesthetic and political, of avoiding the use of digital effects and recent technological developments.[11] The critique of the modern world and its prominent institutions, including money and profit, seems to also take an aesthetic form in his stark, nostalgic and 'anti-modern' filmic style.

At the level of content, aesthetic and production techniques then, Kaurismäki's visual language appears to be 'old fashioned', the counterpart of what the film theorist Steven Shaviro terms as the 'post-cinematic affect' of digital cinematic cultures.[12] For Shaviro, the 'post-cinematic affect' refers to the mediation of '*what it feels like* to live in the early twenty-first century', a subjectivation process filtered through decisive interactions with new media instruments and institutions.[13] Contrary to the ambient sensibility of contemporary neo-liberal configurations, Kaurismäki expresses an aesthetic and a value system that poses as outmoded to the 24/7 contemporary universe of permanent and instantaneous connectivity. Yet we may be able to track another form of contemporariness in Kaurismäki's cinematic approach, a contemporariness related to the need for counter-narratives and inclusive populist articulations within a growing contemporary dystopia marked by the rise of the authoritarian right.[14] Kaurismäki's aesthetic and narrational devices here may actualize contemporariness (rather than merely oppose it) in the spectacular negativity, intimate relationalities and improvisational doings of working-class life.

I explore the one mentioned earlier by looking at the storylines of the so-called Finland trilogy (*Drifting Clouds* (1996), *The Man Without a Past* (2002), *Lights in the Dusk* (2006)), a series of films commenting on the 1990s credit crunch in Finland, as well through selected examples by other Kaurismäki films in which the aforementioned labour-capital dialectic is performed. I discuss how Kaurismäki's ambivalent populism is structured around two representational techniques: the representation of the money-relation as corrupt and the rendering of the working class as a largely benign social force. As we shall see, the first involves the portrayals of the owners of the means of production as socially malicious (a portrayal that passes even at the level of clothing and appearance), while the second encompasses the general workers' relationality, involving instances of comradeship and solidarity as well as pure gender relations customarily filtered through the ideal of a romantic, heterosexual and class-compatible love. Both of these representations involve strong moralizing tendencies, tendencies that however continuously elude becoming didactic as a result of Kaurismäki's general use of absurdity and humour that subverts any 'final' attempt to impose a form of ethical conduct. More precisely, didacticism is eluded, I argue, through a comic and self-subverting pattern of ambivalence overshadowing his films. This pattern refers to the simultaneous existence of two conflicting assumptions present in the filmic narrative: on the one hand, there is a latent parodying of the protagonists' desires as effects of social alienation (consumption, middle-class values, romantic love, pride in their low status work), and on the other, the concomitant presentation of these desires as natural, universal and thus justified and legitimate. These two conflicting assumptions create an absurd effect, an effect that gives rise to a penetrating uncertainty found both in the *Finland Trilogy* and largely throughout his cinematic career. In the last section of this chapter, I discuss a possible reading of these narrational devices in relation to modes of articulation against the current rise of authoritarian governmentalities. The dichotomy between the elites versus the working class is structured in Kaurismäki, I hold, less as a 'subjective' choice but as an objective reality of economic inequality that involves the reliance on wage labour for purposes of social reproduction and the adjacent realities of unemployment, exploitation and the permanent disposability of the labour force. Kaurismäki's characters 'experience' these realities and develop their own responses and strategies through and against them.[15]

Class, Money and the Well-groomed Man

Whether explicitly or implicitly, social class is a recurring reference in Kaurismäki's work.[16] Most of his heroes live an impoverished lifestyle as a result of economic deprivation; they are victims of unemployment, harsh working conditions, lack of social security and exploitable relations with their bosses. References on (the lack of) money then are very frequent and often key to the filmic narrative insofar as they inform the protagonists' daily life, larger aspirations and sense of belonging. Seeing money as a general equivalent, a universally exchangeable commodity offering access to the total pool of commodities and through which one is able to position oneself accordingly in society,[17] allows us to shift focus to the social qualities that money performs as a means of exchange. The capacity of money to generalize consumption, raise status and mark social class, as well as the relations that it initiates, are mostly treated in Kaurismäki as fraudulent and corrupt. The main holders of this capacity, as we shall see, are portrayed as immoral, cold, selfish or as lacking any sense of empathy. Despite its fraudulence, or perhaps precisely because of it, money can enchant, awake passions and lure the working class with promises of individual liberation. Yet money has a further, more mundane function: it is the necessary condition for the social reproduction of the working class. There is often then an ambivalence in Kaurismäki at the heart of the working class' relation with money; on the one hand, we often find a latent parodying of his heroes' alienation who treat money as a vehicle for actualizing a petit bourgeois desire, and on the other, an affirmation of the ordinariness of this desire that augments our compassion towards these heroes' life strategies. The fraudulence yet indispensability of money enables a Foucauldian understanding of power as productive, enabling desire,[18] while the stigmatization of lavish lifestyle as a form of moral degradation promotes an ethical distancing from power that could enact a purer form of relating with the other. Money is then, within Kaurismäki's moral universe, a social institution indispensable for people's life trajectories and simultaneously an instrument of power that needs to be criticized and condemned. In all cases, as discussed in the subsequent section, it is the solidarity *between* workers (solidarity as a relation) that offers a positive glimpse to life against the nightmarish instrumentality of the money-relation.

The significance of the money-relation and its alienating effects on the heroes' lifestyles is a constant trope in all the films I explore. In *Drifting Clouds*, Ilona is a head waitress who loses her job when the restaurant she works for (Dubrovnik) is bought by a big corporation (the Chain). Likewise, her husband Lauri is a tram driver who gets fired as a result of cuts in the transportation company he works for.[19] They both face the harsh experience of unemployment within a precarious and chaotic social environment in which the 'dominant' try to sabotage or exploit their dreams. In the process of their job hunting, the agents of capital and the state perform an absurdly mechanized neo-liberal logic structured around the prospect of money accumulation (and the adjacent modes of individualism, heartlessness and cynicism). For instance, when Ilona asks for a job in another restaurant, the owner replies that 'to be honest, you're too old for a waiter', and when she protests that she is only 38, the boss replies that, 'that's it, you can drop dead anytime [and] you smoke too. Have you any life insurance?' Or when Ilona finds work through the mediation of a shabby job agency, the agent, who is no 'Samaritan' according to his self-description, orders her to empty her bank account within half an hour before he passes her the address of the prospective employer. Likewise, when Ilona asks for a bank loan, the bank manager turns down the 'shoemaker' whom she brought as a guarantor, impassionately replying that 'banks take no risks'. In all these instances, the guardians of access to money, the bankers, the big corporations and the managers are associated with cynicism and lack of compassion. The caricaturing of these guardians substantiates a logic internal to capitalist reason, articulating the often unarticulated grievances of capitalist realism and the disciplinary function of unemployment.

In *The Man Without a Past*, the central hero finds himself in a worse condition; he is denied access to (taxed) money as a result of lacking a legal document to certify his identity (he got beaten up by thugs in the beginning of the film and had forgotten his past). A rogue security guard then takes advantage of his vulnerable situation. The corrupt guard offers the man to stay in an illegal container that lacks basic health facilities, asking him to pay an enormously high rent in return. The amnesiac man goes through a similar phase of unemployment, to that of Ilona and Lauri, and eventually finds work in a construction company where he is eventually rejected because of lacking of legal papers. Caught in a bureaucratic vicious circle, the man is similarly turned down by the social security officers and then by the bank in which he tries to open an account. In this unmanageable (and highly absurd) situation, Kaurismäki shifts focus on the ways that state power, through law and the legal apparatus, controls access to the money-relation and thus the working-class desire, shaping, in essence, one's life coordinates (the man for instance decides at a point to 'exit' the money-relation, albeit unsuccessfully in order to socially reproduce himself by growing vegetables). The anxiety of 'losing' oneself after losing a legal document is here intensified and perpetrated by the rigidity of a total bureaucratic power.

In *Lights in the Dusk*, the hero is a security guard who gets himself into a similar desperate situation. A victim of love, a 'sentimental fool' according to the gangster who trapped him, Koistinen's life trajectory falls victim of the rationale of what we can call 'business-power' (albeit the business is a criminal organization this time) – a social formation that operates through a strictly economic calculus, where morality is absent and everything has a price, and all is bought and sold (Figure 6.1). Koistinen's love for a woman, who was sent by a gangster planning a robbery to the jewellery store he guards, snares him in a chain of dramatic events where he sees love being betrayed, loses his job and in the end is almost killed by the gangster's henchmen.

The sketching of money as a device of corrupt relationality (as opposed to the 'normal' desire for a middle-class lifestyle, work and romantic love) is further augmented by associating its gatekeepers (and especially 'big players' rather than small, local shops) with personality types that are off-putting, if not abhorrent. The association of one's manners, actions and overall style with negative psychological traits expands the battlefield of Kaurismäki's idiosyncratic class hatred to the terrain of clothing and appearance, that is, to how these personality types look like. Linking one's appearance with repulsive qualities then provides a further arena where the binary between the dominant and the dominated is produced. Thus, negative personality traits, such as rudeness, ruthlessness and cynicism, most often assume a particular clothing

Figure 6.1 'Sentimental fool' Koistinen (Janne Hyytiäinen) in *Lights in the Dusk* (2006). © and courtesy Sputnik Ltd.

style that is deemed antagonistic and hostile to the largely benign commonality of the working class. Money is often controlled by what we could call the 'well-groomed men' (money and masculinity seem often to be synonymous); the posh and elegant businessmen or bankers are the archetypical figures raising obstacles in the protagonists' lives. In *Drifting Clouds*, the well-groomed entrepreneurs and prospective buyers of Dubrovnik burst as cold-blooded gangsters into the restaurant outside of its opening hours. Disregarding the workers, they breach the restaurant's rules and order Ilona to get the manager. They are representatives of a big corporation that, as it is later revealed, blackmails the previous (more benevolent and 'local') owner for her inability to repay a loan. They buy the restaurant in a staged auction, a depersonalized arena of value and economic speculation that contrasts with Ilona's human needs to work with dignity and care.

In a similar fashion, the well-groomed boss of Lauri announces that the company is going to be reformed and routes will be cut down by letting the cards decide who will be forced to leave. The casino logic implied in the boss's proposal demonstrates a privileged attitude to life, indifferent to the common anxieties of the working class, and in this case, Lauri, who is about to lose his job. This indifference is contrasted with Lauri's emotional attachment to the job (see next section) and the psychological breakdown that follows. In *Lights in the Dusk*, Koistinen's mundane desires to have a life and find a loving partner are exploited by another archetypical money-figure, the well-groomed gangster. As mentioned earlier, the gangster sends a good-looking woman to seduce Koistinen and steal the security codes for the diamond store Koistinen is supposed to guard. When Koistinen goes to apply for a loan, the slick-looking bank manager rejects his application ('Koistinen … Are you some sort of a comedian? Did you come to cheer us up?') by throwing on top a degrading insult ('Guarantees from trash like you are worthless'). While there is not always a one-to-one equivalence between the clothing style and the abhorrent personality (for instance, in *Ariel*, the head gangster appears with his top shirt buttons open), rudeness and emotional violation is most often associated with a posh clothing appearance. As we shall see in the next section, when the working class assumes more refined clothing, this is associated with a sense of dignity and often craftsmanship in the workplace.

Solidarity, Dignity and Chivalry of the Working Class

Kaurismäki's working-class protagonists seem to occupy a different conceptual universe from these well-groomed men, not only in their looks but also in their manners and general understanding of the world. The binary here is between subjectivities based on altruism and solidarity on the one hand and cruelty and selfishness on the other, or between a broader communitarian approach to life versus one grounded on cynicism, profit and calculation. The vice of the money-relation then is clearly contrasted with the benevolence of relations based on working-class solidarity. The examples of subaltern solidarity in Kaurismäki's films are numerous, most often constructing it as an antidote to the distress brought about by unemployment and social injustice or often by the heroes' own eccentricity and a sense of self-destructiveness. For instance, although disagreements among them occur, the gesture of shared support between Ilona and Lauri throughout their mutual period of unemployment is what encourages them to continue struggling ('What if we fail? ... We will eat the wallpaper, people lived on it before'). And eventually, it is the cooperation with friends, colleagues and old workers of Dubrovnik that brings them back to their feet (they reopen the restaurant in a different venue). The display of solidarity is abundant in the film. When Ilona's new boss refuses to remunerate her for her work, Lauri goes to demand the payment for her (even by attempting to beat up the boss, a move that leads to catastrophic consequences). Or when Lauri mindlessly loses all their money in a casino, Ilona compassionately holds his hand rather than complaining or telling him off. Or, again, when the bank takes their apartment, Lauri's sister accepts them to move in her place, despite Lauri's previous slightly rude behaviour against her. The members of the working class organize a safe space against the violence of power, a space of mutual understanding, altruism and forgiveness towards eccentric behaviour – a benignity that seems to develop directly out of their social marginalization.

The safe space of forgiveness is manifestly portrayed in a scene at the beginning of *Drifting Clouds* when the alcoholic cook of Dubrovnik goes into a psychological breakdown and stabs the bouncer in the hand. Rather than sulking after the incident or plotting to take revenge, the bouncer peacefully shares a smoke with the cook in the backyard. The knifed bouncer even allows in silence the cook to pat him on the back following the news that he had three stitches from the stabbing (later the bouncer helps the cook with his problem of alcoholism and they both cooperate to open the new restaurant as if the incident never happened). In a similar altruistic fashion, an impoverished community living in shipping containers aids the man from *The Man Without a Past* to emerge back to life. There, a poor family with children collects him from the street and voluntarily hosts him until he gets back on his feet despite their obviously desperate economic condition (they also live in a container). Later in the film, this manifestation of goodness, a form of lived idealism, is further displayed by a female social worker of the Salvation Army, herself also living in a run-down apartment, who gives to the man new clothes, finds him a temporary occupation and generally helps him in all his troubles with the law. In a likewise compassionate manner, in *Lights in the Dusk*, Koistinen's female friend who works in a kiosk is the only one to support him when he goes to jail for or when he gets beaten up by the gangster's thugs at the end of the film. This happens despite his previous cold behaviour towards her.[20] In all earlier situations, working-class togetherness develops out of care for the other and is related with feelings of comradeship and solidarity.

The sense of working-class mutuality and understanding also expands into the field of love and romantic relationships. Kaurismäki's ideal love is most usually another crucial safe space from society's cruelty. This involves a traditional, old-fashioned, romantic, innocent, heterosexual and class-compatible understanding of love. As mentioned earlier, again here, Kaurismäki's absurd humour subverts the possibility of presenting this type of relationship as the norm in a didactic or preaching manner. Besides, the desire for traditional love (as all other petit bourgeois desires in Kaurismäki) always balances between social alienation and normality. Most of the working-class men seem to be slightly innocent and sexually inexperienced and are regularly characterized by chivalry and self-sacrifice towards women, that is to say, by values that largely contrast with contemporary (Western) gender roles. This is again opposed to the powerful men's fully commoditized attitude towards women that involves a sense of entitlement and the performance of an instrumental rationality. For instance, contrasting with Koistinen's gentle feelings towards the lady he loves (expressed through a suffering sentimentality and invitations to the movies, concerts and dinners even though his earnings are limited), the gangster's relationship with her is purely instrumental and dominated by his money-power. He insults her verbally, makes her iron his shirts and generally attempts to buy her love. He is patronizing, mocking her fragility and buying her guilty conscience by offering in exchange a salary and travel breaks to 'European capitals'. Koistinen's pure feelings for romantic love are then contrasted with the cynicism of the well-groomed man. Koistinen's altruism and faith in the purity of his feelings even lead him to self-punishment. He accepts to go to jail and refuses to betray his love; he refuses to snitch on her to the police even when he realizes that he has been tricked and framed by her.

Policeman: You've been used.
Koistinen: I don't know anybody.

In the *Man Without a Past*, when the man innocently kisses the Salvation Worker in the cheek after a playful tease, he feels the need to apologize for 'stealing a kiss' and not 'being a gentleman'. In all these instances, there is a certain code that seems to be shared between the deprived, concerning the way that love between a man and a woman should be practised. Love is here accompanied by an 'ethics of commitment',[21] that is to say, a commitment to the ideal of love manifested in relations of trust, altruism and comradeship rather than sexual passion. Sexual passion is generally absent from these relationships, and when it is implied (in other cases), it is mostly associated with feelings of greed and improper behaviour.

Furthermore, apart from being old-fashioned and heterosexual, the ideal love, for Kaurismäki, flourishes principally among members of the same social class, that is, the working class. This is obvious in most, if not all, of his films. To mention just a few examples, in *Shadows in Paradise* (1986) (Figure 6.2), the romance happens between a garbage truck driver and a cashier; in *The Man Without a Past* (2002), between a welder and a social worker; in *Drifting Clouds*, between a waitress and a bus driver; in *Ariel* (1988), between a coal miner and a traffic warden; in *I Hired a Contract Killer* (1990), between a clerk and a flower seller; and in *Lights in the Dusk* (2006), it appears to emerge in the last scene between the security guard and the kiosk worker. Apart from coming from a humble background, these couples assume a similar lifestyle, share similar dreams of building a life together, share dreams of escape and even share similar clothing. When love is sought elsewhere, the result is often disappointing. Same-class relationships articulate the possibility of stitching together a common world, the world of the excluded, a world of selflessness and commutarian bonds. In a semi-anarchist fashion, Kaurismäki constructs this world as not concerned to collectively grasp power but to build interpersonal relations of trust, prefiguring a more ethical world to be. Again, rather than presenting this largely platonic and even puritan understanding of love in didactic terms, that is, an ideal that should be followed by all, Kaurismäki both positions it in the context of general social alienation and petit bourgeois desire as well as conceives it metaphorically as a device for underscoring the value of commitment, altruism and solidarity in the context of a rising neo-liberal cynicism and instrumentality.

Figure 6.2 Ilona (Kati Outinen) and Nikander (Matti Pellonpää) in *Shadows in Paradise* (1986). © and courtesy Sputnik Ltd.

For these working-class heroes, the ethics of commitment is often expanded to include commitment to one's job. There is a work ethic displayed by Kaurismäki's heroes involving what Richard Sennett calls 'craftsmanship', the desire to do the work right and for its own sake (2009).[22] Lauri, for instance, fixes his tie and coat when driving the bus in a display of working-class pride, and Ilona is always well dressed and elegant when working as a hostess. They both seem to take pride in their clothing not because it raises their social status but out of respect for the others, as part of their general dignified attitude to the world. The dignity and pride for one's job happen even in the most seemingly uninspiring occupations. In *The Man Without a Past* (2002), the man feels proud when he eventually realizes that he was a welder in past life, while in *Shadows in Paradise* (1986), Nikonen takes pride in telling that he is a garbage collector and an ex-butcher. In certain cases, there is often a self-realization of one's occupation as inadequate, especially in male workers (Kaurismäki plays again with the stereotypical gender roles here) who seek upward social mobility. In the regular Kaurismäki's style, however, this attempt to escape becomes internally subverted; it is almost absurd and appears both as the effect of general social alienation and as a normal working-class desire. Koistinen asserts to the girl he is in love with that 'it's just temporary. I'm not going to be a guard forever'. However, the futility of this desire is revealed earlier in the film, when he narrates to the kiosk worker friend his plans to set up his own company and drive the big corporation he works for out of business (in a further display of absurdity, the name of the firm would be 'Koskinen Security' because there is 'no sense using your own name nowadays'). The company, as Koistinen asserts, will have 'the most modern equipment money can buy' and his 'workmates will come along' if he asks. Koistinen is broke and a rather unpopular figure in the company, so all this narrative transmits a sense of absurdity, the narrative of a dreamer's (utopian and unrealizable) dream. Similarly, in *Shadows in Paradise*, the dream for upward mobility appears again as unfulfillable, conventional and largely boring. As with Koistinen, Nikonen's friend hopes to make his own garbage collection company and drive the one he works for out of business. However, when he is asked about details, he reveals in full seriousness the comically miserable nature of his motivation ('I am not going to die behind the wheel … Then where? … Behind the desk'). This revelation compels the viewer to see the whole plan in a blatantly comic yet compassionate way as it emanates from a common desire for upward mobility. Here, again, Kaurismäki employs the usual technique of ambivalence. The working-class upward mobility dream involves the opening of small-scale businesses or local initiatives (which do not seem to have the same negative connotations as multinational businesses), but this dream is usually treated superficiality even by the heroes themselves who are unable to assume a proper business mentality or find the capital needed; they are just dreamers, sentimental fools.[23]

Time, Ambivalent Populism and Working-class Desire

An issue relating to the discussion earlier concerns the engagement of these heroes with the question of time (what we do with our time) and more generally the question of the future. The figure of the dreamer can only engage in a fragmented and spontaneous way with these pressing questions for social emancipation. In his text 'Prometheanism and Its Critics', the philosopher Ray Brassier asks 'what does it mean to orient oneself towards the future?' and subsequently adds that ultimately this question comes down to another, simpler question, namely, 'what shall we do with time?'.[24] The questions of time and the future, for Brassier, are significant for building social equality. An abandonment of the engagement with the future means for him the abandonment of the intellectual project of Enlightenment itself. What one is left with is a postmodern relativism devoid of a larger vision about the ways to transforming the world. The abandonment of 'absolutes' in critical thought led, for Brassier, to the 'collapse of communism as a Promethean project'[25] and the relinquishing of possibilities of change to the localized and small-scale experiments. Kaurismäki's romantic and often moralistic attitude against structures of exploitation can be conceived as anti-futuristic, nostalgic and regressive, rejecting modes of networked resistance, connectivity, or the mastering of technological, technocratic or other expert knowledge. His approach with time seems equally stagnating. His heroes do not engage in any kind of carefully planned endeavour but instead rely on the impulsiveness and spontaneity of their desire. They do not *use* their time productively from a Promethean point of view. Rather than accelerating time for creating a more socially equal future, here we have a deceleration, an almost abandonment of the question of productive time. Rather than focusing on a creative engagement with time that could build a more equal futurity, here we have a general rejection of the question of time and the legitimization of repetitive temporalities, grounded on the values of commitment and romantic idealism. It is a counter effort to engage in a *non-productive relation* with time rather than compress and optimize it and generally make it work for 'us' and our future cause. This, for Kaurismäki, seems to be part of a larger effort to rehumanize neglected modalities of doing and being, ranging from neglected temporalities and extending to neglected relationalities or, more crucially, to rehumanize the 'excluded' in general.

One of the main aspects of Kaurismäki's filmmaking effort to rehumanize the excluded consists of an effort to enable feelings of empathy towards the common folk, the working class and generally the 'people' on the grounds of dignity, pride, comradeship, collegiality and solidarity rather than pity and philanthropy. Kaurismäki's rehumanizing of the people, however, differs from realist working-class representations that may involve emotionally loaded moralizations and verge towards the didactic (e.g. Ken Loach) or glorification of the people and their bigger-than-life deeds (e.g. socialist realism). Kaurismäki's effort is more inclusive, encompassing professions and identities beyond the traditional working-class subjects (does a security guard really belong among the oppressed or is he an oppressor himself?) as well as the diverse ways through which these subjects practice an estranged everydayness (trying to follow a petit bourgeois, alienated desire or emotionally burst rather than collectively organize). For instance, when Koistinen expressionlessly and somewhat comically admits, without any hint of self-pity, that 'people don't usually come to talk to us … […] We're human, too', there is a sense of empathy enabled for security workers on the basis of their outcast social status. This empathy comes about on the grounds of the universalizing qualities of dignity and social recognition rather than as a gesture of philanthropy. It is through this effort to rehumanize the people and contrast them with the ruthless bourgeoisie, the 1per cent, that Kaurismäki's approach flirts with what one can name left-wing or progressive populism.[26] In discourse theory (the so-called Essex School),[27] populism is described as a mode of enunciation '(a) […]constructed around the nodal point "the people", and (b) reflect[ing] a perception/representation of society as divided between two hostile camps: the people against the elite'.[28] As a 'thin-centered ideology' (an ideology that can fit different political agendas) that articulates chains of signifiers around the nodal point of the 'people',[29] populism may exist in its right-wing and racist guises (Marine Le Pen, Donald Trump) or as a left-wing and progressive endeavour (Podemos, Syriza, Bernie Sanders, Jeremy Corbyn). This depends on how inclusively the 'people' is each time constructed, for example, from sectarian, national, ethnic or religious terms to pluralistic, internationalist, working class, antiracist and so on. The phrase 'the right of the people', or that the 'right belongs to the people', consists of an obvious violation of the heterogeneity and antagonism found within the people itself, but insofar it is bound with inclusive and pluralistic signifiers, it is in essence a deeply democratic articulation. The exact opposite of populism would be a discursive enunciation structured around notions of 'expertise', 'artistocracy' or 'the elites' who know better than the people – that is to say an essentially exclusive and technocratic form of discourse[30] to which Kaurismäki is explicitly opposed. Kaurismäki, however, as mentioned earlier, advances a working-class populism that continuously undermines itself or perplexes its own validity as true discourse in (what we could call) an ambivalent populist fashion.

While ambivalence is customarily opposed to populism, which relies on the figure of heroic determination, in Kaurismäki, we may be able to discern this unexpected combination. On the one hand, the division he suggests between the 99per cent and the 1per cent, the many and the few, the ruthlessness of capital versus the benevolence of the working class, is a clear populist binary. On the other hand, this binary is constantly undermined by the ambiguity shading the nature of working-class desire. This nature, as mentioned already, is dual; it balances between alienation and normality. If taken to its logical extreme, the duality of this desire involves two contradictory figures: first, the figure of 'normality as alienation' (in an Althusserian fashion, i.e. that the 'normal' desire is already alienated by capitalism and the state apparatuses) and second that of 'alienation as normality' in which the alienated desire is normal (and thus there is nothing else apart from alienated desire). Eventually, in the first case, we are simply left with a totalizing alienation (everything is alienated) and in the second only with a totalizing normality (everything is normal). However, there is never a final resolution between these two extreme figures, between total normality and total alienation, and never a clear indication of which side Kaurismäki chooses. An effect of this ambiguity is the constant parody, irony and ambivalence dominating cinematic time that leads to a regular questioning of Kaurismäki's own intentions. What is often obscured in Kaurismäki's films is his own desire (what he *really* wants to say) regarding the working-class desire: is he critiquing it or asserting it? In this sense, his alleged ethical mandates and moralizing (or his presumed conservativeness) become internally undermined, and while the populist dividing line exists, it may often become porous.

In this sense, as implied in an earlier section, Kaurismäki's moralizing tendencies, involving the idea of commitment, romantic love, solidarity and the rejection of the money-relation, become vehicles of suggesting rather than prescribing a mode of relating with the other. They are less supposed to simply reflect the 'truth' of working-class relationality than to construct a representation in which these tendencies assume a privileged position. It is not so much the issue here whether these may be 'real' or idealized representations of the working class. What is more important is how this construction of the benevolent working class enables a questioning of capitalist realism, of the values, strategies and institutions that maintain its apparatus. The analytical separation between a left-wing and right-wing populism can lead,[31] within a general hegemonic project, to the engagement with forms of artistic and cultural populism enacting counter-capitalist mobilizations. In articulating the humbleness, pride, reclusiveness and familiar desires of the working class, Kaurismäki captures and emits affects of solidarity, dignity and ethical commitment in togetherness that may contribute to such mobilizations.

Notes

1   Andrew Nestingen, 'Aki Kaurismäki – From Punk to Social Democracy', in *A Companion to Nordic Cinema*, ed. Mette Hjort and Ursula Lindqvist (London: John Wiley & Sons, 2016), 291–312.
2   Ibid., 293.
3   Aki Kaurismäki in Simon Hattenstone, 'Seven Rounds with Aki Kaurismäki', *The Guardian*, April 2012. https://www.theguardian.com/film/2012/apr/04/aki-kaurismaki-le-havre-interview
4   Yiannis Stavrakakis, 'The Return of "the People": Populism and Anti-Populism in the Shadow of the European Crisis', *Constellations*, 21, no. 4 (2014): 505–517 and Alexandros Kioupkiolis, 'Podemos: The Ambiguous Promises of Left-wing

Populism in Contemporary Spain', *Journal of Political Ideologies*, 21, no. 2 (2016): 99–120.

5   Christian Fuchs, 'Donald Trump: A Critical Theory-Perspective on Authoritarian Capitalism', *tripleC: Communication, Capitalism & Critique*, 15, no. 1 (2017): 1–72.

6   Nestingen, *'Aki Kaurismäki – From Punk to Social Democracy'*.

7   Nick Dyer-Witheford, 'Red Plenty Platforms', *Culture Machine*, 14 (2013): 1–27.

8   Nick Srnicek and Alex Williams, *Inventing the Future: Postcapitalism and a World Without Work* (London and New York: Verso, 2015).

9   Michael Hardt and Antonio Negri, *Multitude: War and Democracy in the Age of Empire* (New York: Penguin, 2005). Brian Holmes, *Unleashing the Collective Phantoms: Essays in Reverse Imagineering* (New York: Autonomedia, 2008).

10 Peter Schepelern. 'The Element of Crime and Punishment: Aki Kaurismäki, Lars von Trier and the Traditions of Nordic Cinema', *Journal of Scandinavian Cinema*, 1, no. 1 (2010): 87–103, 96.

11 Andrew Nestingen, *The Cinema of Aki Kaurismäki: Contrarian Stories* (New York: Columbia University Press, 2013).

12 Shaviro Steven, *Post Cinematic Affect* (London: John Hunt Publishing, 2010).

13 Ibid., 3.

14 This contemporary reading of left-wing populism largely lies on a (re)reading of the work of Ernesto Laclau. Some examples can be found at Owen Jones. 'The Left Needs a New Populism Fast. It's Clear What Happens If We Fail', *Guardian*, November 2016, https://www.theguardian.com/commentisfree/2016/nov/10/the-left-needs-a-new-populism-fast

15 Furthermore, I avoid an interpretation based on the discourse on 'Finnishness' or on Kaurismäki's presumed exotization of Finnish national traits, interpretations that have produced some common critiques against his work, scholarly or not. Kaurismäki's exaggerated take on 'Finns' is here seen as contingent upon the larger values he performs and needs to be viewed as part of this larger context.

16 Sanna Kivimäki, 'Working-class Girls in a Welfare State: Finnishness, Social Class and Gender in Aki Kaurismäki's Workers' Trilogy (1986–1990)', *Journal of Scandinavian Cinema*, 2, no. 1 (2012): 73–88. See also Nestigen, *The Cinema of Aki Kaurismäki: Contrarian Stories* and Nestingen, *Aki Kaurismäki – From Punk to Social Democracy*.

17 Karl Marx, *Capital: Volume 1* (London: Penguin, 1976), 188–244.

18 Michel Foucault, *The History of Sexuality* (New York: Random House, 1978).

19 'Firing' is a constant motive, forcing Kaurismäki's heroes to navigate the world without jobs (also found for example in *I Hired a Contract Killer, Shadows in Paradise* or *Ariel*).

20 In *Shadows in Paradise*, for instance, the supermarket cashier takes the initiative to bind Nikander's bleeding hand.

21 Alain Badiou, *Ethics: An Essay on the Understanding of Evil* (London and New York: Verso, 2002) and Simon Critchley, *Infinitely Demanding: Ethics of Commitment, Politics of Resistance* (London and New York: Verso, 2014).

22 Richard Sennett, *The Craftsman* (New Haven: Yale University Press, 2008).

23 The only exception is perhaps the opening of the new restaurant when all the community of previous workers cooperated.

24 Ray Brassier. 'Prometheanism and Its Critics', in *Accelerate: The Accelerationist Reader*, ed. Robin Mckay and Armen Avanessian (Berlin: Urbanomic, 2014): 486–487, 469.

25　Ibid., 469.
26　Stavrakakis, 'The Return of "the People"'.
27　Ernesto Laclau, *On Populist Reason* (New York and London: Verso, 2005).
28　Yiannis Stavrakakis, Ioannis Andreadis and Giorgos Katsambekis, 'A New Populism Index at Work: Identifying Populist Candidates and Parties in the Contemporary Greek Context', *European Politics and Society*, Vol. 18, no. 4 (2016): 1–19. http://dx.doi.org/10.1080/23745118.2016.1261434
29　Laclau, *On Populist Reason*.
30　Stavrakakis, 'The Return of "the People"', 506.
31　Stavrakakis et al. argue that 'right-wing populism is exclusionary and identity-focused, while left-wing populism is more inclusive and pluralist'. Stavrakakis et al., 'A New Populism Index at Work: Identifying Populist Candidates and Parties in the Contemporary Greek Context'.

Chapter 7

THE CULTURAL TECHNIQUES OF GESTURE IN AKI KAURISMÄKI'S PROLETARIAN TRILOGY

Angelos Koutsourakis

Introduction

Aki Kaurismäki has stated his passion for making films that can generate meaning with minimum dialogue and suggested that early cinema had a unique capacity to develop the storyline out of images: 'I was watching all kinds of silent movies to educate myself and to study the language. It was then that I started to understand the people that said cinema had died when they put sound to it.'[1] Kaurismäki argued that the era of the silent cinema gave rise to a film language that rendered dialogue unnecessary. He has also noted that his films include many elements from Buster Keaton and Charlie Chaplin, while elsewhere he mentioned similarities with Japanese cinema, due to his preference for an aesthetics of 'reduction'.[2] Kaurismäki confers importance on a *performative* minimalism, which stresses gesture and non-psychological character portrayal. This element is coupled with moments of visual excess such as colourful compositions and cult diegetic music that add an anti-realist dimension to the narrative. Similar representational approaches have been the stock in trade of modernist art cinema, but what distinguishes Kaurismäki is that his elliptical style does not resist the medium's storytelling function but simplifies it and allows the narrative to emanate from the images and the actors' performances.

Kaurismäki's style is grounded upon visual strategies that give preference to the autonomy of the shot at the expense of intensified continuity. In this way, the shot highlights the corporeal interactions between characters even when there is very little movement within the frame. This particular aspect of his work evokes early cinema practices, since to recall Béla Balázs, he frames the actors in such ways that the situations speak for themselves.[3] Early cinema was a gestural cinema and, as Jean Epstein pointed out in 1921, it was a cinema that relied on showing things rather than telling by employing an 'aesthetic of suggestion'.[4] For Epstein, gestures in early cinema are not conclusive but suggestive. Similarly, Rudolf Arnheim observes that the story before cinema's transition to sound was developed out of postures and facial expressions that condensed dramatic action.[5] Indeed, suggestion and dramatic condensation are visual schemes relevant to Kaurismäki, not least because many of his early films are less than 80 minutes of screen duration. There is also something unique about the performance style employed in his films, and this uniqueness rests on a certain degree of deliberate gaucheness in the acting.

A question may indeed be raised on the function of such an 'aesthetic poverty' regarding performance, and taking into account the filmmaker's interest in characters living on the margins of society, one may conjecture that the form is not only in service of the content but also serves the films' thematic interests. The social themes are addressed through a minimalist aesthetic that underscores corporeal interaction and physical action. In this chapter, I discuss Kaurismäki's proletarian trilogy (*Shadows in Paradise* (1986), *Ariel* (1988), *The Match Factory Girl* (1990)), and I suggest that an emphasis on the characters' gestures can help us connect aesthetic with political questions and understand broader 'cultural techniques' and the 'techniques of the body' – terms that I will qualify later. My argument is prompted by the films' form and content, since in this body of films the characters seem to be placeless and unable to orient themselves in a social environment that is changing fast.

While the idea of gesture as mediation can be traced in Bertolt Brecht's writings on the social *Gestus* and Giorgio Agamben's writings on gesture as a process of making things visible that defies the fixity of the image, the context for the thoughts discussed in this chapter is indebted to German Media Theory.[6] The concept of cultural techniques refers to operations that minimize discussions of human agency in favour of questions of the mediation of everyday life. Bernhard Siegert explains that cultural techniques question canonical approaches to human agency, prioritizing instead 'chains of operations' and 'technical objects'. As he writes:

> Thus the concept of cultural techniques clearly and unequivocally repudiates the ontology of philosophical concepts. Humans as such do not exist independently of cultural techniques of hominization, time as such does not exist independently of cultural techniques of time measurement, and space as such does not exist independently of cultural techniques of spatial control.[7]

Siegert's argument underlines the agency of a series of social 'operations' and is very much consistent with German Media Theory's thesis that machines and media are not simply instruments with which humans communicate things, but they also mediate humans and affect the very processes of communication. Siegert explains that the term 'cultural techniques' also includes gestures and 'body techniques', which are processes of subject construction.[8] Sybille Krämer and Horst Bredekamp clarify this further by explaining that cultural techniques 'can be understood as skills that habituate and regularize the body's movements and that express themselves in everyday fluid practices'.[9] In a way, cultural techniques point to the prioritization of structures, cultural, technological and social, rather than individual agents. Kramer's and Bredekamp's point evokes implicitly Marcel Mauss's 'techniques of the body', while Siegert mentions him explicitly to explain how certain operations, such as swimming and walking, are not the product of mental processes but describe the ways that bodies become 'docile'.[10] For Mauss, the human body is a medium that transmits socially and culturally encoded actions. Even when it comes to biological operations, the body does not perform movements independently of the social context. Instead, the body is the repository of cultural and social operations that are the product of conscious and unconscious training.

Referring to his anthropological research on how gestures and postures vary among different societies, Marcel Mauss suggested that learnability and education are key processes that are at times perpetuated unconsciously. As he writes:

> What takes place is a prestigious imitation. The child, the adult, imitates actions which have succeeded and which he has seen successfully performed by people in whom he has confidence and who have authority over him. The action is imposed from without, from above, even if it is an exclusively biological action, involving his body. The individual borrows the series of movements which constitute it from the action executed in front of him or with him by others.[11]

Mauss's point is strikingly similar to Brecht's motto that human education is a theatrical process in the sense that the individual copies gestures and expressions after encountering situations.[12] It is fair to conjecture that cultural techniques and the techniques of the body point to the ways corporeal interactions are determined by specific social spaces. But this requires a shift of attention from the actions themselves to the empirical details that throw light on the ways actions are executed. Cornelia Vismann phrases this lucidly and argues that cultural techniques invite us to study the operations that take place irrespective of the acting subject as well as the ways these operations are reproducible and learnable.[13]

Kaurismäki's proletarian trilogy relies on a filmic composition that privileges gestural relationships, and this aspect of the films can offer us an insight into the cultural techniques and the techniques of the body as reproduced by his working-class characters. As I will explain, such an emphasis on the gestural study of operations does not necessarily imply the complete disappearance of agency nor does it suggest the subject's passive compliance. This is also suggested by Bernhard Siegert, who explains that cultural techniques do not simply 'colonize' but 'decolonize' bodies as well – a point to which I shall return later on.[14]

Mechanization and Work Alienation

Before proceeding to the main corpus of the argument, I will spend some time summarizing the films' stories and the historical context under which they were made; both are instrumental to understanding how the characters' corporeal interactions point to historically induced cultural techniques. *Shadows in Paradise*, the first film of the trilogy, tells the story of Nikander, a lonely garbage collector (Matti Pellonpää), whose colleague and friend dies before achieving his dream to start a private waste-removal company. Nikander's life seems to have no purpose, and he only gets to meet another friend, Melartin (Sakari Kuosmanen), after spending a night in jail. His life changes after meeting a supermarket cashier, Ilona (Kati Outinen), who has been doing numerous precarious jobs. They start going out, but their relationship suffers from their shyness and inability to connect. The film ends on a positive note, when Nikander convinces Ilona to give their relationship a second chance. Ilona quits another precarious job and joins him on a trip to Tallinn. *Ariel*, the second part of the trilogy, focuses on Taisto (Turo Pajala), a coal miner who is forced to move to Helsinki following the closure of the countryside mine, where he works, and his father's suicide. His first experiences in Helsinki are far from positive, since he is beaten and robbed and thus forced to work precariously to afford to pay for a room in a cheap motel inhabited by people on the margins of society. He enters into a romantic relationship with Irmeli (Susanna Haavisto), a single mother working four jobs to raise her son, but his good luck does not last long, since he ends up in jail for a crime he did not commit. In jail, he meets Mikkonen (Matti Pellonpää) with whom he manages to escape prison, planning to leave abroad with Irmeli. Encouraged by two underworld criminals, they end up robbing a bank but after the robbery, Mikkonnen is injured fatally. In the end, Taisto, Irmeli and her son manage to board on a ship to Mexico and leave the country. Finally, *The Match Factory Girl* tells the story of Iiris (Kati Outinen), a factory worker leading a grim life in which she has to take care of her withdrawn mother (Elina Salo) and stepfather (Esko Nikkari). The monotony of her everyday life makes her seek a romantic relationship. When she meets Aarne (Vesa Vierikko), she believes that her life has some direction, but the latter rejects her after a one-night stand. Iiris realizes she is pregnant and tries to reconnect with him, only to be rejected once again. She unsuccessfully attempts to commit suicide, and this alienates her from her parents, who force her to leave the house. In the end, she decides to take revenge by poisoning Aarne and her parents for all the suffering they have inflicted upon her.

The characters in the proletarian trilogy are individuals who have first-hand experience of engaging in labour that does not ascribe them social status but working insecurity and social alienation. All the films implicitly address the changes in the social and economic landscape that took place during the 1980s. In the 1960s and 1970s, Finland experienced economic prosperity which can be attributed to its astute foreign policy, since the country had trade relations both with the Soviet Union and with Western European countries, as an associate member of the European Free Trade Association. Collective bargaining, work benefits, workplace protection and social welfare were key facets of the country's affluence.[15] The country's Cold War neutrality allowed it to benefit from its special relations with the Soviet Union (known also as Finlandization) and its ability to form economic partnerships with other key European economies.[16] By the 1980s though, as historians observe, Finland started looking West, and Harri Holkeri's government elected in 1987 proceeded to a "'controlled structural change'" so as to deindustrialize and deregulate the economy. By 1989, the property bubble exploded, leading to a long recession in the 1990s. The recession was also heightened because of the decline in exports following the collapse of the Soviet Union.[17]

It is during these important economic changes that these three films take place. We can certainly identify the historical context within their stories; working flexibility and insecurity figure importantly in the first two films (Ilona in *Shadows in Paradise*, and Irmeli and Taisto in *Ariel* are examples of workers coming to terms with the changes in the labour market). Furthermore, there is a certain mistrust of public institutions (as evidenced in the characters' encounters with the state, for instance, Taisto's trial in *Ariel*), and the old generation seems unable to adapt to the new market reality (evidenced by Nikander's deceased colleague in *Shadows in Paradise*, Taisto's father in *Ariel* and Iiris's unemployed parents in *The Match Factory Girl*).[18]

Characters in these films do not seem to be totally integrated in the social environment of the time and are unable to orient themselves in the changing economic landscape. Alienating labour plays its role here, and the labour processes of mechanized work follow the characters in their private lives too. The opening of *Shadows in Paradise* provides a good example (Figure 7.1). The film opens showing a group of workers clocking in, and the camera eventually focuses on Nikander and his workmate. What follows are images of the two of them while mechanically emptying garbage bins. The extra-diegetic music in the background adds a sense of rhythm to the actions on screen; at some point, the scenes of work are interrupted and the camera cuts to a restaurant in which both characters are having lunch. They still carry themselves as if working, something that is intensified by the mechanistic way they are eating and by the fact that there is no dialogue between them. In the scene that comes immediately after that, the camera cuts back again to scenes from their working routine. The repetitive gestures of work point to the characters' alienation from their work, but what is important is that this sense of alienation is perpetuated when they engage in leisure activities too. These are the markers of the cultural techniques of automated work and alienation that the characters are unable to do away with in their personal lives. On his first date with Ilona, Nikander takes her to a bingo game. The atmosphere there does not differ much from a disciplinary work environment; the caller of the game reads the combination of letters, and the players without much enthusiasm participate in the game

Figure 7.1 Nikander (Matti Pellonpää) in *Shadows in Paradise* (1986). © and courtesy Sputnik Ltd.

by crossing their lines and at times shouting bingo. Nikander plays passively without even establishing eye contact with Ilona. He is unable to get rid of the rigid working techniques of his body even during his free time. Ilona realizes that, and after a few minutes, she decides to leave.

This scene invites parallels with Marx's writings on the alienation of the worker. Marx's thesis rests on the argument that when the worker fails to relate to his or her labour, he or she is losing him/herself and acts only freely outside labour activities. Self-estrangement is thus the reduction of social life to 'animal activities'. What does Marx mean here? He suggests that the loss of individuality at work ends up reducing other 'human functions' to 'animal activities'. The worker feels at home only when eating, drinking and having sex, but not during his labour. Marx does not contend that leisure activities like the former ones are not 'human', but when dissociated from other forms of social activity, for example, labour, they become 'exclusive ends' and perpetuate alienation.[19] What the aforementioned scene though suggests is a different form of alienation according to which the worker ends up acting as if he/she is always at work. Nikander's body – and his colleague's in the opening scene – has turned here to a medium carrying out alienating mechanistic operations outside his work. A corollary to this is that we are invited to reconsider questions of culture beyond the distinctions of human and non-human as mentioned by Marx earlier. In fact, such an approach allows us to better comprehend the concept of cultural techniques, whose very foundation is the blurring of the boundaries between the human and the non-human. As Siegert explains:

> Cultural techniques inevitably comprise a more or less complex actor-network that includes technical objects and chains of operations (including gestures) in equal measure. The 'human touch', the power of agency typically ascribed to humans, is not a given but is constituted by and dependent on cultural techniques. In this sense, cultural techniques allow the actors involved to be both human and nonhuman; they reveal the extent to which the human actor has always already been decentered by the technical object.[20]

The technical objects here are the bodies, which are colonized by work operations during leisure time, and the capital, which is the precondition for the mechanization of the workers' physical movements.

Within these parameters, one needs to emphasize the ways cultural techniques refute distinctions between mind and body. In an ironic scene in the beginning of the film, we get to see Nikander's workmate telling him that he wants to open his own private waste-collection business. As he says, 'the banks and the state will support us'. Later on, he returns to the subject and elaborates on the idea in more detail. In a series of shot-reverse-shots, the characters deliver their lines in a deadpan way. The gesture here is produced by the cuts and the inexpressive delivery of the characters' lines. At some point, the camera returns to him, and he reveals to Nikander the business's watchword: 'reliable garbage disposal since 1986'. When Nikander retorts that is the slogan of the business they already work for, he responds: 'that's why it catches the eye'. This passage reveals the structural relations of alienation and, to evoke Lauren Berlant, the cruel optimism of the neo-liberal era, that is, the attachment to objects that are problematic.[21] Nikander's colleague has fallen for the neo-liberal belief in capital, hoping that it can alleviate his social hardship. Ironically, in the subsequent sequence, he dies while performing work duties. His death is framed by the camera as being part of the working routine. We see him collapsing, and then the camera cuts to an image of garbage being disposed, followed by Nikander's reaction shot. The sequence concludes with the camera framing the surrounding shabby landscape. Ironically, the worker has been consumed by the cultural techniques of capital on a literal and metaphoric level – literally because his body collapses while performing his work and metaphorically because he dies while having previously voiced his total faith in capital.

Alienating labour here is represented as an automatic operation that has inhabited both the body and imagination. This implies that labour is also a cultural technique. Frédéric Lordon phrases this, albeit implicitly, when aiming to answer the often-posed question, why individuals continue subjecting themselves to alienating labour and oppressive working conditions.

Reconciling Marx and Spinoza, Lordon suggests that the key to answering this question is to understand the historically defined 'desires', which are far from individual ones but the product of social relations of production. Within the capitalist neo-liberal economy, the dominant desire is the struggle to maintain one's being, and this translates to continue being in employment. Work becomes the precondition of affective fulfilment, and herein lies the complexity of Lordon's argument, which suggests that affects are also not subjective but the product of determined social relations. Citing Spinoza, Lordon illuminates the ways affects and desires are collective and provide a way of interpreting and acting in the world even against one's social interests. As he says, 'human beings are passionate automata'.[22] The term 'automata' corresponds with the very foundation of the concept of cultural techniques, according to which human beings execute operations that problematize notions of individual agency.

For Lordon, the difference between Fordist and neo-liberal societies is that the former organized labour on the premise of the affective joys of consumerism that compensated for the alienating work that individuals had to endure, whereas in the neo-liberal landscape, to be in work constitutes an affective desire in itself. This formulation corresponds with the foregoing passage with Nikander and his colleague, so from its opening sequences, the film provides an insight into the ways subjects negotiate their existence within the restructured Finnish economy, something evident in *Ariel* and *The Match Factory Girl* too. In the latter two works, this is expressed by placing emphasis on individuals who are also low on the economic scale and fail to come to terms with labour and emotional flexibility. The cultural techniques of alienated work have thus their effect on the characters' interpersonal relationships.

A closer look at the first 9 minutes of *The Match Factory Girl* can corroborate this. In the film's opening sequence, the camera registers a factory during the production process. Emphasis is placed on mechanized labour. We see machines cutting logs, refining them, producing matches and crating them in small boxes. It is only after 3.5 minutes of screen time that the camera registers the central character, Iiris (Kati Outinen), and initially we only get to see the lower part of her body and not her face. The effect is that the character is filmed as if she is part of the machinery surrounding her, and when we get to see her face, she is shown repeating a series of mechanized movements, inspecting and arranging matchboxes in the assembly line; behind her, a worker higher in the hierarchy observes her tactlessly. Later on, after finishing her shift, Iiris heads home, and the cultural techniques of alienated labour are emphatically reproduced in the labour required from her in the house she shares with her parents (Figure 7.2). We see her cooking and preparing the table for the family. Initially, we only see the lower part of her body, emphasizing again the mechanized aspect of her activity, and this highlights the ways her labour in the house is no less estranged than her low-wage work. When dinner is served, the family hardly exchanges any words; the characters' detachment from each other is further highlighted

Figure 7.2 Iiris (Kati Outinen) and her parents in *The Match Factory Girl* (1990). © and courtesy Sputnik Ltd.

when the mother (Elina Salo) reaches for Iiris's plate and grabs a piece of meat. In the scene that comes immediately after this one, we cut to the living room, where the mother is indifferently watching television news reporting on the Tiananmen Square massacre, while her stepfather (Esko Nikkari) is sleeping. The camera pans to the right and captures Iiris making herself up to go out, and through a sound bridge, we get to hear the report on the Tiananmen Square massacre.

The sequence mentioned earlier is emblematic because it condenses a series of historically defined relationships without the aid of dialogue or voice-over (the only exception is the TV news report from Tiananmen Square). What come into critical focus here are the techniques of hominization in a changing social and political environment. One might retort that the opening sequence evokes a Taylorized society, but it is initially striking that with the exception of Iiris and her supervisor, there are no other workers captured by the camera. We thus encounter a working space in which the workers are overshadowed by machines.[23] This can be read as a comment on the eventual disappearance of traditional blue-collar work. Satu Kyösola comments on the staging and suggests that the distinguishing feature is that Iiris 'is an absent presence' as if the image refers to a time past.[24] But Kaurismäki's concern with the machinization of life is also an index of his interest in the historical roots of the medium in the industrial era, its capacity to capture the rhythms of everyday life as well as its ability to provoke gestures that confound the boundaries between the real and the narrative universe.

One may recall Walter Benjamin's writings on Charlie Chaplin as an actor whose gestures merge the alienating rhythms of everyday life as well as the automated gestures provoked by the film apparatus. For Benjamin, the technological aspect of the film image cannot be separated from its industrial/ technological origins, and this has a profound effect on the movement of the body on screen.[25] Pasi Väliaho has pushed this argument further, drawing attention to the medium as the product of 'generalized mechanization that was presented by modern technological media in conjunction with increased capitalist power'.[26] The film medium, as he suggests, does not just represent corporeal movements but becomes embedded in them, since it transforms the body's movement on screen and potentially outside the boundaries of the screen.

Väliaho's argument is that by doubling gestures, the image becomes a gesture in itself. By automating corporeal movement, it exposes the body as a mediated entity that carries with it operations originating in technological processes of capitalist production. To return to the factory scene, one needs to note that the gesture in the image is mainly generated by the movement of the machines, whereas Iiris stays for the most part motionless; she occasionally extends her hands to rearrange the match boxes in the assembly line. This visual arrangement serves as a token of the expendability of the worker and the ways her body has been seized by the rhythms of capital. The mise en scène here attests figuratively to the individual's subordination to a whole nexus of capitalist tempos, and as Jonathan Rosenbaum insightfully observes, Iiris is framed by the camera as 'an object among objects'.[27] For Rosenbaum, the film's visual rhetoric recalls Fassbinder's practice, which intended to show how social conditions relegate working-class characters to the status of 'objects' instead of individuals. This comparison with Fassbinder helps to highlight the ways characters carry the labour conditions of exploitation in their social interactions.

Commenting on the relationship between workers and machines in industrial societies, Vilém Flusser argues that the individual turns into an 'attribute of the apparatus', since the machine in the production process is the norm while the workers are expendable. Flusser observes that unlike the optimistic Enlightenment narrative of the individual being able to liberate herself through machines, the individual turns out to be a 'property of the apparatus', because he or she has not learned how to live outside the rhythms of capital.[28] To extend Flusser's argument in the post-industrial, neo-liberal era, I would posit that the individual adopts the alienating operations of capital in her private life, making it difficult to distinguish between labour operations and leisure time. This is affirmed in the aforementioned sequence in the shift from the public space of work, that is, the factory, to the private working-class setting. Alienation is here part and parcel of a reality in which human relationships are no longer founded upon trust or acknowledgement of a shared class status. Iiris's domestic work is performed in the same estranged way as her waged labour, while the body language between her and her bitterly marginalized parents demonstrates an attitude of mistrust and exploitation within the domestic environment. Hence, the corporeal interactions between the characters are the outcome of operations prescribed by alienating conditions of labour (in the case of Iiris) and unemployment (in the case of her parents).

These operations question the individual's agency as well as its ability to construct meaningful relationships, a historical reality heightened by the large-scale changes in employment in the post-industrial world. Guy Standing's discussion of the ways in which working instability produces relationships that cannot be founded on cooperation and trust situates the problem succinctly. For Standing, this epitomizes the ways that people on the lower scales of society do not develop relations of solidarity, because these relations require some sense of stability, which is currently absent.[29] The present conditions of working flexibility have their effect on the individuals' psyche, their social interactions and communication. Similarly, Jennifer Silva explains how the narrative of individualism and depoliticization has been appealing to young working-class people, whose 'coming of age' does involve neither the joining of social groups nor the consciousness of belonging to a class.[30]

The absence of any connection or solidarity with other victims of social oppression is captured in the characters' manifest indifference towards the news report from Tiananmen Square. They watch the news indifferently, but the crucial element is the ways that television does not simply represent but mediates too, conditioning the responses of the viewers. Later on, when the news reports on the famous Beijing protester, the camera alternates between the characters and the news images. In the passage that follows, the camera locates the spectators in the factory, framing Iiris's lower body while she arranges products on the assembly line. This association of two different visual materials alludes to themes of media agency. The automation of the subject's movement in the factory is compared with the automation of her spectatorial labour, making a comparison between cultural techniques of alienated labour and spectatorship.[31]

In *Ariel*, it is also in everyday gestures that we can observe the individual's dissociation from the changing social environment. Indicative in this respect are the gestures of smoking. Satu Kyösola remarks that smoking in Kaurismäki's films is a motif, which is used to point towards moments of social bonding as well as detachment from the world. It is the repetition that assigns it with meaning, and as she suggests, 'smoking encodes the repetition of gesture, something mechanical and rhythmic'.[32] Such a representation of smoking as a mechanical repetition helps us understand it as a gesture that carries social weight and demonstrates the characters' uneasiness in the new changing social landscape. Yet it is the technicity of the gestures that can help us identify the social context, since their representation does not subscribe to direct cause and effect explanations.

The character's uneasiness and inability to process changes in the Finnish environment is given full sway in two important scenes in *Ariel*. The first one takes place in one of the first sequences of the film in which Taisto has a conversation with his father following the closure of the mine. Within a medium shot, the camera captures both characters and approaches them as the father starts a conversation with Taisto. He notifies him that he intends to give him his car and advises him to leave the village and try to make a living in Helsinki. Ultimately, the camera closes up to the car keys that the father hands to his son and to a packet of cigarettes on a table. This is followed by a series of shot-reverse-shots, and then Taisto's father takes a gun from his pocket and heads towards the toilet. Taisto, obviously confused, lights a cigarette nervously. A gunshot is heard, but he does not look surprised. The camera follows him as he moves slowly towards the bathroom. Then, framed in a medium shot, we see Taisto gazing at the off-screen dead man. The scene concludes as Taisto apathetically puffs another smoke.

The gesture of smoking here does not operate as a reaction shot. The actor and the filmmaker emphasize its technicity, that is, its mechanical operation. Thus, its function within the scene is not necessarily communicative. This non-communicative function of the gesture chimes neatly with Flusser's definition of gesture 'as a movement of the body' 'for which there is no satisfactorily causal explanation'.[33] For Flusser, gesture is not necessarily the expression or representation of a state of mind. A gesture can instead be seen as something that enacts a state of mind, and here the questions of humanness and agency are again confounded. Gesture is inscribed within a context of automatism, and this brings us back once again to the ways the body is mediated and produces gestures which are simultaneously human and technical. Add to this the fact that smoking as addiction has social connotations and cannot be subsumed under individual and psychological explanations. In Taisto's case, the mediated element in his mechanical gesture of smoking is that this is not simply an internalized gesticulation, whose meaning can be determined by resorting to a definite psychological explanation. Smoking is thus coded as a corporeal gesture that responds to an estranged social environment.

A similar mechanized gesture of smoking is evidenced when Taisto goes to the docks of Helsinki, hoping to get some day-to-day labour following his assault by two vagrants. When he arrives, the camera frames him as being part of the group of workers, who are waiting to see if their name will be called by the supervisor. A sudden close-up of his face follows as he lights a cigarette. A series of cuts follow, capturing the docks supervisor, Taisto and the group of workers. Taisto continues smoking almost motionless even when he is offered work, and this staging conveys a feeling of social banality. Kaurismäki's modus operandi corresponds with the Bressonian idea of highlighting gestures so as to investigate the reasons that trigger them. As in Bresson, the exploration of causes does not imply providing definite conclusions. The causes are to be discovered in the minute corporeal movements that produce a sense of social mise en scène. It is not accidental that Bresson speaks against cinema as a mode of 'reproduction', privileging a cinema of 'discovery'.[34] In Kaurismäki, this approach to representation is emphasized in scenes of ostensive gestures, whose framing does not always convey narrative information but emphasizes their quotidian aspect and underscores their mechanical execution. The gesture of smoking in his social mise en scène is not a psychological trait of the characters, but a form of mediation, a cultural practice that sets the characters apart from their environment.[35]

Consequently, Kaurismäki's stress on quotidian gestures de-individuates his characters so as to reveal the social weight of their actions. Moments of humour also participate in this process of de-individuation and social critique. Some fine examples of humour can be seen in the previous discussed sequence between Nikander and his colleague, when the latter formulates his 'business plans'. Similarly, Taisto's response to his father's death has a tragicomic dimension that complicates the representational process. In the first example, Nikander's colleague sounds like a mouthpiece for the social reality that oppresses him, and in the second one, Taisto's confusion betrays a broader inability to deal with the seriousness of the situation, as well as the difficulty in processing changes on a personal and a social level. Finally, in *The Match Factory Girl*, a series of socially encoded actions are framed in a humorous manner; one may recall here Iiris's night out at the disco, where she is shown consuming numerous bottles of orange juice, having not succeeded to be asked to a dance by any of the local men. Another humorous scene takes place when Aarne visits her house in the presence of her parents; a combination of embarrassment and gaucheness adds an absurdist humour to the sequence, making us notice the class distinctions that set the characters apart.

Humour here invites us to see the actions on screen as strange; this defamiliarizing effect of humour and the comic has been noted among many by Hegel, Brecht and Arnheim. For Hegel, the comic produces a dissolution of subjectivity, drawing our attention not only to the characters but also to their external circumstances, while Brecht in an equally Hegelian fashion thought that the comic has the potential to create a sense of distance and make one see obvious situations from a different perspective. Similarly, Arnheim has elaborated on Charlie Chaplin's comic effects and their ability to produce 'dramatic contradictions'.[36] The moments of humour in Kaurismäki's trilogy serve an analogous purpose, since they draw attention to situations that are far from being individualistic, but they carry social implications. Gender hierarchies, class divisions and an apolitical understanding of the social environment by Nikander's colleague are among the many social aspects brought to the surface by means of such an absurdist humour.

Techniques of the Body

As mentioned in the beginning of the chapter, any discussion of cultural techniques does not automatically suggest individual passivity, since mediation is a dynamic process. Furthermore, as already pointed out, the study of cultural techniques does not focus only on the body as subject to operations that are oppressive but also on the ways cultural techniques can have a liberating effect and can 'decolonize' bodies.

While currently discussions of media's ability not simply to represent, or inform, but also to 'transform' are widespread, one significant contribution that highlighted media's agency was offered by Marcel Mauss in a text written in 1935.[37] The title of Mauss's text is 'Techniques of the Body', and it was concerned with analysing the processes through which individuals learn to use their bodies. For Mauss, the body is an 'instrument', and through an analysis of different corporeal gestures, he demonstrates the technicity of the body, its dependency on technical and media processes. In one often-quoted part of the text, Mauss describes his experience at a hospital in New York and his astonishment after observing the gestures of the nurses.

As he says:

> A kind of revelation came to me in hospital. I was ill in New York. I wondered where previously I had seen girls walking as my nurses walked. I had the time to think about it. At last I realised that it was at the cinema. Returning to France, I noticed how common this gait was, especially in Paris; the girls were French and they too were walking in this way. In fact, American walking fashions had begun to arrive over here, thanks to the cinema. This was an idea I could generalise. The positions of the arms and hands while walking form a social idiosyncracy, they are not simply a product of some purely individual, almost completely psychical arrangements and mechanisms.[38]

Mauss describes here the trainability of corporeal behaviour or, to put it more clearly, the ways the body is modulated by social processes. Pasi Väliaho comments that the Austrian novelist Joseph Roth expressed similar puzzlement when encountering the gestural behaviour of the residents of a German provincial town. Roth was surprised to see how people could 'absorb' gestures and facial expressions of movie characters.[39] These comments shed some light on the broader idea of contemporary German Media Theory and its core thesis that media do not simply communicate information, but they also alter our ways of being in the world.

In *Shadows in Paradise* and *Ariel*, there are some significant passages that suggest the changeability of corporeal postures and gestures stemming from the characters' encounters with different forms of media and cultural practices. In *Shadows in Paradise*, Nikander's apprehensive and shy attitude changes after accidentally finding a tango record on a landfill site and after practising his English language skills during a community course. A telling index is the modulation of his corporeal behaviour following an English language class. The camera locates him at a booth desk while listening to an English man's sentences, which he subsequently translates into Finnish. The English audiobook includes a sentence that reads: 'it's funny, it's very funny. And it's a lot of fun too to be in love'. He pauses the cassette player and translates the text. When he rewinds the cassette to listen to the text, he listens to the same sentence again. Determined, he removes his headphones and heads to find Ilona. This shift in attitude is demonstrated in the following sequence, when he meets up with her. Despite the fact that she is accompanied by another man, her new boss, he initiates conversation and asks her to accompany him on a trip. When she refuses, he throws down his cigarette and retorts – in an unusually confident way – in English: 'ok, see you'. Towards the end of the film, he decides to revisit Ilona at her workplace. Within a medium shot, the camera frames them facing each other. He asks her to give their relationship a second chance and follow him on a trip to Tallinn. Ilona's employer enters the frame and stands between them, but Nikander hardly acknowledges him. When the former insults him, Nikander assumes an ostensive pose, grabs him physically and asks him laconically to leave. He then encounters Ilona, and when she asks him whether they will be able to survive, he responds in determined English: 'small potatoes'. This sense of empowerment is also figured in another memorable sequence earlier in the film, where Nikander is framed spending time on the beach with Ilona; the latter has just confided him that she has stolen money from her former employer to take revenge on him for having made her redundant. We see both of them listening to music and gazing at the sea. The rock tune in the background is a love song, and suddenly Nikander's rigid posture changes, and he embraces and kisses Ilona who acquiesces. Again, there is a mechanistic depiction of the gesture, and the implication is that the body's changeability is motivated by the diegetic music.

These sequences attest to the body's capacity to respond to stimuli and absorb different corporeal techniques. While in the previous section, the sequences mentioned from the film centred on Nikander's alienation and the colonization of his body from the rhythms of capital, in the aforementioned passages from the film, we notice how the body adopts different techniques that somehow allow the character to radically alter his composure and attitude. While Mauss, for the most part, was concerned with revealing how techniques of the body tend to produce bodies that are disciplined, something different takes place here, where the character's encounter with another language modulates his behaviour. This is plainly shown whenever he cites English sentences, since his disposition is overtly altered. Kaurismäki's representation of the character's changeability reveals the dynamic aspect of corporeal techniques and has an optimistic tenor, since he does not solely show the body as being imprisoned in an alienated world but also its potential to change. In this context, body techniques are not static but performative, and the technicity of the body is not a code word for alienation but can equally lead to empowerment.

Such an empowering potential of technicity is also illustrated in *Ariel*. Following Taisto's and Mikkonen's escape from prison, the film borrows generic formulas from gangster B-movies. Importantly, Taisto and Mikkonen seem also to carry themselves as movie characters, something that chimes with Mauss's example mentioned earlier of people adopting body techniques from the cinema. This absorption of body techniques from cinematic cultural stereotypes accords with the characters' changeability. In one of the first sequences following their escape, Taisto visits the car yard where he had been deceived by the owner to sell his car at a very low price. Initially, the camera frames Taisto and Mikkonen in a medium long shot as they enter the yard. Within a static shot, we can observe the characters' gestures and costumes that recall pictorial elements from gangster films. From now on, the film's visual and narrative architecture changes and consciously includes iconic references to gangster movies. This is also an instance of self-reflexivity that shows further Kaurismäki's cinephilia and specifically his repeatedly stated admiration for B-movies and the films of Samuel Fuller. Moreover, the characters within the diegesis act in such a way as if they are consciously copying visual stereotypes from gangster films. Taisto, who has been hitherto represented as shy and apprehensive, becomes resolute and dynamic after attiring himself in clothes and sunglasses that carry generic cinematic connotations. This is also exemplified later on when he and Mikkonen make a deal with two members of the underworld, who agree to offer them fake passports so that they can escape abroad. While Mikkonen takes charge of the negotiations, Taisto, wearing his sunglasses, remains expressionless and performs gestures in a deadpan manner when asked to confirm his agreement. Later on, when he realizes that he and Mikkonen have been framed, he acts after putting on his sunglasses and carrying himself in a performative way. His performative technicity is highlighted because while waiting for his partner outside the criminals' shelter, he is shown acting nervously. In the following passage, he enters the building, glasses on, with a gait that communicates will power, and by the end of the sequence, he shoots the underworld thugs. The contrast between these two passages is noticeable; the actor performs Taisto's apprehension in the first instance through an acting style that emphasizes physical restraint; in the second example, he employs a highly mannered acting style, but here his gesture exemplifies physical fluidity, making evident the performative element in his postural change and behaviour.

One is inclined to concede that the characters feel so alienated from the world that the copying of cultural stereotypes, gestures and visual elements from the world of cinema has an empowering and utopian effect. They do not adapt to an alienating environment, but they accomplish small-scale changes, demonstrating that there are not only techniques of the body that serve to assimilate individuals to normative behaviour but also others that allow them to construct alternatives. From this perspective, we can see how the body's dependency on medial and technical processes does not involve a passive being in the world. Mauss's thesis that the body is technologically constituted does not subscribe to a different form of ontology, according to which the technological aspect of being suppresses the natural one; it highlights instead its medial construction and its potential for change. One may consider here Iiris's gesture of smoking in *The Match Factory Girl*. In the only scene where she is shown smoking, having finished her cigarette, she decides to carry out a series of murders against those who have manipulated her. Smoking here is not a lethargic gesture, as it is the case with other characters in Kaurismäki's films but a dynamic one. It highlights not only the character's detachment from the world but also her desire to act.

One needs to note that this film marks a departure from the optimistic tenor of the two preceding parts of the proletarian trilogy. In both *Shadows in Paradise* and *Ariel*, there is an underlying romantic optimism that, despite the changing and inhospitable social environment, the subjects can initiate interpersonal relationships, which can help them cope with institutional dysfunctions, oppressive labour conditions and structural inequalities. According to Andrew Nestigen, individuals in these films tend to believe that they can amend oppressive conditions to their own benefit.[40] Nikander and Ilona ignore the difficulties of the future by reuniting and travelling to Tallinn. Similarly, Taisto and Irmeli leave the country and seek a better life in Mexico. Certainly, the films' endings ironically rework the clichéd generic patterns that consolidate the formation of the heterosexual couple. Retrospectively, this romantic optimism can be understood as an index of a 'cruel optimism', which translates to a problematic belief in 'the narrative of good life', that is, the potential to bend structural conditions of injustice and project 'social-democratic fantasies' into a changing economic environment.[41] Cruel optimism describes the withdrawal to narratives of the self and the belief that happiness can be achieved even in the most adverse social conditions. It appears then that *The Match Factory Girl* stands out for its capacity to offer a counterweight to cruel optimistic narratives. Iiris's gestural behaviour towards the end of the film points to collective operations of political resignation but also of anger. Family, romantic relationships and work interactions cannot fulfil the vacuum of life produced by oppressive regimes of economic injustice. In the absence of collective political action, the recourse to narratives of the self does not seem to provide a pathway to change, and this is the reason why Iiris's interpersonal relationships are doomed to failure. Instead, Iiris's murderous tirade is symptomatic of the breakdown of sociality in neo-liberal capitalism, whose irreconcilable contradictions cannot be ameliorated by subscribing to a narrative of normative optimism. Thus, this trilogy of films prefigures many themes elaborated in the contemporary cinema of precarity as exemplified in the films of the Dardenne brothers, Olivier Nakache and Eric Toledano, Stéphane Brizé, and Laurent Cantet. A key feature of the films produced by these various filmmakers is the stress on gestures and the quotidian rather than dramatic verbal communication aiming to capture the subjects' traumatic assimilation into the regimes of neo-liberal capitalism. Gesture becomes a significant bearer of meaning because it emphasizes the violence inflicted by capital both on the mind and the body of those positioned low on the economic scales. In many respects then, Kaurismäki's trilogy could be renamed as that of the 'precariat', precisely because it heralds aesthetic, formal and thematic elements typical of the contemporary cinema of precarity.

Acknowledgements

I am grateful to the editor, Thomas Austin, for his insightful comments and suggestions for this chapter. I would also like to thank Jussi Parikka and Thomas Apperley for introducing me to writings on cultural techniques.

Notes

1   Jochen Werner, 'Talking Without Words: Aki Kaurismäki's Rediscovery of the Virtues of Cinema', *Journal of Finnish Studies*, 8, no. 2 (2004): 68.

2   Andrew, Nestigen, *The Cinema of Aki Kaurismäki: Contrarian Stories* (London and New York: Wallflower Press, 2013), 147; Pietari Kääpä, 'The Working Class Has No Fatherland: Aki Kaurismäki's Films and the Transcending of National Specificity', *Journal of Finnish Studies*, 8, no. 2 (2004): 83.

3   Béla, Balázs, *Theory of the Film: Character and Growth of a New Art* (London: Dennis Dobson Ltd, [1952] 1970), 69.

4   Jean Epstein, 'Cinema and Modern Literature', in *Jean Epstein: Critical Essays and New Translations*, ed. Sarah Keller and Jason N. Paul (Amsterdam: Amsterdam University Press, [1921], 2012), 271–276, 273.

5   Rudolf Arnheim, *Film as Art* (Berkeley, LA, London: University of California Press, 1957), 228.

6   Giorgio Agamben, 'Notes on Gesture', in *Infancy and History: The Destruction of Experience*, trans. by Liz Heron (London and New York: Verso, 1978), 139.

7   Bernhard Siegert, *Cultural Techniques: Grids, Filters, Doors, and Other Articulations of the Real*, trans. by Geoffrey Winthrop-Young (New York: Fordham University Press, 2015), 9.

8   Ibid., 193.

9   Sybille Krämer, Horst Bredekamp, 'Culture, Technology, Cultural Techniques – Moving beyond Text', *Theory, Culture and Society*, 30, no. 6 (2013): 27.

10   Siegert, *Cultural Techniques*, 14.

11   Marcel Mauss, 'Techniques of the Body', *Economy and Society*, 2, no. 1 [1935] (1973): 73.

12   Bertolt Brecht, 'Two Essay Fragments on Non-professional Acting', in *Brecht on Theatre*. ed. Marc Silberman, Steve Giles, and Tom Kuhn (London and New York: Bloomsbury, [1939] 2014), 210.

13 Cornelia Vismann, 'Cultural Techniques and Sovereignty', *Theory, Culture and Society*, 30, no. 6 (2013): 87–88.

14 Siegert, *Cultural Techniques*, 14.

15 Jason Lavery, *The History of Finland* (Westport, CT, London: Greenwood Press, 2006), 147.

16 Fred Singleton, *A Short History of Finland* (Cambridge: Cambridge University Press, [1989] 1998), 153.

17 Lavery, *The History of Finland*, 155–158.

18 For more on the historical context and the films, see Toiviainen 'The Kaurimäki Phenomenon', 28.

19 Karl Marx, *Early Writings*, trans. by Rodney Livingstone (London: Penguin, [1844] 1974), 327.

20 Siegert, *Cultural Techniques*, 193.

21 Lauren Berlant, *Cruel Optimism* (Durham and London: Duke University Press, 2011), 24.

22 Frédéric Lordon, *Willing Slaves of Capital Spinoza and Marx on Desire*, trans. by Gabriel Ash (London: Verso, 2014), 17.

23 Kaurismäki has also reflected on the dwindling of labour, commenting that technological development renders the workers unnecessary. See Schepelern, 'The Element of Crime and Punishment', 94.

24 Satu Kyösola, 'The Archivist's Nostalgia', *Journal of Finnish Studies*, 8, no. 2 (2004): 55.

25 Walter Benjamin, 'The Formula in Which the Dialectical Structure of Film Finds Expression', in *The Work of Art in the Age of Its Technological Reproducibility, and Other Writings on Media*, ed. Michael W. Jennings, Brigid Doherty, and Thomas Y. Levin, trans. Edmund Jephcott, Rodney Livingstone, Howard Eiland, and Others (Cambridge, MA and London: Harvard University Press [1935] 2008), 340.

26 Pasi Väliaho, *Mapping the Moving Image Gesture, Thought and Cinema Circa 1900* (Amsterdam: Amsterdam University Press, 2010), 31–32.

27 Jonathan Rosenbaum, 'Wallflower's Revenge [THE MATCH FACTORY GIRL]', http://www.jonathanrosenbaum.net/1993/02/wallflower-s-revenge/, last accessed 31 March 2016.

28 Vilém Flusser, *Gestures*, trans. by Nancy Ann Roth (Minneapolis and London: University of Minnesota Press, [1991] 2014), 16–17.

29 Guy Standing, *The Precariat: The New Dangerous Class* (London and New York: Bloomsbury, 2011), 22. Richard Sennett has brilliantly demonstrated that late capitalism's commitment to short-term goals and immediate return of profit has equally impacted members of the salariat class, bringing into conflict the individuals' institutional roles with their personal lives. Whereas commitment and trust are values considered irrelevant in the neo-liberal working environment, they are necessary for the formation of 196 sustainable social and personal connections, and this contradiction makes even better-paid workers feel insecure and isolated. See Richard Sennett, *The Corrosion of Character: The Personal Consequences of Work in the New Capitalism* (London and New York: W. W. Norton & Company, 1998), 20.

30 Jennifer M. Silva, *Coming Up Short: Working-class Adulthood in an Age of Uncertainty* (Oxford: Oxford University Press, 2013), 84.

31 Geoffrey Winthrop-Young explains that watching television is a cultural technique too, since it involves technological competence and skills in decoding information. See Young, 'The Kultur of Cultural Techniques', 381.
32 Kyösola, 'The Archivist's Nostalgia', 57.
33 Flusser, *Gestures*, 3.
34 Robert Bresson, *Notes on Cinematography* trans. by Jonathan Griffin (New York: Urizen Books, 1975), 32.
35 In *The Match Factory Girl*, there is an interesting scene, when Iiris's boyfriend visits her household. Both parents act in an introverted and shy manner, which is heightened by the fact that Aarne's gesture of smoking is a gesture of separation from their working-class household. His gesture makes Iiris's parents more nervous as if they are examined. This is another example of how the execution of a gesture situates a character – here from a different class background – at odds with the surrounding setting.
36 G. W. F. Hegel, *Aesthetics: Notes on Fine Art*, Vol. 2, trans. T. M. Knox (Oxford: Oxford University Press, [1935] 1975), 1199; John Willett, *Brecht in Context* (London: Methuen, 1984), 86; Arnheim, *Film as Art*,146.
37 Sarah Kember, Joanna Zylinska, *Life after New Media: Mediation as a Vital Process* (Cambridge, MA and London: MIT, 2012), 37–38.
38 Mauss, 'Techniques of the Body', 72.
39 Väliaho, *Mapping the Moving Image*, 105.
40 Nestigen, *The Cinema of Aki Kaurismäki*, 108.
41 Berlant, *Cruel Optimism*, 25.

Chapter 8

KAURISMÄKI'S MUSICAL MOMENTS: GENRE, IRONY, UTOPIA, REDEMPTION

Andrew Nestingen

There are some great moments that conclude Aki Kaurismäki's films. Their magnitude arises at least in part from the narrative that precedes them. It is hard to watch the life of a gritty protagonist swirl into chaos. Often the only thing that makes the narratives tolerable is the music, irony and allusive humour – if not the math jokes. The concluding moments, however, qualify the irony and often offer sincerity and redemption. The humour is ironic and arch in the 1980s films but became increasingly sentimental in the films since *Kauas pilvet karkaavat* (Drifting Clouds, 1996). When Kaurismäki's conclusions reward their characters with redemption, and a flash of hope, in a moment of concluding music, the viewer is interpolated into an affective experience and also rewarded for hoping on behalf of the character. Joined affectively, there is a hope for something better, a utopian impulse amid the dreariness and the grit.

How do Kaurismäki's films generate these intense affective conclusions, and how can we make sense of them? Studies of Kaurismäki have not considered affect much. Neither have critics paid much attention to the films' formal construction, as Jaakko Seppälä has pointed out in undertaking an ambitious and sorely needed formalist reading of Kaurismäki's cinema.[1] This article's thesis is that the redemption that typifies the conclusions of Kaurismäki's films is best understood as the concluding instance in a series of 'musical moments', a term elaborated by Amy Herzog.[2] The musical moment, she argues, inverts the dominance of narrative to privilege music, creating intense, meaningful affective instances.[3] In a typically Kaurismäkian twist on a conventional form, these musical moments can be understood as an inflection of film genre – the film musical. These elements are combined to create an affectively intense ending, which highlights utopian notions of community and intensity.

Musical Moments

Kaurismäki's films end big through music, but these big musical endings draw their power, and some ironic ambiguity, from earlier 'musical moment' scenes in the films. That is, the concluding scene is part of a series of linked scenes, a pattern of narrative organization. This logic may be likened to the musical genre in which formal distinctions are drawn in the 'number' scenes to establish oppositions, which create narrative tension that can be overcome to produce a concluding emotional payoff or, in Kaurismäki's case, the sense of redemption.

A good example of such narrative organization can be seen in *Ariel* (1988). The story could be related by its key songs, whose lyrics narrate the emotional oppositions around which the film is organized. At the film's conclusion, the protagonist Taisto Kasurinen (Turo Pajala) and his newly wedded wife Irmeli (Susanna Haavisto), and her son Riku (Eetu Hilkamo), flee to Helsinki's East Harbor to board the *Ariel*, bound for Mexico. As a launch transports them through the dusk, non-diegetic music begins to play, 'Saateenkari vie maahan satujen' (Somewhere over the rainbow, way up high). Taisto, Irmeli and Riku are finally united and safe. They have escaped unjust, dystopian Finland for a second chance, a fantasy world of blooming flowers, fluttering bluebirds and lemon drops, 'over the rainbow'.

The otherworldly light in the lyrics also alludes to the figurative language of a musical moment earlier in the film, the musical montage of Taisto's road trip south from the mining town Salla, set to the tune of Rauli Badding Somerjoki's 'Valot' (Lights). In Somerjoki's song, light signifies absence and longing, rather than illumination and unity. The song plays as Taisto drives across snowy landscapes in the traditional journey of the Finn from the north, seeking work and a second chance by migrating to the south.[4] This musical moment is organized around Somerjoki's lyrics. A lonely narrator sings about the light produced by his beloved for whom he longs. She is the 'brightest light' (valo kirkahin). Her luminescence allows him to live in the darkness of evening shadows: her love illuminates his world. Yet she is not present, and so the figurative light also stands for her absence. In 'Over the Rainbow', the longing has changed, and light is now present. The narrator, like Taisto, wants light and knows that 'dreams really do come true'. Light has come to stand for unity, underscored by the shift from Somerjoki's minor key to the C major of 'Over the Rainbow'. The figurative language of the two songs, and the figure of light in particular, works according to an expressionist aesthetic principle, exteriorizing Taisto's inner world in terms of light. In so doing, the music and lyrics can be understood as musical moments.

What does Herzog mean by the term 'musical moment'? She theorizes the concept in her book *Dreams of Difference, Songs of the Same*. She writes, 'music, typically a popular song, inverts the image – sound hierarchy to occupy a dominant position in a filmic work. The movements of the image, and hence the structuring of space and time, are dictated by song'.[5] By contrast, music is often 'unheard melody' in Claudia Gorbman's formulation, especially through the ubiquitous inclusion of non-diegetic music.[6] 'Nondiegetic scores typically map themselves onto the rhythm of the image, supporting the flow of narrative action without interrupting it […] the music stabilizes the image and secures meaning while remaining as unobtrusive as possible,' writes Herzog.[7] In the musical moment, 'this hierarchy is inverted and music serves as the dominant force in the work.'[8] Marked out through extra-diegetic amplification, for example, obtrusive lyrics, live performance or combination with distinctive sounds, in the musical moment, music and sound come to signify. In *Ariel*, they signify a longing for unity, and then unity realized.

Kaurismäki uses sound frequently in his films, not least to create musical moments. An instance of his signifying use of sound is evident in the opening sequence of *Tulitikkutehtaan tyttö* (The Match Factory Girl, 1990). Critics have frequently described the film as realist in style. Yet sound in the opening shows how sound and music work to signify. The film opens on a silent, black screen with an epigraph in white, 'He ovat takuulla kuolleet siellä kaukana metsän keskellä kylmään ja nälkään' (They have surely died of cold and starvation far away in the middle of the forest). The epigraph fades to a credit reel, in the same lettering, which rolls above a subtle use of non-diegetic, or really extradiegetic, sound. One can hear intermittent gusting wind for 35 seconds, before a cut to a shot of a log in the match factory. The image of the log marks a cut in the soundtrack: the sound transition from the blowing wind to the interior sounds of the production line, inside the match factory. The sound of the wind is thus connected to the sounds of the factory in which the viewer soon meets protagonist Iiris (Kati Outinen) working the line. Like the children of the epigraph, she is figuratively dying of cold and starvation. Associative sound editing gives expression to this notion, which is at that heart of the film. While this credit sequence is not technically music, or a musical moment, sound works in the way music does elsewhere in the film in Kaurismäki's musical moments. The hierarchy of image and sound is inverted, and sound conveys meaning. Iiris is figuratively 'starving and freezing', abandoned by her mother, who is in thrall to her stepfather. Sound makes evident that Iiris is isolated and alone in an urban forest, living in a dystopia.

The film follows up with some key musical moments, which voice other sentiments. The most obvious of these is one of the most memorable scenes in Kaurismäki's body of work, the dance-hall scene in which Iiris seeks a dance partner during a tango evening. The scene is built around a set of oppositions, which tie together multiple story worlds: the story of Iiris and her parents, the story of Iiris's quest to find a romantic partner, the story of Iiris's interaction with the dystopia she inhabits. The scene begins on the last, with TV images of student demonstrators at Tiananmen Square in Beijing being attacked by soldiers. The camera pans from these to an image of Iiris applying makeup, 'backstage', donning her costume, before she ventures out to the dance hall, where she seeks a partner. As her costume suggests, and the staging of the scene underscores, the dance hall is a fantasy space. The performance of Reijo Taipale further reinforces this dimension: he sings 'Satumaa tango' (Storyland Tango) on stage, behind the proscenium arch, an artificial, expressionist background behind him. These layers are more subtly present in the context of the words of Taipale's song. 'Aavan meren tuolla puolen jossakin on maa / missä onnen kaukorantaan laine liplattaa' (Somewhere beyond the ocean lies a land / where waves wash the happy shore). The overt fantasy of these lyrics, Iiris's dance costume and the proscenium that marks off the performance signal the film has entered a fantasy space, a 'storyland'. The scene gives expression to Iiris's wish. She wishes to reach that land but cannot: 'vanki olen maan / vain aatoksin mi kauas entää / sinne käydä saan' (I am a prisoner of this earth / and only in my dreams / may I visit). What awaits her in the land is a one and only beloved. The song's lyrics invert the image, dominated as they are by the visually uninteresting images of the Taipale performing. Yet the lyrics themselves express Iiris's innermost affective state, what exists beneath her costume. Indeed, the viewer can now see that the filmmaker has shown Iiris donning her costume to create a mask, which can then be dropped to reveal her true self in the musical moment – with its live music, quirky musical choice, live performance and emphasis on lyrical expression. The musical moment is built on contrasts that work to express the sentimental feelings and in particular longings of a character who cannot realize these feelings within the dystopian world she inhabits.

Elements of the Musical

The scene in *The Match Factory Girl*, and the scene of Taisto's drive south to the music of Rauli Badding Somerjoki, can be understood as musical moments, but they also show a close relationship to the film musical. Such scenes can be understood as what Jane Feuer calls the 'wish ballet', insofar as each announces the protagonist's wish or dream, but they also delineate plural diegetic spaces in the film.[9] Feuer writes that the wish ballet is a key scene in the MGM musicals of the 1930s and 1940s, as they 'emphasize either the wish of the dreamer (the *Pirate* ballet, the first dream ballet in *Lili*) or they represent a tentative working out of the first problems of the primary narrative'.[10]

In *The Match Factory Girl*, and other Kaurismäki films, it is evident that there is always a musical moment scene, usually early in the film, in which the protagonist's dreams are given expression through music. Our focus so far has fallen on the content of the dream. Yet there is another dimension. In Kaurismäki's films, conventions of the musical help organize the narrative structure, as well. The premise of Feuer's argument about the wish ballet is that it depends on a delineation between diegetic worlds. The wish ballet not only defines the protagonist's dreams and their aims but also works to establish and distinguish contrasting narrative worlds. The wish ballet occurs in the fantasy space, which is juxtaposed to a reality space, structuring other scenes. Taisto's garage collapses, and he empties his bank account in the reality scenes, but the music and its lyrics indicate Taisto is in a dream space. So, too, we move from Iiris's alcoholic parents and the scenes of brutality at Tiananmen Square to strains of 'Satumaa Tango' and its expressive lyrics. Distinct narrative worlds of reality and dream with their alternative codes are established. Feuer describes the coding of story worlds to music and dance as a dialectic of narrative and number, as does another key scholar of the musical, Rick Altman, as we will see.

The subtle but effective delineation of these worlds, by way of musical moments and the conventions of the musical, has not been discussed by critics. Yet it is the structure that makes possible the prevailing reading of Kaurismäki's characters as fully human.[11] For example, Lauri Timonen writes, 'The distinguishing mark of Aki Kaurismäki's cinema is its "double-vision," which seamlessly juxtaposes present and past, in which the latter stands as the measure of the former. Once things were better in the world and among people, and since things have declined, maybe forever.'[12] The late Peter von Bagh often praised Kaurismäki's films for their humane, moral values.[13] In such criticism, the emphasis is on people. But how is it that the films' characters are perceived as 'people'? It is through the attribution of dream and desire to character, which happens through musical moments and the delineation of diegetic worlds, that such readings are possible. They say few words, they show little affect and their actions are unremarkable. But we are subtly given access to their dreams worlds in ways that give expression to it and so construct their humanity for the viewer.

The dream world is juxtaposed to a cinematically and culturally allusive reality, which itself also includes multiple story worlds. For instance, a narrative world of the present, represented by contemporary costuming and other mise en scène, and a narrative world of the past, represented by outdated costuming and mise en scène. As an example, Laitakaupungin valot (Lights in the Dusk, 2006). the outdated apartment of Koistinen (Janne Hyytiäinen) and the contemporary styling of the crime boss Lindholm's (Ilkka Koivula) apartment place them in different worlds. Further, the location of the film in the late-modern built environment of Helsinki's Ruoholahti neighbourhood stands in contrast to nostalgic places, inhabited and visited by Koisitinen, such as the Finnish fast-food kiosk he frequents where the film ends. Another such example is the distinction between the costuming of police officers in *Le Havre* (2011): the heavily armed, contemporarily outfitted officers who persecute Marcel (André Wilms) and Idrissa (Blondin Miguel) differ from the old-fashioned attire of Police Inspector Monet (Jean-Pierre Dardin). Henry Bacon has emphasized these coded differences in the films' mise en scène, arguing that there is a poetics to it, a sort of moral geography.[14]

Rick Altman is in consensus with Jane Feuer on the dualism of the musical. He argues that the structure of the musical organizes a series of pairs, writing that the film musical 'has a dual focus, built around parallel stars of the opposite sex and radically divergent values […], [which depends on] the resolution of their differences'.[15] Resolving the differences between the worlds is the definitive feature of the musical. The musical develops the relationship through scenes in which the poles of reality and fantasy are marked out through music, dance, colour design, dialogue and editing. Feuer writes, 'musicals are built upon a foundation of dual registers, with the contrast between narrative and number defining the musical comedy as a form'.[16] Song, and all it stands for, ultimately 'synthesizes' the opposing poles, replacing opposition with unity and harmony.

Many other filmmakers in the art film tradition construct their films around a structure of multiple diegesis. Indeed, the term 'multiple diegesis' comes from Peter Wollen, who used it 'to refer to the heterogeneous narrative levels in JeanLuc Godard's post -1968 films'.[17] Wollen writes that in *Weekend*, 'characters from different epochs and from fiction are interpolated into the main narrative [...] instead of a single narrative world there is an interlocking and interweaving plurality of worlds'.[18] This structure is also obvious in Lars von Trier's films, which often use formal differentiations to distinguish between narrative worlds. In *Riget* (The Kingdom, 1994), for example, handheld 16 mm cameras are used to shoot the narrative sequences in the Royal Hospital, while 35 mm fixed camera is used to shoot scenes in the dish-washing station in which two dishwashers with Down syndrome act as a chorus, commenting on other narrative action. So, too, in *Dancer in the Dark*, Linda Badley notes the way in which formal differentiations distinguish narrative worlds:

> In the scenes in [Selma's] trailer, for instance, [the camera] lurches between Bill and Selma in tight close-up that evokes her cramped financial straits and failing vision. In contrast, the musical sequences [...] are signaled by a vibrant rush of color (enhanced by transferring the video to a high quality film stock), a shift from monaural to stereophonic sound, and from subjective camera to an omniscient visual field created by one hundred cameras placed in various positions.[19]

The connection between multiple diegesis in von Trier's general production and his musical *Dancer in the Dark* points to a connection emphasized by Feuer. The multiple diegesis of the art film is also present in the musical but used for a different purpose. In the art film, multiple narrative worlds contribute to an aesthetic and philosophical exploration of the cinematic language we use to represent contemporaneity and history, which can never be identical with these. By contrast, argues Feuer, in the musical, 'heterogeneous levels are created so that they may be homogenized in the end through the union of the romantic couple'.[20]

Since the beginning of his career, Kaurismäki's films have been organized around the kinds of oppositions noted by Feuer and Altman, albeit restrained and minimalist, not spectacular as in the musical. What we find over and again is that diegetic music in particular gives expression to a central character's fantasy world. Often, the song lyrics seem to express the character's dreams, as our examples have shown. These stand in contrast to the problems the character is confronting elsewhere in the film.

What we have in Kaurismäki then is a filmmaker who draws strongly on the art film tradition to create a spatial and representational poetics, as suggested by Bacon.[21] Yet at the same time, present in his films as well is an authorial consciousness that looks to classical Hollywood, including the film musical genre, to find narrative and formal inspiration. In doing the latter, Kaurismäki draws on the musical, which provides a plural narrative structure, which creates tension that can be resolved in the films' redemptive endings. Seen from another analytical angle, the musical moments establish heterogeneous story words, which the films 'homogenize' in their conclusions, through music as well as the union of the romantic couple, generating the sense of redemption with which the films conclude.

Irony and Utopia

One of the problems with this argument is that Kaurismäki's films are bristling with irony, which qualifies the redemptive dimension significantly. What is more, this irony is often present in what I have argued are the films' redemptive endings. If a viewer is searching for redemption, or national sentiment, problems arise. Anu Koivunen writes, the 'mixture of national sentiment, politics and irony characterizes [Kaurismäki's cinema] resulting in a spectator address that is highly ambivalent for audiences in search of "national sentimentality".[22] *Ariel's* conclusion, for instance, is so excessive in its narrative resolution and musical choice as to undermine the sense of redemption. It is hard for the viewer to respond to the narrative action as credible. So, too, *The Match Factory Girl*. The film ends with Iiris poisoning the lover who has rejected her, an innocent bystander, and her parents, concluding with her apparent arrest at the match factory. What is more, the multiple story worlds of these films tend to emphasize metanarrative commentary. The relationships between the story worlds make possible a kind of commentary in which action in one comments on the other. The musical moments are an example of this dynamic in which fantasy is in part a comment on the reality the character lives in other parts of the film. The music does not state meaning literally but implies it through sound and lyrics. This signification allows for metanarrative commentary, as it implies meaning about related action. Thus, music has notable ironic potential, for the commentary in the music may be about a depicted narrative world. As such, it is figurative and allusive, rather than direct and literal. Yet while the irony may be, and often is, present, its primary function is to qualify a utopian charge in Kaurismäki's films. The irony seeks to keep the redemptive dimension from becoming sentimental. By leavening the redemptive strand with irony and humour, the redemption and utopianism become more approachable and emotionally durable.

Kaurismäki's signature irony is evident from his first piece of film work *Valehtelija* (The Liar, 1981), directed by his brother Mika. Aki wrote the screenplay and played the male lead, Ville Alfa. The film is at once sincere, absurd and ironic. The protagonist Ville Alfa is an aspiring writer for whom everything needs to be subjected to critique. But he speaks in nonsensical dialogue, 'Is Kari there? No? Is he dead? He's in the army? Then he's surely dead.' He keeps the phone in his fridge. And he gets in many ironic jabs, responding to a friend's praise of France's philosophical culture, saying, 'the promised land of existentialism is Finland'.

The film has multiple narrative worlds: the world of youthful aspiration, the reality of the Helsinki in which Ville lives, the world of love, and the world of music and expression. The last is powerfully displayed in a wish ballet-style scene that draws the oppositions of fantasy and reality in a way that recalls the film musical. Ville Alfa walks into a nightclub, where Juice Leskinen Slam is performing, a seminal Finnish rock band of the 1980s, now a classic. The camera slowly zooms in on Leskinen delivering a riveting performance, radiating authentic energy, singing his hit 'Mies joka rakastaa itseään' (A man who loves himself). The song voices what is in Ville's head and his heart, a vital expression of authenticity in which narcissism, self-doubt and hope all blend. The aspiration to authenticity, however, is drained by the city Ville inhabits. The film ends on Ville's apparent death, shot down in an armed robbery of a flower store. His beloved Tuula (Pirkko Hämäläinen) arrives after he has died, but he bats his eyes and gives her a wink, as the film concludes. Ville has acted authentically, and yet, as the wink indicates, it is an ironic achievement, for the status of his death is itself uncertain. Already here, despite the director credit going to Mika, we see the combination of irony and aspiration, or redemption, which will figure in the later films as well. The live musical performance which gives full-throated expression to the fantasy and dreams of the protagonist is a musical moment, and wish ballet, which the film's conclusion turns on, in its ironic affirmation of Ville's authentic action to which he aspires in the musical moments.

Kaurismäki's early film *Calmari Union* (1985) combines much of the same absurdism, irony and aspiration to authenticity, as a gang of actors and musicians make an odyssey across Helsinki, which ends in their deaths one by one. To a much greater extent than Kaurismäki's other films, *Calmari Union* is a film of multiple story worlds. Its dramatis personae is made up of thirteen Franks and one Pekka, each of whom traverses the city, headed for the same goal, but each in his idiosyncratic way. The film overcomes their different journeys and deaths with a rousing ensemble performance of the number 'Pahat Pojat', (Bad Boys), an 'anthem' performance that overcomes the posing, styling and ridiculous humour of the film. As Altman suggests, the musical performance and their union resolves their differences, and it is rock and roll and their love of popular culture that brings them together. The absurdity and irony ease the powerful expression of unity and community, which the performance expresses, and which carries a utopian charge.

In his article 'Entertainment and Utopia', Richard Dyer argues for a dialectical understanding of some of the generic elements of the musical under analysis in this article. He argues that song and dance, as both representational and non-representational forms (lyrics and dance, for example), offer forms and sensibilities that furnish 'temporary answers to the inadequacies of the society which is being escaped through entertainment'.[23] Where there are pervasive experiences of 'dreariness (monotony, predictability, instrumentality of the daily round)' utopian entertainment offers 'intensity (excitement, drama, affectivity of living)'; where there is 'fragmentation (job mobility, rehousing and development, high-rise flats, legislation against collective action)', utopian entertainment offers 'community (all together in one place, communal interests, collective activity)'.[24]

As Dyer admits, such a schema oversimplifies the relationships of representation. Yet Dyer helps us identify in musical moments the structure of utopian elements in Kaurismäki's cinema. Over and again, the musical moments we have analysed foreground intensity, a sense of drama and authenticity in living that alienated characters long for in the films. So, too, Kaurismäki's films often feature moments of community, coded as live musical performances, in which an audience gathers in one place and experiences together a rousing anthem like 'Pahat pojat', or an eccentric performance by Joe Strummer, as we see in *I Hired a Contract Killer* (1990), as well as all variety of other performances. These are musical moments, as well in many of the films, but also expressions of utopia in which community counters fragmentation, and intensity counters dreariness and alienation. Yet at the same time, the irony and absurdity of the films take the edge off the utopian charge, admixing it with entertainment in ways that make it approachable and less polemic.

Utopian Conclusions

Two films pull together the elements under analysis, Kaurismäki's 1996 film *Drifting Clouds* and the 2011 film *Le Havre*. In *Drifting Clouds*, after being laid off from the Restaurant Dubrovnik and the transportation authority, the protagonists Ilona (Kati Outinen) and her tram-driver husband Lauri (Kari Väänänen) experience a downward spiral, which is reversed in an abrupt turnaround. A former employer provides a loan, the couple establishes a restaurant with their former colleagues and it catches on. Lauri and Ilona step onto the restaurant's portico at a busy moment and gaze skyward, a sincere utopian expression of community against the economically caused fragmentation that has determined the action of the film. The film's title song, 'Kauas pilvet karkaavat' ('Drifting Clouds'), begins to play in another number by Rauli Badding Somerjoki. Ilona and Lauri have experienced redemption through coming together with each other and their community, which the song celebrates by conjuring as a concluding fantasy, happiness and escape.

The conclusion is set up by several musical moments, and a wish ballet, early in the film. There is a long dance scene from the closing-night party of the fittingly named Dubrovnik. The restaurant goes out of business during the economic depression Finland suffered in the early 1990s. The patrons gather a final time, entertained by the Tango singer Markus Allan. The scene is made up of intercut long shots of Allan performing, and the restaurant patrons dancing, with medium close-ups of the restaurateur Ms. Sjöholm and her staff watching, including protagonist Ilona. 'Kohtalon tuulet rakkani vei / ja takaisin koskaan saavuta ei […] minua täällä enää ei näy' (Fate swept up away my beloved / and I cannot return / and I will be gone from here). It is an elegiac final evening. The wish expressed is for community and intensity, in Dyer's terms, and yet that is slipping through the employees' and patrons' fingers as the scene plays. Medium close-ups and long takes are combined with direct camera angles to capture the melancholy staff, making the lyrics of the song the collective expression of their internal emotional state. Dream and fantasy have run their course, and one can only look back in melancholy at a lost dream. The restaurant itself is a story world, now lost. Indeed, another restaurateur to whom Ilona speaks tells her that Dubrovnik belongs to a bygone, post-war world. The conclusion's affirmation of community and intensity shows how Ilona, Lauri, and their colleagues and friends overcome these different story worlds and the contradictions between them to affirm a utopian urge. They are together, they work together and they look forward together, as they do in the concluding shot of the film.

Le Havre tells the story of Marcel, Arletty and Idrissa. The last is a youth who is an undocumented migrant in Le Havre. Marcel and his friends band together to provide for the boy and provide him money to be smuggled to England. His wife Arletty is hospitalized with a terminal illness at the same time. The band that aids Idrissa is tied together by a utopian impulse for community. At the same time, the utopian impulse seems to erase any critical sense of the colonial backdrop to the story. For once again, we have a 'white savior' story, the story of a benevolent white protagonist acting on behalf of a character of colour, who cannot help himself. Still, the film uses the combination of wish ballet and redemptive ending. The wish ballet involves Le Havre rocker Little Bob (Figure 8.1). The characters recruit him to the project of raising funds for Idrissa to escape. A live musical scene of Little Bob's performance depicts a utopian sense of intensity and community, which arises from the unity of the performance. Although Little Bob's performance is idiosyncratic, the typical irony of Kaurismäki's cinema has diminished.

The emphasis on community returns at the end of *Le Havre*. The state has persecuted Idrissa and Marcel, with the exception of Inspector Monet, who has helped Idrissa escape, and exhibits kindness and practicality. After Idrissa escapes to the UK, Marcel and Arletty return home to cherry blossoms, unity and Kaurismäki's favourite band The Renegades, playing 'Matelot'. In a twist of fate, Arletty has survived her terminal diagnosis, and they can recall their separation and longing from a position of togetherness and unity. 'Matelot'

Figure 8.1 Little Bob and his band performing in *Le Havre* (2011). Photographer: Malla Hukkanen. © and courtesy Malla Hukkanen and Sputnik Ltd.

narrates a wish for unity as the singer on land imagines a beloved sailor gone to sea: 'matelot, matelot / Where you go my heart goes with you'. The sailor is in one sense the undocumented refugee Idrissa, whom Marcel has helped escape France for England but whom he now thinks of and misses. Yet at the same time, the scene celebrates unity, and indeed solidarity, of Marcel and Arletty and their neighbours. The cherry blossoms in the yard offer an abstract reinforcement of the wish for unity. The French number, 'Les temps de cerises', was a theme of the Popular Front of the 1930s, which imagines a better future for workers as time of cherry blossoms. The number was also performed in Kaurismäki's 1999 film *Juha*. So, too, this scene emphasizes the utopian unity and community of the protagonists, and their unity with the community. Their redemption is palpable because it has been set up in a structure of musical moments, multiple story worlds and an ultimate synthesis of the differences to forge a utopian vision.

Noting and analysing the musical dimension of Kaurismäki's films helps answer a fundamental question about his cinema. Why is there so much music in his films and so many live musical scenes in the films, an apparent excess without clear rationale? The 'number' scenes are crucial to building and making emotionally authentic and balanced the redemption offered in the films' conclusions. The elements of the musical help delineate story worlds, which can be brought together in unity at the end of the films. This abstract moral language emphasizes the importance of a universalist ethic of moral community, solidarity and inclusiveness. At the same time, as we see in *Le*

Havre, the emphasis on unity can overlook painful historical relationships, which persist even in Euro-American film culture. This quality has certainly lent itself to the national readings of the films in which the redemption is understood in terms of Finnishness and national self-understanding. As Finland becomes a more multicultural society, that universalism can become problematic, even as it can be important. Kaurismäki's big endings affirm harmony and togetherness, a sorely needed value in what seems to be an increasingly divided world.

Notes

1   Jaakko Seppälä, 'Doing a Lot with Little: The Camera's Minimalist Point of View in the Films of Aki Kaurismäki', *Journal of Scandinavian Cinema*, 6, no. 1 (2016): 5–23.

2   Amy Herzog, *Dreams of Difference, Songs of the Same: The Musical Moment in Film* (Minneapolis, MN: University of Minnesota Press, 2009), 5.

3   Ibid., 7.

4   See Anu Koivunen, 'Do You Remember Monrepos? Melancholia, Modernity and Working-class Masculinity in *The Man Without a Past*', in *Northern Constellations: New Readings in Nordic Cinema*, (ed.) C. C. Thomson (Norwich: Norvik Press, 2006), 133–148; also see Tommi Römpötti, *Vieraana omassa maassa : suomalaiset road-elokuvat vapauden ja vastustuksen kertomuksina 1950-luvun lopusta 2000-luvulle* (Jyväskylä: University of Jyväskylä Press, 2012).

5   Herzog, *Dreams of Difference*, 7.

6   Qtd. in Herzog, *Dreams of Difference*, 6.

7   Ibid.

8   Ibid.

9   Jane Feuer, *The Hollywood Musical* (Bloomington, IN: Indiana University Press, 1982), 74.

10   Ibid., 84.

11   See, for example, Lauri Timonen, 'Päämme päällä ja sisällämme moraalilaki', in *Suomen kansallisfilmografia, 1996–2000*, Vol. 12, ed. Sakari Toiviainen (Helsinki: Edita, 2005), 54–62; Lauri Timonen, *Aki Kaurismäen elokuvat* (Helsinki: Otava, 2006); Sakari Toiviainen, *Levottomat sukupolvet: Uusin suomalainen elokuva* (Helsinki: Finnish Literature Society, 2002); Peter Von Bagh, 'Aki Kaurismäen elokuvat kertovat ankarasta arjesta ja ihmisarvosta', *Lapin Kansa*, 4 March 2003; Peter von Bagh, 'Aki Kaurismäki ja suomalainen todellisuus', in *Suomen kansallisfilmografia, 1986–1990*, Vol. 10, ed. S. Toiviainen (Helsinki: Edita, 2002), 138–145; and Peter Von Bagh, *Aki Kaurismäki* (Helsinki: WSOY, 2006).

12   Timonen, 'Päämme päällä ja sisällämme moraalilaki', 57.

13   Von Bagh, 'Aki Kaurismäki ja suomalainen todellisuus'; also see Von Bagh, *Aki Kaurismäki*.

14   Henry Bacon, 'Aki Kaurismäen sijoiltaan olon poetiikka', in *Taju kankaalle: Uutta suomalaista elokuvaa paikantamassa*, ed. Kimmo Ahonen et al. (Turku Kirja Aurora, 2003), 88–97.

15 Rick Altman, 'The American Film Musical: Paradigmatic Structure and Mediatory Function', in *Genre: The Musical: A Reader*, ed. Rick Altman (London: British Film Institute), 197–207, 201–202; also see Rick Altman, *The American Film Musical* (Bloomington, IN: Indiana University Press, 1987).

16 Jane Feuer, *The Hollywood Musical*, 68.

17 Ibid., 68.

18 Qtd. in Feuer, *The Hollywood Film Musical*, 68.

19 Linda Badley, *Lars von Trier* (Champaign, IL: University of Illinois Press, 2011), 92.

20 Feuer, *The Hollywood Film Musical*, 68.

21 Bacon, 'Aki Kaurismäen sijoiltaan olon poetiikka'.

22 Anu Koivunen 'Do You Remember Monrepos? Melancholia, Modernity and Working-class Masculinity in *The Man Without a Past*', in *Northern Constellations: New Readings in Nordic Cinema*, ed. C. C. Thomson (Norwich: Norvik Press. 2006),133–48, 134; also see Pietari Kääpä, 'The National and Beyond: The Globalisation of Finnish Cinema in the Films of Aki and Mika Kaurismäki, 1981-1995' (unpublished PhD dissertation, School of Film and Television Studies, University of East Anglia, 2008).

23 Richard Dyer, 'Entertainment and Utopia', in *Genre: The Musical: A Reader*, ed. R. Altman (London: British Film Institute, 1981), 175–189, 183.

24 Ibid., 185.

Part III

PERFORMANCE

Chapter 9

LEVELS OF TYPIFICATION IN AKI KAURISMÄKI'S
DRIFTING CLOUDS

Henry Bacon

In all fiction characters appear to varying degrees like fully rounded personalities as well as somehow representative types. In very rough terms, it may be said that individuation makes characters interesting and evokes sympathetic reactions, while typification establishes their story functions and the relevance of their exploits and predicaments. Typification often but not necessarily entails a degree of caricaturization.[1] Aki Kaurismäki's *Kauas pilvet karkaavat* (Drifting Clouds, 1996) is a particularly interesting case in that there is an exceptionally wide range of typification all the way from classically realistic to fairly broadly caricatured characters. Kaurismäki's considerable achievement in this film is the way he is nevertheless able to create aesthetic unity within which characters on different levels of typification serve the thematic concerns and affective impact of the film.

Functions of Narrative Typification

Types in fiction stand for something more general than an individual, either to ensure narrative clarity, to make a point about human behaviour and social relations or for expressive purposes – and these may well combine in a variety of ways. The degree of typification may be a measure of narrative economy: the more central characters tend to be rounded by a range of character traits that make them interesting and induce spectatorial engagement. Lesser characters are likely to have mainly functional roles, in which case there may simply not be any need to develop them to any significant degree.[2] The crucial question is the narrative weight and relevance of the different traits that emerge through characterization.

In real life, social contexts provide us with relevance structures which have a major role in controlling what kind of traits in our fellow humans capture our attention. In fiction, this process is more crystallized because of our awareness of the nature of the story we are following and what we think are the thematic concerns the story exemplifies. More or less conscious classification of a film in terms of, say, genres, auteurs or ideological contexts is highly likely to guide our recognition of types and their narrative cum thematic functions. Yet, even within any such schema, the character may appear more or less individuated. Both in real life and in fiction, there may appear to be a continuum from the merely stereotypical to fully individuated, but more often the way we conceive of real persons as well as fictional characters is more dialectical: individuation can be seen as a process of increasing refinement in applying categories as heuristic devices that in turn may be modified as they expand in use.

Fictional characters, irrespective of the degree of typification, can be seen as instances of modelling human behaviour. Paul Ricoeur has suggested that mimesis on the whole should not be understood as imitation, as this word, particularly in connection with Aristotle's *Poetics*, has customarily been translated. Mimesis is an act of composition and construction, and thus it does not consist simply of duplicating reality. Rather, it is an instance of metaphoric redescription of a less-known domain – say, some underexplored aspect of human reality – in the light of relationships within a fictitious but better-known domain – typically, a more or less canonical story format.[3] Mimesis can thus be understood as modelling in a similar sense as is the creating of a scientific model with the aim of capturing the relevant features of the object of description in a medium that makes these features more easily perceptible and manageable. The idea of mimesis as modelling applies to all the types of typification in fiction and transcends traditional notions of realism in fiction. This is particularly important notion in the case of an author with a highly idiosyncratic style such as Kaurismäki. The locations, props and characters appear weirdly but meaningfully out of place, vaguely suggesting a time, place and a social setting, but simultaneously avoiding anchoring to any specific historical situation. A film can enhance our knowledge of the visual world not only when it is set in locations unfamiliar to us, but also by presenting familiar locations or types of locations in ways which show them, perhaps both literally and figuratively, in a new light or from an unfamiliar point of view. Aki Kaurismäki has shot many of his films on-location in Helsinki in a way which renders the city recognizable for anyone living here, yet uncannily anonymous, as if out of kilter, leaving the characters strangely out of place in this world. That Helsinki can be shot like this, as if through the eyes of its socially displaced characters, implies that it can also be thus experienced.

Kaurismäki's milieus, particularly in *Drifting Clouds*, stand in a special kind of metaphorical relationship to real Helsinki: the diegetic world both is and is not Helsinki. A similar pattern can be discerned also regarding temporality, where the mise en scène makes the story appear in some sense to be taking place in the contemporary world, yet somehow in the past, as if in the 1970s or even 1950s. What Ricoeur writes about metaphors in language is applicable also to this kind of audiovisual rhetoric: 'In service to the poetic function, metaphor is that strategy of discourse by which language divests itself of its function of direct description in order to reach the mythic level where its function of discovery is set free.' Furthermore, 'we can presume to speak of metaphorical truth in order to designate the "realistic" intention that belongs to the redescriptive power of poetic language'. The latter notion leads to the concept of tension which is 'extended to the referential relationship of the metaphorical statement to reality'.[4] Following this, it could be argued that for someone who knows Helsinki, recognizing it yet realizing how it has been, as if, displaced as the setting of *Drifting Clouds*, the film produces a metaphorical tension between the indexical and the symbolic aspects of the filmic discourse, where the indexical as manifested in the iconic stands for literal interpretation of the events taking place in Helsinki, and the way this has been cinematically achieved, distancing or defamiliarizing that city at times to the point of reducing it to anonymity, making that 'literal' interpretation of time and place impossible. Correspondingly, the film both is and is not social realism. It relates to very real social problems, but its truth about those issues is poetic rather than statistical; the characters are truthful figures in respect of figuratively treated social phenomena rather than socially representative types, say, in the sense propounded by the literary historian György Lukács.

In exploring how a film models human affairs, it is good to keep in mind Bordwell and Thompson's warning about trying to assess characters merely in terms of realism. What really matters is how a certain style of acting functions in the total context of filmic means employed. Thus, the criterion of an actor's success is whether he or she 'looks and behaves in a manner appropriate to his or her character's function in the context of the film … [rather than] whether or not she looks or behaves as a real person would'.[5] *Drifting Clouds* serves as a perfect case study of how this kind of appropriateness can be achieved when the characters appear to occupy quite different positions on the line from a fully rounded individual to plain caricatures.

Setting and Style in Drifting Clouds

As in most of Kaurismäki's films, the sets in *Drifting Clouds* are relatively austere, emphatically unglamorous. However, more clearly than in his previous films, there emerges an almost systematic use of prominent single-colour surfaces, often combined with complementary colours (red/green, blue/orange). Sets and props give scanty and somewhat conflicting cues as to when the story takes place. The news broadcast heard as Ilona is cleaning the apartment is of 1995, the time of the film's making, and both main characters becoming unemployed echoes the severe recession Finland suffered in the 1990s. However, furniture, vehicles and other props vaguely suggest an earlier era, possibly the 1970s. The rather bleak sets appear slightly stylized but can conceivably be taken as realistic in terms of the partial openness of the time frame. The film begins at a restaurant and ends in another one. The former appears somewhat faded, the latter emphatically even less glamorous. Neither suggests clearly a particular era but both hark back to bygone days.

The camerawork appears stationary, although there is a number of small slow pans and track-ins to facial reactions. Editing is slow, and outdoor scenes often consist of single, fairly tightly framed shots. There is even a sense of confinement as editing is not used to any significant degree in creating diegetic space. The effect is further emphasized by fairly elliptical narration and the avoidance of establishing shots that would ease recognition of exact locations.[6] As was pointed out earlier, this leads to a certain quasi anonymity of the city, which can just about be recognized as Helsinki but which appears somewhat 'displaced'. The style of acting further strengthens this effect, making the characters appear somewhat displaced from society.[7] Kaurismäki relies very much on his actors' ability to convey the impression he is after. Characters' reactions are not constructed to any significant degree by editing, for example by the interplay between facial expressions and object shots – one of the few exceptions is when Lauri at his workplace draws a card, a three of clubs, and realizes he has lost his job. One rather delicate stylistic flourish occurs in the rather long wordless sequence as the orchestra plays at Restaurant Dubrovnik on its last evening: There is a sequence of the faces of the workers looking at the orchestra and the dancing crowd. It constitutes kind of a communal point-of-view shot pattern. But on the whole, there are relatively few shot-counter-shot patterns as Kaurismäki in this film prefers to use two shots. The scene at the employment agency is effectively captured by a single shot in which Ilona and the agent sit opposite to each other.

The generally restrained style of delivering dialogue and the severe economy of expressing feelings could be seen as a mild caricature of the stereotypical Finnish subdued manner of communicating. Character behaviour is sometimes explicable only in retrospect, and often we have to infer what has happened just before. In seeking to understand the characters, we have to detect certain details about them on the basis of briefly passing cues. On the other hand, the limited range of obvious expressions might tune the spectator to observe the more fine-grained reactions on the actors' faces.[8] Also, there is a range of styles of acting and a corresponding gamut of character typification. This enables Kaurismäki to create a highly idiosyncratic cinematic poetics suspended between social realism and the kind of abstraction which allows him to explore more ethical alternatives to the existing social order.[9] In an interview at the time of the film's premiere, Kaurismäki stated that in modern society the 'enemy is invisible', and thus he had to invent something more universal.[10]

On the whole, there is a certain obviousness in Kaurismäki's characters. One feature of social behaviour that seems to be almost completely absent from *Drifting Clouds* is pretension. Characters tend to be either naively candid or brutally honest. There is no 'social performance' or assuming of roles intended to manipulate or mislead other people. Thus, one concern familiar from a lot of fiction as well as real life does not occur here: we don't have to worry about what people's real intentions are behind their ostensive behaviour. Their body language might cue us to their innermost feelings, but it doesn't 'give away' anything because they have nothing to hide.[11]

The obviousness of the characters is strengthened by the use of music. Non-diegetic Tchaikovsky extracts create atmosphere and indicate their feelings in a polarizing fashion, that is, suggesting affects not otherwise obviously present in the story; songs, both diegetic and non-diegetic, function in a more parallel fashion.[12] Kaurismäki's use of music in guiding spectator affects is actually quite unusual. Whereas Ilona is first introduced accompanied by only the diegetic sounds of the restaurant dining room, in the chef's first scene, the unexpected use of a dramatic passage from Tchaikovsky's Sixth Symphony heightens the sense of implausibility of what is going on in the kitchen. This is an important point as there is a sudden shift from Outinen's restrained, seemingly realistic acting to the caricatured ravings of the alcoholic chef. Later on, Ilona gets her share of the Tchaikovsky symphony, a more lyrical passage, as she joins her husband Lauri (Kari Väänänen[13]) as he is completing his shift as a tram driver. The noble music places their relationship slightly above the everyday world they live in.

However, despite the discreetly fairy-tale-like aura of Kaurismäki's realism created by a number of stylistic devices, it should be appreciated that at least in *Drifting Clouds*, there are fairly distinct levels of characterization. Four levels can be discerned on the basis of the degree to which the characters appear as types and how this typification functions narratively. The way the spectator can be assumed to make sense of this range is based on the same schemas that guide our perception of people in real life, but they are being put into quite different use in this aesthetic context. From this quite elaborate structure of typification emerges Kaurismäki's highly idiosyncratic way of modelling the human condition with a vague reference to a certain particular situation – unemployment in Finland in the 1990s – but which transcends the confines of a single social context and emerges as a more general statement about struggling within a callous economic system and finding a ray of hope in genuine solidarity, not only within a class but also across social differences. These levels will now be analysed in increasing order of caricaturization.

Mrs Sjöholm

We meet Mrs Sjöholm (Elina Salo), the owner of Dubrovnik Restaurant, for the first time as she tells the head waiter Ilona to let in the men to whom she is forced to sell her restaurant. She is outwardly calm but clearly in an emotional state. She immediately appears distinctly more rounded than the other characters. Salo's style of acting derives from her long experience in her profession. She started her career in the 1950s, during the studio era. Kaurismäki probably has tender respect for her achievements and perhaps he decided that her talent could be put to better use than trying to make her adhere to the kind of acting style Kaurismäki had cultivated for years in his earlier films.[14] Be that as it may, Sjöholm appears as a fully rounded individual. She represents a certain class of people whose life and communal function change because of the inevitable social process that is going on: she is a small-scale entrepreneur having to give way to a well-networked chain that takes over her business. Her barely contained emotions as she is forced to close her restaurant and dismiss all her faithful employees give the film nostalgic resonance, emphasized by the fairly long music sequence full of nostalgia on the closing night.

The contrast between the way Mrs Sjöholm and the other characters are depicted becomes explicit in the scene in which Sjöholm explains the financial state of her restaurant to Ilona. Sjöholm relates her situation with bitter irony yet by her facial expressions and voice she also conveys a sense of resignation. Ilona, even as she expresses her sympathy, does so in a restrained fashion, finding rather absurd explanations for the financial troubles the restaurant faces: 'The customers are getting old and can't drink as much as they used to.' Sjöholm would qualify as a socially representative type as defined by Lukács, but Ilona, while retaining a distinct sense of being a sensitive personality, responds in a mildly farcical fashion. Importantly, though Ilona as well as some other characters have several of these comic lines, they never undermine the sense of the seriousness or the emotional content of the situations the characters find themselves in. This kind of delicate fusion of toned-down melodrama and farce is the very core of Kaurismäki's art. Here it allows for the contrast between the characters not to appear discordant: both Salo and Outinen express similar emotions, even if conveyed in slightly differently calibrated acting styles.

During the nostalgic tango on the last evening at Dubrovnik, there is a track-in to a close-up of Mrs Sjöholm, giving gentle emphasis to her sorrow. She then disappears from the film only to reappear like a deus ex machina when all hope for the protagonists, Ilona and Lauri, appears to be lost. After Lauri's attempt to win money at a casino has predictably failed, Sjöholm and Ilona reencounter by chance at a beauty parlour where Ilona is trying to find employment. The difference between Salo's and Outinen's acting re-emerges as the women go to a bar. They have a few drinks, and Sjöholm even boasts about having been able to drink many men under the table in her youth: 'Men just pretend they can drink a lot.' Ilona thinks this is because of their inferiority complex. She may well know, having attended at various points throughout the film to all of the key male characters as they have succumbed to severely drunken states. Sjöholm is looking for a new challenge in her life and offers to finance Ilona's restaurant with the idea that Ilona will eventually buy the restaurant. This is Kaurismäki's capitalism with a human face. Large chains and corporations represent the inhumanity of big enterprise, but capitalism just might be somehow benign if it is worked out in terms of the ordinary people acting together as a community.

Ilona and Lauri

Ilona is the first character we are introduced to as she is seen working as a head waiter. After guiding some people to a table, she stands by a wall and there is a track-in to her thoughtful, concerned face. This cues us to observe, even care about her as a person with a degree of interiority. In many ways, she and her husband Lauri are more rounded characters than the two prominent members of the staff, chef Lajunen and doorman Melartin.

Nevertheless, apart from Ilona's workmates and Lauri's sister – who appears only very briefly, first for the sake of a single joke and later on to serve a single plot function – Ilona and Lauri are not shown as having any social relationships. In typical Kaurismäki fashion, the couple appears faintly naive and not well in touch with modern life. As Lauri introduces Ilona to his surprise purchase, a television set, he is boyishly excited about the remote control. Her rather listless comment is only: 'It even has colours.' Through this medium, the real world makes a brief intrusion into their home: we hear a news broadcast covering topics such as the war in Chechnya and the siege of Sarajevo. Thus, the news connect the story to the time of the film's making, 1995.[15] As Ilona asks worriedly about the method of payment, Lauri consoles her by saying the first instalment will only be in the spring. Judging by the soundtrack (the television image is never shown), Lauri does find some more entertaining programming, but Ilona only suggests going to bed. Lauri agrees. Next morning as Ilona is cleaning the house, equally depressing news is announced from different parts of the world. She sits down, and dejectedly drops the hose of the vacuum cleaner, as if burdened by the horrors that the 'new' medium brings to her home.

Ilona and Lauri are slightly ill at ease in modern society. Eventually they come to know how the system works, but this almost leaves them despondent. They have a strong sense of pride – Lauri in particular bitterly resists applying for unemployment benefit – and a strong sense of solidarity – they support both each other and their workmates, even Lajunen who completely succumbs to alcoholism. As compared to principal characters in mainstream cinema, they have a fairly narrow range of emotional expression. Only, when shoved out from the safe life they have happily lived, they appear increasingly melancholy as their hopes for a decent life appear to fade away. Perhaps the most salient feature of the way Ilona and Lauri emerge as characters is the snappy, laconic, at times comically unlikely dialogue delivered in relatively deadpan fashion even when the situation could be loaded with emotion. This is only slightly relaxed when for a moment things appear to turn out for the better. Lauri comes back home as Ilona is cooking. He has a bunch of flowers and says: 'Let's eat the soup later in the autumn. I bought some cutlets.' He has got a job driving tourist buses to St Petersburg. 'Aren't you jubilant?' he asks. 'Of course. When do you begin?' But there are only the faintest external signs of jubilation in their own very modest scale: they do smile.

Then a subtly emotional moment follows. After Lauri leaves for his new job, there is a wordless scene with Ilona standing next to a photograph of a little boy. Her face expresses sorrow, but to a large extent it is for the spectator to project emotions on her – or even to figure out that the little boy in the picture must be a child the couple has lost. This is followed by a scene which in a touching way combines sadness with slapstick. Lauri returns home and says that he has been rejected from the job and has lost his professional driving licence because he is almost deaf in one ear. Then, totally erect, he falls straight down on the floor. Ilona lies down next to him and presses her head against his shoulder, but even at such tender moments, facial expressions are tightly controlled. Here and elsewhere, the acting style has a touch of the absurd and keeps sentimentality at bay. Kaurismäki has developed this style to be his hallmark,[16] and in *Drifting Clouds*, it is an integral component of the characterization of the more caricatured characters. Against this, certain very finely graded and fleeting expressions and gestures create a sense of vulnerability and solidarity. The sense of communion between Ilona and Lauri seems almost stronger when they both stare in the same direction than at the rare moments when their gazes actually meet. We see them together in their kitchen, both looking straight to the left. The dialogue is laconic to the extreme. As he tears up the application for unemployment benefits and throws the pieces in the kitchen sink, she asks how they are going to pay the bills. He says he will sell his car, but Ilona remains sceptical. 'It's a fine car', claims Lauri, 'a Buick'. He then sets fire to the application form. Standing or gently leaning against a cupboard in a fairly erect posture, they appear to be stoically facing a seemingly hopeless situation. But in another scene quite early on, we have seen Lauri falling into a slumped posture.

Ilona succeeds only marginally better than Lauri in the job market. The work she gets through a shady employment agency turns out to be at a bar where she is expected to do alone everything needed to run the establishment. This she does to the point of putting on a performance in order to convey the impression of someone else working in the kitchen – giving orders to the kitchen and then sneaking in there to do the cooking herself. Outinen is at her most expressive, next to tears, when she tells Lauri about the bar: 'It's a lousy hole.' She has been stripped of all that has remained of her professional pride. Nevertheless, she makes a brave effort to raise the standards at the bar.

Kaurismäki does not strive to meet the sort of criteria Georg Lukács ascribes to realism, where 'the central aesthetic problem of realism is the adequate presentation of the complete human personality' or to depict the inner life of his protagonists by portraying them 'in organic connection with social and historical factors'.[17] With some extension of the definition, this may be said to apply to Mrs Sjöholm. However, Christopher Prendergast's view of the nature of literary typification as 'a form of imaginative naming, whereby the characteristic or "essential" features of the social process are picked out and gathered into a single expressive moment of a peculiarly intense and concentrated kind ("the specific figure which concentrates and intensifies a much more general reality")')[18] applies well to Ilona and Lauri. The difference lies in moving to a more universal level that Kaurismäki mentioned in the interview while making *Drifting Clouds*.[19] To some extent, this could be said also about the portrayal of Mrs Sjöholm, but the marked difference in the style of acting detaches Ilona and Lauri further away from any more precisely defined social reality, making them exemplars of social processes on a slightly more universal level.

Importantly, although Outinen's and Väänänen's acting style veers towards caricaturization, it does not preclude spectatorial engagement with their predicament. Fairly early on, we see Lauri come to work only to hear that there will be layoffs. The manager of the tram company says that routes have to be reduced (not a very plausible prospect in a major city, but it serves well enough to suggest the dire economic circumstances in Finland in the 1990s). The manager, played by Solmu Mäkelä, a popular magician of bygone years, lets cards decide which of the men will lose their jobs. As Lauri sees he has picked a three of clubs, there is a track to a close(er)-up, just like the first time we saw Ilona and when Mrs Sjöholm came to have one more look at her dear old restaurant. It functions quite conventionally as Lauri appears to take in the implications of this blow of fortune. Yet his face could well be described as expressionless. Andrew Nestingen sees this as an example of Kaurismäki's use of minimalist, affectless acting style which serves to de-emphasize the traumatic aspect of becoming jobless: 'By minimising the trauma, through use of acting style and cinematography, the depiction differentiates Kaurismäki's characters as misfits, and even losers, at the same time as they maintain their dignity and humour.'[20]

Acting in Kaurismäki's films is often described as expressionless. This is of course a relative issue. As Lauri tells Ilona that he has already been laid off for a month, we certainly do not see the kind of stereotypical reactions on their faces that we might expect in a standard realist film – even a Finnish one. His style may be seen as a partial stylistic loan from Robert Bresson, although for quite different thematic purposes. Bresson seeks to evoke a response to his characters' spiritual condition in an emphatically non-melodramatic fashion that does not attempt to give the spectator any such state of mind as immediately evident. Rather, he uses formal means to suggest that there is a dimension which reaches beyond the everyday experience which is at the brink of being dissolved into meaninglessness.[21] Also Kaurismäki keeps melodramatic impulses at bay by not having his characters react particularly strongly in any obvious way even to quite drastic – melodramatic – turns of events, but his project appears somewhat less ambitious. Although the situation the characters are in and how they feel about it are quite obvious, there is no Bressonian suggestion of transcendence, exceeding the contingencies of the every day. Instead, there is a purely mundane re-establishment of communality achieved through solidarity that exists beyond obvious verbal manifestations – a gentle tap on the shoulder will do. Nestingen observes that Kaurismäki makes a 'conscious effort to eliminate both the overtly aestheticized performance [he] sees in Bresson, but also method acting, which constructs narrative by linking plausible emotion, goal-orientated motivation, and action'.[22] This invites the spectator to make a bigger effort to understand what the characters stand for and what kind of emotional issues it entails than when being entertained by more ordinary mainstream cinema. It is also a matter of emotional economy. There is none of what Andrew Klevan has called 'theatricalization of the character', histrionic behaviour, as one of the key elements of melodrama.[23] The only one to do so in *Drifting Clouds* is Lajunen in his alcohol-induced fit of madness. Otherwise the characters are rather 'untheatricalized' as regards their reactions to their social predicament. At times, however, their mental state is made evident by other cinematic means. After a sequence in which Ilona's attempts to find a job have been frustrated, there is a dramatic track-out from her. As when we saw her on the tram Lauri was driving, it is night. But now a tram passes between her and the camera and does not stop to pick her up. This time an extract from Tchaikovsky's Sixth gives resonance to her expression of dejection.

Finally, Ilona's persistence, strong sense of communality and Mrs Sjöholm's faith in her allow her to start a new restaurant. Continental á la carte is good, but Ilona insists that there must also be simple food in big portions so as to cater for the working men employed nearby. The restaurant is named Työ (Work). Ever so slowly on the first day, the new restaurant begins to attract customers and Ilona begins to feel more confident. A telephone call from Helsinki Wrestler's Society, making a reservation for thirty people, consolidates their prospects for the time being. The film ends with Ilona and Lauri silently looking up to the sky as the theme song concludes the film (Figure 9.1).

Figure 9.1 Lauri (Kari Väänänen) and Ilona (Kati Outinen) in *Drifting Clouds* (1996). © and courtesy Sputnik Ltd.

The Kitchen Staff

Character construction in cinema almost always begins with the physical appearance of the character as incarnated by the actor and calibrated by his or her talent for expressing belonging to a certain type or class of people. Likewise, makeup and costuming are more than likely to have social connotations that will be recognized by the target audience. Usually we are also quickly cued to assess the narrative significance of a character, the degree of subjectivity that is to be rendered, as well as what kind of narrative function he or she is likely to have. Depending on how rounded the characters are destined to be, this initial impression is either valid throughout the film, or character traits and finer shades of characterization are developed as the story proceeds. Sometimes, for dramatic reasons often tied to genre, we may be led astray in mentally constructing the characters.

Kaurismäki follows this pattern without any significant deviations. Acting style may be ostensibly similar, but the narrative prominence of each and every character determines how much depth they are given. Whereas Ilona is immediately indicated as possessing a degree of interiority, the chef Lajunen (Markku Peltola) and doorman Melartin (Sakari Kuosmanen) appear first of all and throughout the film as types created with only a few bold strokes based on physical types. They form almost a Laurel and Hardy couple, one lean, the other stout. The contrast is stretched even further as Amir, a rather small fellow, has to put on Melartin's big jacket as he temporarily assumes the role of the doorman.

Lajunen and Melartin are significantly more caricature-like than Ilona and Lauri, partly because they have much less screen time and partly because their predicaments are narratively subordinate to the existential situation in which Ilona and Lauri find themselves in. Their reactions to events are crystallized in small gestures often with little or no verbal support, giving the impression of simple, naive and rather helpless, good but marginal people. They are the stuff that the mildly fantasmatic Kaurismäkeän communality is made of. In Lajunen's first scene, this entails a degree of comedy which signals that even occasional aggressive behaviour should not be taken too seriously if a person is basically a good fellow.

Neither Lajunen nor Melartin is given any context that would either round them as characters or make them stand for anything more general – apart from the effects of boozing. The first thing we learn about Lajunen is that he has alcohol-induced fits of violent madness. When the sturdy Melartin fails to tame him and only gets a wound in his hand, Ilona disarms the madman of his big kitchen knife and then orders everyone back to work – the humbled chef included. Both struggles take place just off-screen. As Ilona ties a bandage round Melartin's wounded hand and tells him to go and have it stitched, Melartin delivers his first line: 'What if there'll be a riot? Amir is pretty fragile.' An unlikely prospect, as it seems to be a soporifically quiet evening at

Dubrovnik restaurant. The crucial point is that the line is delivered and received in deadpan fashion, indicating that within this fictional universe, the line is not taken as a joke. The scene also establishes Ilona as a resourceful professional who commands the respect of her subordinates. They in turn appear more or less unable to manage in their professions without harming others or getting harmed, were it not for her firm guidance.

After losing his job as Dubrovnik is closed down, Lajunen resorts to alcohol without restraint. Midway through the film, he happens to visit the bar Ilona briefly works in. He is really badly off track and quickly drinks the beer he has ordered after stiffening it with a dose of vodka. He says his hands are in such a bad condition that he can't even make porridge. Then he leaves saying he will go as far as vodka will carry him. Apart from a degree of professionalism somewhat casually established in a fleetingly short scene as the menu of the new restaurant is being decided, Lajunen has no other particular characteristics. More important is his function in demonstrating the magnanimity of other characters. Melartin just taps him on the shoulder to indicate that he bears no hard feelings despite having had his hand wounded by the chef madly wielding his kitchen knife. Ilona in turn twice gives Lajunen the opportunity to continue working despite his increasingly severe alcohol problem.

Melartin also drinks heavily after losing his job. There is a fair degree of humour and even pathos in the depiction of Melartin, particularly in a scene where Ilona meets him outside a bar. He is already drunk and admits he can't even pay his bill, but she nevertheless joins him for a drink. The scene takes place with 'Con rauco mormoria' from Händel's Rodelinda playing, giving an ironically sublime aura to the encounter. Inside the bar, Melartin asks Ilona to buy one more full bottle. She agrees, now that they have met after a long time. Melartin delivers to great effect a number of those amusingly absurd lines – now about the miserable state of restaurant life and the behaviour of youngsters.

There is nothing more for us to learn about Melartin or Lajunen as the film proceeds, Melartin is a somewhat more salient character, and he has the plot function of encouraging Ilona to start her own restaurant. Neither of the men is depicted as having any kind of social background apart from the band of homeless drunks to which Lajunen belongs until Lauri and Melartin come to take him into rehabilitation. When they meet again after Lajunen has recovered, not a word is needed or uttered.

Social Types

The men Ilona meets when seeking employment – restaurant manager (Esko Nikkari), employment agent Ronkainen (Sulevi Peltola), Forsström the bar owner (Matti Onnismaa) and the bank manager (Aarre Karén) – stand for social types, caricatures which embody aspects of Kaurismäki's social criticism by frustrating Ilona's attempts at starting anew. They have no other story function, and their range of expression is strictly limited to conveying their narrative and thematic functions with just a few telling gestures. The cynical restaurant manager bluntly tells Ilona that she is already too old to have much prospects in the restaurant business. In this scene, there is one of the very few slightly extended shot-counter-shot patterns in this film. It takes place on the 180-degree line with the characters looking almost directly into the camera. The manager is absolutely stone-faced, even saying things such as: 'To be honest, for a waitress you are already quite old.'

'I'm 38', she replies. 'Well, that's just it. You might drop dead any time.'

Ilona makes another attempt to find a job through a private employment agency. The agent is sitting in an office furnished with only bare essentials. He is another stone-faced figure but with slightly more revealing behaviour. When Ilona tries to show him her recommendations or when she says she hasn't got enough money to pay the fee demanded, Peltonen indicates with just a light gesture of hand that such things are not important. He is clearly in the business of taking advantage of the desperation of the unemployed. He promises Ilona a job, but she has only half an hour to find the money. This she does by emptying her bank account.

The restaurant owner, employment agent and the bank manager who appears when Ilona tries to get a loan for the restaurant, all represent social institutions who work according to their own modes of operation and interest. They will only tell Ilona why she does not fit the contemporary requirements of business life. Ilona encounters them in 'typical' situations – applying for a job or a bank loan – and these scenes secure the film's position as a statement about the unemployment of the 1990s.

Forsström, the bar owner has more scenes and screen time than the other characters in this category, but that does not make his character any more rounded. He thinks nothing of making Ilona do all the work in his bar. Soon enough it becomes blatantly obvious that he is very far from being an honest or even barely competent businessmen. He doesn't leave enough money in the till for Ilona to pay for the delivery of beer. As a car arrives outside the bar, Forsström tells Ilona not to reveal anything about him and then runs away. Tax officials raid the place, and Ilona realizes that there is no bookkeeping, let alone receipts of taxes or pension contributions paid. The only social context Forsström is given are the hoodlums who eagerly assume the task of beating Lauri as he comes to demand for Ilona's salary. They are even more caricatured than the man himself. They merrily suggest throwing Lauri into the sea: 'It would be fun.' And they laugh.

Summary: Characters as Tokens and Types

In *Drifting Clouds*, a considerable variety of characters in terms of the degree of typification function in a manner which, in Bordwell's words, appears 'appropriate to his or her character's function in the context of the film'.[24] Kaurismäki ensures the aesthetic unity of the film by not letting Mrs Sjöholm interact to any considerable degree with other characters than Ilona. Ilona in turn is the only one who interacts with characters of all levels of typification – in fact, with all the other character of the slightest prominence. She is the pivot round which the film is organized both plotwise and stylistically. Mrs Sjöholm appears as a fully rounded individual who represents a certain class of people in a historical situation in which the traditional values it represents appear hopelessly old-fashioned – measure of success and the attached values being now determined by financial concerns related to increasing centralization of finance and enterprise. This pattern is only briefly referred to, and interest is focused on immediate human concerns. Salo's fairly brief yet touching performance together with the final evening sequence has the important function of making this development appear like a genuine loss.

The more stylized performances of Ilona and Lauri exemplify this social process in a more intense and concentrated way. Their loss is a question of economic means and self-respect. Taking slight distance from the norms of what is recognized as realistic acting allows Kaurismäki to give a discreetly absurdist kick to the situation he depicts. Thus, without any loss of the sense of social relevance, he is able to treat his themes in a wryly humorous way.

The restaurant staff appear more caricatured than Ilona and Lauri partly because they have much less screen time and partly because their predicaments are subordinate to the existential situation in which Ilona and Lauri find themselves in. They also provide a dose of comic relief, which again, without distracting from the seriousness of the existential situation depicted, serves the purpose of handling it in an entertaining and thus more involving way.

The characters referred to earlier as social types embody aspects of Kaurismäki's social criticism by frustrating Ilona's attempts at starting anew. They have no other function, and their range of expression is strictly limited to conveying their narrative and thematic functions by quite minimalistic means. They complete the analysis of the social situation by extending the range of treatment to sarcastic depiction of the way society is developing. Importantly, they do not have the last word, as Mrs Sjöholm's reappearance in the story opens up the prospect of enterprise on a genuinely human level, fortified by a sense of solidarity among working-class people. However, at this point, at the very end of the story, the faintly fairy-tale-like quality of the narration, deriving to a significant extent from the way the social situation is depicted by means of varying degrees of caricaturization, reminds us of the wistfulness of this narrative solution.

Notes

1   Often typification and individuation are treated simply as polar opposites between which there is a continuum. However, we should bear in mind that our perception of an another person, real or fictional, always begins with some kind of initial classification which may then be refined by more subtle classifications if we get to know that other person or character more intimately. Such classifications also structure our relationship with people closest to us. Typification and individuation should thus be seen as dialectically interrelated. I explore the ranges of individuation and typification in my forthcoming article preliminarily titled 'Being typical and being individual'.

2   It should be appreciated that great actors in small roles have created some truly memorable characters by evoking just a few or even just a single telling trait. In *Drifting Clouds*, Sulevi Peltola's contribution as the employment agent belongs to this category.

3   According to Ricoeur: 'Metaphoricity is a trait not only of lexis but of muthos itself; and, as in the case of models, this metaphoricity consists in describing a less known domain – human reality – in the light of relationships within fictitious but better known domain – the tragic tales – utilizing all the strengths of "systematic deployability" contained in that tale. As for mimêsis, it stops causing trouble an embarrassment when it is understood no longer in terms of "copy" but of redescription' (Paul Ricoeur, *The Rule of Metaphor – Multi-disciplinary studies of the creation of meaning in language*. Translated by Robert Czerny with Kathleen McLaughlin and John Costello (London and Henley: University of Toronto Press, 1978), p. 244)

4   Ricoeur, *The Rule of Metaphor*, p. 247.

5   Bordwell and Thompson, *Film Art*, 160–161.

6   The main exception is Johanneksenkirkko church, which can be seen briefly in the background as Ilona enters a telephone booth.

7   I have developed this theme in my articles 'Aki Kaurismäen sijoiltaan olon poetiikka' and 'Deforming Helsinki on Film'.

8   Regrettably, this does not always work out like thus. In analysis class, I have sometimes encountered a degree of resistance to Kaurismäki's art, based on the perception that his actors are too stolid and unexpressive.

9   More precisely, Andrew Nestingen sees the juxtaposition of 'symbolically archival objects, images, and music with symbolically contemporary material, [as] creating contrasts which interrogate the ethical and moral systems on which the contemporary social order rests' (*The Cinema of Aki Kaurismäki*, 25).

10   *Aki Kaurismäki*, HS 27 February 1996; Helena Ylänen, "Elokuvan viimeinen romantikko - Aki Kaurismäki palasi rehellisen työn ja todellisen työttömyyden Suomeen." Helsingin Sanomat 27.1.1996.

11   A slight exception is that Lauri reveals to Ilona about being laid off only a month after the event.

12   The underlying notion here is the division of film music according to whether it functions in a parallel, polarizing or contrapuntal fashion, that is, whether it simply expands the feelings or atmosphere that can be found in a given

scene; otherwise, it brings some such new dimension or offers some kind of counterpoint.

13 The leading male role was originally intended for Matti Pellonpää, but he passed away just before shooting of the film. He was to have had the role that eventually went to Kari Outinen, and Kari Väänänen was allocated the role originally intended for her (Von Bagh, *Aki Kaurismäki*, 159). This gave Outinen her first role as a strong character, in marked contrast to the way she appeared victimized in *The Match Factory Girl*. Although Kaurismäki has said that she fitted the original role well (ibid.), the script must have changed significantly, as Ilona can hardly be imagined going to Forsström's den to demand the payment of her spouse's salary. The photo of a little boy Ilona gazes in the scene after Lauri has gone to his new job, suggesting that she and Lauri have lost a child, is of Pellonpää.

14 Salo's roles in other Kaurismäki films such as *Hamlet Goes Business* (1987) and *The Match Factory Girl* (1990) are much more caricaturized.

15 Nestingen, however, points out that although the news items are genuine and were broadcast in November 1995, they did not occur on the same day (*The Cinema of Aki Kaurismäki*, 101).

16 Part of its roots can be found in the early films of Aki's brother Mika, particularly in *Arvottomat* (The Worthless, 1982), in which Aki appeared as an actor.

17 Georg Lukács, *Studies in European Realism. A Sociological Survey of the Writings of Balzac, Stendhal, Zola, Tolstoy, Gorki and Others* (London: The Merlin Press, [1950] 1972), 7–8.

18 Christopher Prendergast. *The Order of Mimesis: Balzac, Stendhal, Nerval, Flaubert*: Cambridge University Press, 1986, 32.

19 Aki Kaurismäki, HS 27 February 1996; Helena Ylänen, "Elokuvan viimeinen romantikko - Aki Kaurismäki palasi rehellisen työn ja todellisen työttömyyden Suomeen." Helsingin Sanomat 27.1.1996.

20 Nestingen, *The Cinema of Aki Kaurismäki*, 45.

21 This applies particularly to *Pickpocket* (1959), at the very end of which the protagonist is transported from a profound sense of meaninglessness ('Why live?') to a sense of meaning regained as his girlfriend comes to visit him in the prison, and a seemingly trivial perception ('Something illuminated her face … ') is elevated by subtle cinematography, editing and, above all, music heard for the first time after a long interval, to the point of suggesting a fundamental spiritual transformation. Paul Schrader in his *Transcendental Style in Film* offers an analysis of the formal means through which this is achieved so convincingly. David Bordwell, in turn, in his *Narration in the Fiction Film*, explains in terms of cognitive theory why viewers and critics find in this work an element of transcendence (1985, 305).

22 Nestingen, *The Cinema of Aki Kaurismäki*, 45.

23 Klevan, *Disclosure of the Everyday*, 16.

24 Bordwell and Thompson, *Film Art*, 160–161.

Chapter 10

MASQUERADING, UNDERACTING AND SCREEN PERFORMANCES IN *HAMLET GOES BUSINESS*

Ulrike Hanstein

The second act of William Shakespeare's play *The Tragedy of Hamlet, Prince of Denmark* features a speech by the character Polonius in which he announces the arrival of a group of actors at Elsinore. Polonius delivers an eloquent eulogy on the players' prodigious powers to perform all sorts of dramatic texts: 'The best actors in the world, either for tragedy, comedy, history, pastoral, pastorical-comical, historical-pastoral, tragical-historical, tragical-comical-historical-pastoral, scene individable or poem unlimited' (2.2.394–98).[1] Polonius's speech accumulates, combines and recombines the classical genres, and he self-consciously refers to the various traditions of dramatic texts. Moreover, this intertwining of different genres alludes to Shakespeare's play itself, which was also published under the title *The Tragical History of Hamlet, Prince of Denmark* in the First Quarto in 1603 and the Second Quarto in 1604–1605.[2]

In the production notes on his cinematic adaptation of Shakespeare's play, *Hamlet liikemaailmassa* (Hamlet Goes Business, 1987), Aki Kaurismäki conspicuously links terms of dissimilar filmic codes and visual styles. He characterizes his film as a 'black-and-white, underground, B-movie, classical drama'.[3] Kaurismäki's playing with preconceived understandings of different film forms and corresponding modes of production in the American film industry aptly marks his eclectic and idiosyncratic filmmaking practice. In a book chapter on Kaurismäki's body of work, Andrew Nestingen elaborates on the filmmaker's 'contrarian style'.[4] Nestingen introduces this term to describe the films' contradictory combination of elements from different time periods and various cultural frameworks. For Nestingen, the contrasts between the visual design and the disparate musical idioms and popular songs assembled on the soundtracks introduce 'temporal disjuncture[s]'[5] into the film form. Nestingen's insights regarding the nostalgic expressions that underpin the inconsistent and anachronistic renderings of the films' story worlds certainly hold true for Kaurismäki's diminutive film version of *Hamlet*.

Kaurismäki's film turns Shakespeare's ambiguous and convoluted drama into a succinct farce. *Hamlet Goes Business* does not delve into the personal crisis of Hamlet, the melancholic. Neither does the film stress the drama's political conflict. Instead, the film plot transposes the play's paramount scenes from historical Elsinore to contemporary Helsinki. *Hamlet Goes Business* portrays an upper-class industrialist family, driven by unscrupulous business interests and selfish desires. The film constructs the dramatic conflict between power and moral virtue in social rather than personal, psychological terms. Some props and costumes in the film clearly invoke the time and place of the film's production. Nevertheless, the film's imagery and mise en scène seem to be haunted by ghosts from classical Hollywood movies and from modern *auteurist* visions of film. Moving through a range of expressive and minimalist forms, the film's unique blend of small-scale play, film noir, farce, *Lehrstück* and action-revenge plot resists any clear-cut categorization. In *Hamlet Goes Business*, the most pronounced and striking contradiction evolves from the tension between hyperbolic dramatic action, the screen performers' blatant underacting and ostentatious cinematic mise en scène through the shots' highly stylized composition.

In the following, I want to discuss the ways in which *Hamlet Goes Business* investigates the theme of theatricality using cinematic means by foregrounding the intricate relationship between masquerading, play-acting and film acting. As a first step, I will briefly touch on different modes of adapting *Hamlet* for the screen in order to situate Kaurismäki's particular approach in the tradition of Shakespeare films. Next, I turn to the alterations in adapting the play, which support the strict narrative economy of Kaurismäki's film plot and refashion the tragedy as a social parable of our – post-industrial and economically volatile – times. Finally, I discuss three scenes from the film in order to demonstrate how *Hamlet Goes Business* breaks away from conventional practices of character impersonation, which includes the visible expression of feelings and passionate responses.

Kaurismäki's film presents deadpan characters and underacting performers, surrounded by a few evocative objects and a shadowy decor. Nevertheless, the audiovisual film form highlights particular moments and adds dramatic effects by means of the camera's canted framing and dynamic movement as well as the brief musical passages on the soundtrack. In order to engage with the film's displaced and delegated expressivity, this chapter explores the intricate relations between the actors' performances, the props and settings, and the shots' visual dramatization, which calls attention to itself and supports the film viewers' awareness and appreciation of the images' theatrical duplicity.

Cinematic Visions of Hamlet

Among the eighteen feature-length films that Kaurismäki has directed and produced so far, five films are adaptations from plays and novels by European writers. Besides Shakespeare's *Hamlet*, Fyodor Dostoyevsky's *Crime and*

Punishment (1866), Jean-Paul Sartre's *Les Mains sales* (1948),[6] Henri Murger's *Scènes de la vie de bohème* (1847–1849) and Juhani Aho's *Juha* (1911) have been sources for films by Kaurismäki. Interestingly, Kaurismäki reworked these literary texts thoroughly and altered the particulars of the original compositions. Thus, the adaptations clearly stand out as distinctive expressions of his personal filmmaking style.[7] The stories and dramatic incidents are presented chronologically in a succession of brief scenes, which interpret the characters' social background and relationships and condense their conflicting aspirations. Like all of his films, Kaurismäki's literary adaptations introduce a distinctive tone and rhythm of dialogue.[8] The characters are involved in terse and laconic exchanges, whose highly inventive verbal humour and poetic diction are closer to written language than to the usage of words in everyday interaction. The film's narrative and stylistic composition relies on visual gags, unspeaking characters, everyday routines and gestures, and elaborate compositions of shots, which most often show few objects and plain spaces surrounding the characters in the frame.

Among the literary works which Kaurismäki has adapted for the screen, Shakespeare's *Hamlet* is the text with the most significant tradition in film history.[9] Certainly most film adaptations of *Hamlet* are inventive negotiations of complementary theatrical and cinematic codes. Since the 1960s, several prestigious productions have aimed at balancing artistic sophistication and popular appeal by making the most out of a star cast of distinguished theatre actors and advanced recording technology. In 1964, *Richard Burton's Hamlet* was screened in movie theatres across the United States on two days only. The film consists of images recorded at three theatrical performances – with live audiences – of John Gielgud's *Hamlet* production at the Lunt-Fontanne Theatre in Manhattan. For the film's production, a multiple camera setup using a process of videotape recording called Electronovision was employed, which allowed for high-resolution images while using available light. The edited video images were transferred to film for the theatrical release. *Richard Burton's Hamlet* foregrounds the sense of immediacy, which is rooted in the linear progressing and simultaneously unfolding time of enactment and viewing in the theatre space. And the film combines this evocation of 'liveness' with the heightened and nuanced visual and vocal rendering of the actors' expressive performances that is facilitated by the recording technology.

Kenneth Branagh's 1996 *Hamlet* film also seeks to merge theatrical traditions with the visual opulence of film-specific techniques. Branagh's movie runs for nearly 4 hours. For the DVD release, it was promoted as the 'first-ever full-text film of William Shakespeare's greatest work'.[10] This complete text version was shot on 65 mm negative film for 70 mm projection. Branagh cast distinguished stage actors (such as Derek Jacobi) and Hollywood stars (Charlton Heston, Jack Lemmon). The film production thus strove to harmonize diverse acting traditions from high culture and popular entertainment, and it amassed celebrities in order to appeal to international audiences.

On the one hand, film adaptations of *Hamlet* are shaped by – and contribute to – the transmission and interpretation of Shakespeare's text across time. On the other hand, films developed from Shakespeare's play always interact with their contemporaneous film culture – its genres, its visual styles and narrative techniques, its progressive artistic impulses, or industrial modes of production. With regard to movies based on *Hamlet*, Harry Keyishian suggests considering the particular cinematic forms in the context of film history and the cultural imaginations of popular genres. Keyishian demonstrates the importance of cinematic traditions in his discussion of three *Hamlet* films, which he classifies as 'Olivier's *film noir*, Zeffirelli's action-adventure, and Branagh's epic'.[11]

Apart from films which stage Shakespeare's text, a number of thematically complex films have been produced that appropriate only key elements from *Hamlet*. For example, Edgar G. Ulmer's *Strange Illusion* (1945) and Akira Kurosawa's *The Bad Sleep Well* (1960) are loosely inspired by the play's intertwined conflicts of murder and revenge. Ulmer's *Strange Illusion* with its visually inventive uses of shadows, superimpositions and distortions presents the mental turmoil of an adolescent protagonist after his father's sudden death. The story of the teenager's crisis is part of a suspense thriller plot, which revolves around a serial killer of rich widows, who woos his mother. Kurosawa's *The Bad Sleep Well* transposes some elements of Shakespeare's revenge tragedy onto the corporate culture in Japan in the late 1950s. The film's protagonist Koichi Nishi (Toshiro Mifune) seeks to take revenge for the death of his father, who committed suicide in order to cover up a massive corruption scandal. Kurosawa portrays bluntly the stifling social conventions and ruthless economic rationales that allow evil to prosper in business as well as politics. In the cold and dispiriting world of high-ranking officials and tycoons, it is only the protagonist who struggles with his conscience over the justification of his actions.

Briefly, both *Strange Illusion* and *The Bad Sleep Well* present an isolated protagonist and his divided consciousness, as he is driven by suspicions and torn between action and introspection. Both films depict a distraught protagonist in pursuit of clearing up a crime, and they vividly express the character's entrapment in a menacing, immoral environment. In addition, Kurosawa's film unfolds the protagonist's highly ambivalent, loving and destructive relationship to a young woman (an Ophelia-like character). Nourishing the plot conventions of a film noir and acutely portraying an upper-class social sphere ruled by greed, betrayal and corruption, Kurosawa's impressive film reverberates throughout Kaurismäki's adaptation of *Hamlet*.

From Play to Plot to Film Performance

In a published text, Kaurismäki points out that he developed the dialogue for *Hamlet Goes Business* while shooting the film – based on the Finnish translation of *Hamlet* by Veijo Meri.[12] In his concise revision of the play, Kaurismäki leaves out most of the minor characters. Thus, the film plot concentrates on the character of Hamlet as the energetic and manipulative core of the drama. In addition, the plot reshapes the pivotal dramatic situations in order to effect swift pacing and straightforward direction of the narrative. The film's modified rendering of the dramatic incidents results in a succession of compact scenes, which curtail significantly the length and intricacy of the characters' interactions in comparison to Shakespeare's work.

Kaurismäki's wry reworking of the play assumes that viewers are au fait with all the visual icons, famous scenes and significant lines of the play from previous stage and film productions of *Hamlet* if not from the fact that they have long since entered popular culture. In order to illuminate the ways in which the film invokes and reinterprets the drama, I want to consider the film's beginning, the main characteristics of the devised plot, and the visual cues of places and settings, which specify where and when the action takes place.

Introducing neither the setting nor the main characters of the film, the first shot of *Hamlet Goes Business* shows a puppy on a leash, which is tied to one leg of a grand piano. Filmed from a low height, the images show the dog restlessly circling around under the piano. The dog whimpers and apparently witnesses the underhand dealings of a man. As viewers, we initially see only the man's legs in the unlit background of the shot, as he enters the room. The following shot shows the formally dressed man from the waist upwards (Esko Salminen) as he walks towards the camera. Sidelight creates highly dramatic contrasts between his bright face and shirt collar and the engulfing darkness in the shot. On the film's soundtrack, slow instrumental music (a piece by Dmitri Shostakovich) supports the images' ominous tone.[13] After a brief superimposition, which introduces the film's title 'Hamlet LIIKEMAAILMASSA', we see the man moving across the dark room.

The next shot – filmed from a high angle – shows a bathroom. The man enters, approaches the washbasin, takes a tumbler out of a medicine cabinet on his left and pours some alcohol from a small flask into the glass. The shot directs the viewers' attention to the man's measured gestures, which are reflected and thus doubled in the image by a mirror on the wall. After that, a close-up singles out the man's face: he looks determined, but otherwise his face does not reveal any emotion. Then, a series of brief shots captures the man's malicious act: he takes a small flask out of the cabinet – as viewers we can read 'Myrkkyä' and 'Gift', the Finnish and German words for 'poison', on the flask's label – and pours some poison into the glass. Finally, he adds an ice cube to the fatal drink.

The next shot shows a dimly lit, long corridor. Due to the scene's dominant backlight, the man first becomes visible as a silhouette while he walks towards the camera, carrying the tumbler in his right hand. He sits down in an easy chair in a small anteroom. A woman (Elina Salo) enters the anteroom from the left side. She carries a small tray with a glass. She puts down the tray on a wooden side table and kisses the man passionately. The kissing couple is presented in a medium close-up. With a tilting movement, the camera then turns downward and reveals the man's left hand as he replaces the glass on the tray with the poisoned drink that he brought along. The camera moves back and shows the figures from the chest up. Seemingly, the woman has not noticed the man's trick.

The woman says, 'Not here, Klaus! He might hear.' He replies, 'All right, Gertrud. Later.'[14] As viewers of the film we might be puzzled, because we don't know of any character named 'Klaus' in Shakespeare's drama. Nevertheless, we conclude from the brief dialogue and the incidents shown so far that the film depicts an encounter of Gertrud and Claudius. Further, we infer from the presented action that the poisoning of Gertrud's husband, Old Hamlet, is about to happen. By means of portraying Klaus's secret schemes and Gertrud's perfidious act, the film's beginning builds up suspense, which is intensified by the viewers' knowledge of the characters and the incidents in Shakespeare's play.

Gertrud leaves Klaus to bring the poisoned drink to her husband (Pentti Auer), who sits alone in his study. Differing considerably from the dramaturgy of Shakespeare's play and presenting visual evidence of the crime, a close-up shows Hamlet's father as he gulps down the fatal drink. Abruptly, his eyes widen. On the soundtrack, highly dynamic instrumental music (Shostakovich, again) suddenly starts. Although the character's body movements appear rather restrained – a medium shot captures the man as he rises from his chair and clasps his throat with both hands – the music evokes a fierce sense of emotional turmoil and urgency. Instead of exploiting the grisly scene of poisoning, the film immediately cuts to a long shot, which presents the facade of a huge building in neo-baroque style at night. Apparently, this old and splendid building is the stage for the hidden tragedy of passion and betrayal.

Like a theatrical performance, Kaurismäki's film begins with the entrance of a character. While Shakespeare's play is preoccupied with secret machinations, trickery and the protagonist's contradictory impulses to act or refrain from action, Kaurismäki's film brings about a drama by markedly visible gestures, which set in motion the main events. At the film's beginning, the images present a series of small acts and only a few interior spaces. Every gesture, every shot and every spoken word is integral to the story. The visual presentation of Klaus's scheme to kill Old Hamlet is punctuated by close-ups, which isolate the poison, the tumbler, the ice cube, the kissing, the tumbler on Old Hamlet's desk, his right hand approaching the tumbler and his face as he is drinking and suddenly becomes aware of the fact that he is going to die. On the one hand, the film plot clarifies the complicated composition of Shakespeare's play, the characters' ambiguous attitudes and duplicitous verbal exchanges. On the other, the cinematic presentation of a seemingly simple and explicit story is a ruse to strengthen the startling effect of the final twist of the plot.

Immediately after the murder of Old Hamlet, his son (Pirkka-Pekka Petelius) is introduced. Hamlet strolls around a kitchen, cuts a thick slice off a joint of ham and devours it greedily. The character's name is not mentioned in this brief scene.

Nevertheless, the pun on his name – he says, in Finnish, a line that translates as 'Ham, let me' – makes it clear that the well-dressed, vigorous, Finnish-speaking ham eater stands for the melancholy Dane. The story of *Hamlet Goes Business* is set in Helsinki in the 1980s. After his father's death, Hamlet is the majority shareholder of the family-run business, which is founded on shipbuilding and a sawmill. Despite Hamlet's disapproval, Gertrud marries her brother-in-law Klaus. At night, the ghost of Hamlet's father appears to Hamlet and demands that Hamlet avenge his murder. Hamlet offends his childhood friend Lauri Polonius (Kari Väänänen) and pesters Lauri's sister Ofelia (Kati Outinen) with his improper advances. Ofelia is only attracted by Hamlet's wealth and wants him to marry her.

Acting as the company group's new director, Klaus wants to sell the shipyard and the sawmill to a Swedish firm, which plans to shut down both operations. Hamlet frustrates Klaus's plans. In order to learn more about Klaus's treachery, Hamlet feigns madness and melancholia. He invites Gertrud and Klaus to see a play. The actors demonstrate in dumbshow how Old Hamlet was murdered. Hamlet shoots Polonius (Esko Nikkari), who is spying on a conversation Hamlet is having with his mother. Rejected by Hamlet, Ofelia swallows a large number of pills and drowns in her bathtub. Klaus takes advantage of Lauri's sorrow for his dead father and sister.

Together, Klaus and Lauri inject a roast chicken with poison to kill Hamlet. Unsuspectingly, Gertrud takes a piece of chicken and dies. Klaus lures Hamlet into his study, where Lauri attacks him with a large cooking knife. Hamlet smashes Lauri over the head with an old wooden case radio and shoots Klaus. Hamlet then covers up his crimes by making the scene look as though Lauri and Klaus have killed each other.

With everyone dead, Hamlet wants to get rid of the company group. He prepares a contract for selling the shipyard and the sawmill to the Swedish corporation. Hamlet confesses to having murdered his father to the family's driver Simo (Hannu Valtonen). Acting on instructions from the union, Simo is determined to prevent Hamlet from selling the sawmill. He poisons Hamlet. Eventually, Simo and his girlfriend, the maid Helena (Mari Rantasila), leave the industrialists' villa and take the dog, who briefly appeared at the beginning of the film, with them. The final shots of *Hamlet Goes Business* are devoid of any living beings. A series of medium long shots and medium shots displays some machines running at the sawmill. On the soundtrack, a slow song (*Muuttuvat laulut*), performed by Estonian singer Georg Ots, begins and continues for the film's closing credits. At the end, the jobs at the sawmill have been saved. Most of the characters are dead, and there is no loyal friend of Hamlet left to tell his story.

Clearly an erratic combination of serious and comic elements, *Hamlet Goes Business* transforms the main conflicts of Shakespeare's play into a present-day tale of capitalist treachery and working-class solidarity. This audacious transposition allows the filmmaker to treat the dramatic situations more lightly and to motivate the quite absurd reversals in the presentation of the main characters. For instance, in Shakespeare's play, Claudius is filled with remorse after the dumbshow and attempts to pray (3.3.36–72).[15] Instead, Kaurismäki's film presents him drinking in a pensive mood.[16] Further, extravagant stage props like foils, rapiers and the poisoned cup of wine with a pearl in it are replaced by common objects: in *Hamlet Goes Business*, a cooking knife, a radio and a poisoned roast chicken are used as deadly weapons. Revising Shakespeare's play into a familiar, everyday story world, Kaurismäki also slightly modifies the characters' names to amusing effect (from Claudius to Klaus and from Laertes to Lauri Polonius).

The loose and irreverent relationship of Kaurismäki's film to Shakespeare's drama is most pronounced in the characters' dialogues. The overall length of Shakespeare's play as well as the emotional tone and ornate Early Modern English of the text challenge conventions of cinematic storytelling, which rely on narrative clarity and explicit psychological motivation. *Hamlet Goes Business* foregrounds this incompatibility of the period poetic text with codes of realism and presents Shakespeare's original only on a few occasions. Given the elevated style of the sentences extracted from the original play, the appropriated lines are clearly marked as quotations for the film's viewers – it seems as though sometimes the characters can't find the right tone and fall unintentionally into outmoded theatrics when they adopt roles in order to deceive one another.

Hamlet Goes Business overtly demonstrates mismatches between the drama's elaborate poetic voices and the modern everyday visual surroundings in which the characters speak and interact. This strategy of simultaneously integrating and displacing the poetic text is evident in a scene 39 minutes into the film.

Hamlet walks into the lobby and feigns madness in his exchange with Polonius. To Polonius's question 'What are you reading?' Hamlet responds: 'Words, words, words', while he is reading a comic. Here, the solemn tone of the well-known phrase is undermined by the scene's visual presentation – the prop is displayed as a significantly inappropriate detail. In an earlier scene in the film, we find a different strategy of presenting and unsettling Shakespeare's text: Polonius says farewell to Lauri, who leaves for Sweden, and gives him some parting advice. Shakespeare's play unfolds a series of commonplace precepts (1.3.54–80). In Kaurismäki's film, Polonius gives advice on gallant and moral behaviour first but ends his speech on an amoral, laconic punchline: 'Buy clothes as good as you can afford, stylish, not gaudy. Clothes make the man and the Swedes have a most selective taste. Never lend money, you'll lose both your money and your friend. If you ever borrow, don't pay back too soon. The lender may die and save you a lot.' Here, the character's speech plays with the well-known text and switches to a surprising ending. Evidently, contradictory impulses are manifest in the film form: at times, the characters' speeches and gestures move along with the original text; at other times, the actors' performances and their engagement with the visible surroundings move against the profundity and cultural status of the literary work.

In *Hamlet Goes Business*, the imagery's attachment to a specific location plays a defining role in constructing a coherent space for the dramatic incidents. The film was shot on location in the Fennia Building, a former Grand Hotel near the Central Railway Station of Helsinki. The Fennia Hotel opened in 1899. A landmark of the built environment, the splendid building evokes a bygone era of the city's past. In *Hamlet Goes Business*, the mood of the narrative and the visual style – low-key lighting and spaces absorbed into shadows – recall the dark cities of film noir. In film noir, the protagonist's activity of walking links movement and perception to the tangible details of ominous urban spaces. But *Hamlet Goes Business* displays but a few views of the urban space. The visual presentation of Helsinki's actual architecture is limited to a view of the Central Railway Station and a small number of indistinct streets and undefined places. Kaurismäki's film predominantly explores enclosed, dimly lit interior spaces. The details of the decor conspicuously articulate the main characters' social milieu. As backgrounds for the characters' encounters, the domestic spaces appear solid and compact. The wooden furniture, the sofas, the drawn curtains and a few evocative objects generate the subdued atmosphere of a bygone period of bourgeois lifestyle.

The characters' diminished mobility within the sumptuously furnished rooms, the slowed-down dynamics of the camera's long takes and canted shots from high-angle positions generate an atmosphere of enclosure and non-action. The characters' dialogues are often presented in medium long shots or medium shots. The film for the most part refrains from conventional shot-reverse-shot patterns for dialogues, which would emphasize facial expressions, and it sometimes shows characters not looking at each other while speaking or listening to one another, for example, when Polonius gives advice to Ofelia on how to lure Hamlet into marriage. Thus, the camera's distance from the characters and the lack of eyelines, which would establish links between them, charge the views of the characters with the sense of their insurmountable isolation. The actors' detached positions within the shots and their distance from the camera mark the characters out as inscrutable individuals, who conceal their desires from one another.

The visible details of the decor offer a vague sense of the time of the action for the film's viewers. Given the design of the furniture, lamps, cars and common objects, the characters' surrounding environment integrates styles from the 1940s to the 1980s. The actors' costumes display inconsistent trends, too. While the materials, styles and patterns of the younger generation's clothes (Hamlet, Ofelia, Lauri, Guildenstern, Rosencrantz) were up to date at the time of the film's production, the dresses, costumes and suits of Gertrud, Klaus and Polonius appear more timeless. The only overt reference to contemporary popular culture is a scene where Hamlet, Rosencrantz and Guildenstern have a drink in a bar and listen to a live performance of the Finnish rock band Melrose.

Revealing Duplicity and Reinterpreting Performance

In Shakespeare's *Hamlet*, we find the principles of dramatic action and acting –
that is, the means of the theatrical mode of presentation – reduplicated within
the play. The play is composed as an investigation of Hamlet's acts of self-
conscious role playing and self-aware introspection. The sequence of dramatic
incidents interrogates acts of masquerading, which effectively transform the
relationships between the characters and reveal each person's true disposition
to others. Thus, Shakespeare's play prompts a pronounced self-scrutiny of
conceptions of theatricality, staging and acting. To explore the ways in which
Hamlet Goes Business translates this preoccupation with theatricality and
acting into the film's sounds and images, I shall take a closer look at the screen
performers' nuanced activities, which are tied to tangible surroundings and
shaped by the film medium's means of visibility.

In his works, Kaurismäki has assembled an unconventional repertoire of
characters and elaborated a unique approach to film acting. The recurrent
working-class or bohemian characters are specified by gestures and
performance details, which indicate their social milieu. The characters
appear as types with fixed attributes and a specific iconography. They come
across as being representatives of social classes rather than psychologically
complex, plausible personalities. The film viewers' recognition of these types
is supported by the recurrence of a small number of screen performers,
who play similar roles in several films (Kati Outinen, Matti Pellonpää, Elina
Salo, Esko Nikkari, Kari Väänänen).[17] In striking contrast to models of
storytelling in Hollywood cinema that are based on characters who grow in
self-knowledge and eventually overcome internal conflicts as well as external
obstacles, the personages in a Kaurismäki film are shown as unshakeable and
quite unchanging. The characters are depicted as learning slowly through
failure and as resourceful in finding and sustaining new kinds of sociability.
In Kaurismäki's films, which present workers and the unemployed, the
actors' muted performances contribute to the characterization of the
isolated protagonists, who communicate through gestures and reserved
expressive attitudes rather than through explanatory verbal exchanges. At
times, the protagonists' incapacity to display or declare their feelings rises to
melodramatic moments of blocked communication and misunderstanding,
which encourage the viewers' strong affective alignment with the solitary
characters. At other times, the characters' failure to express their feelings and
interact with others exposes their insecurity as a light and amusing matter.
The characters' ineptitude to act congruent to common codes of expressive
behaviour then brings out their failure in everyday acts of social role playing
as comedy.

In *Hamlet Goes Business*, the at times underplayed and at other times
exaggerated performances foreground the bourgeois characters' utter lack of
genuine feelings and moral sensibilities. In an exchange between Polonius and

Ofelia, for instance, the latter explains that she sometimes feels that Hamlet really likes her. While viewers might expect an emotional enactment to reinforce the meaning of Ofelia's words, the actor, Kati Outinen, sits unmoving on a sofa and delivers her lines in a flat tone of voice. Her unblinking eyes and her impassive face do not indicate or project any emotion which would portray a sensitive character. The tension between the meaning of the spoken words and the deadpan performance clearly invites the film viewers' awareness of the actor's skilful impersonation of a quirky, highly indifferent character.

Originating in American slang, the word 'deadpan' has been used since the 1920s in reviews of stage and film performances to characterize a blank or impassive face, look or behaviour.[18] In her discussion of the understated screen acting in Wes Anderson's films, Donna Peberdy gives the following definition: 'Deadpan is commonly used to refer to a lack of expression (facial, vocal, bodily) or immobility.'[19] Peberdy draws on Michael Kirby's observation that even a 'motionless performer may convey certain attitudes and emotions that are acting' in order to substantiate her understanding that the most restrained screen performance involves the actor's skilful execution of small acts of pretence.[20] As Peberdy explains: 'Motionless does not equate with emotionless [...] and deadpan functions in a number of ways to call attention to character emotion, despite its relatively expressive "lack".'[21]

In *Hamlet Goes Business*, the understated performances contribute to the personages' characterization as heartless, superficial and unscrupulous in their double-dealing. Of the main characters only Lauri Polonius is presented as acting out feelings. Eighteen minutes into the film, there is a scene with a confrontation between Lauri and Hamlet. After the intertitle 'A terrible quarrel', Hamlet and Lauri are shown in a brightly lit room, sitting at a small table facing each other. Lauri wants a new office. He complains that his current office can only be entered through a closet and does not have a phone. Hamlet promises to take care of the matter. After that, Lauri rebukes Hamlet for pestering Ofelia. Abruptly, Hamlet jumps to his feet. He shouts 'Bastard!', quickly slaps Lauri's right and left cheek, breathes hard and declares in a loud voice and a more composed manner, 'You don't give me orders!' Then he throws Lauri out. A medium shot shows Hamlet sitting at the table as he spitefully proclaims: 'The closet is your new office.'

Suddenly, the film cuts to a canted medium shot of a corridor. Filmed from a low-angle position, we see a door rapidly opening on the left. The surprising visual motion is underlined by the loud music, which sets in on the soundtrack (the chosen part from Shostakovich's symphony is a rhythmically complex and fast-paced section for drums and strings). Lauri bursts into the corridor, quickly closes the door behind his back and leans against it. He fiddles with his tie as though he has difficulties in breathing. The camera had stayed with Hamlet as he delivered his final line. Given the delayed display of the words' devastating effect on Lauri and his isolation vis-à-vis the camera, the performance of distress rises to an overly dramatic crisis. Lauri approaches the camera, which starts tracking backwards with him through the corridor. Baffled and crushed, Lauri presses his right hand clenched into a fist against his forehead. His gaze anxiously wanders down the corridor to make sure that nobody sees his misery. When Lauri has moved into the foreground, he props his hands on a front desk, slumping in a way that suggests he is completely exhausted from the confrontation with Hamlet. Without looking at the secretary, who is sitting at the desk, Lauri says in a low voice, 'I want to see the president. I've been insulted.' While the receptionist calls Klaus, Lauri gets a small battery-powered razor out of his jacket pocket and frantically starts to shave his cheeks and chin. The next shot shows Lauri in Klaus's office. Lauri is presented at the centre of a medium long shot – his torso dominates the frame – as he whines about his work being disrespected. In striking contrast to the shot's composition, Lauri seems unable to hold his ground. He shyly lowers his eyes, and his fashionable yet much too short tie evokes the ridiculously inappropriate ties that contributed to the grotesque elegance of Oliver Hardy's screen performances. While Lauri speaks, Klaus turns away from him and prepares a drink for himself. Polonius is present in Klaus's office, too. He plays around with a radio, whose noises interfere with Lauri's speech.

Looking for support, Lauri is eventually humiliated by Klaus and Polonius as well. Polonius scolds Lauri for his vague and petulant complaints and brusquely demands, 'Get to the point, son. Don't babble like a small girl.'

The scenes, which introduce Lauri, humble the character through the comical shift from his restrained performance to his flamboyant expression of agitation. In striking contrast to Shakespeare's noble and vigorous rendering of Laertes, the character of Lauri exudes vulnerability. His annoying subservience is most strongly articulated by his gesture of shaving before entering Klaus's office. Lauri's hasty gesture reveals that he aspires to be seen as a solid employee by the company's powerful manager.

In this scene, the character's exaggerated attempt to comply with social standards unintentionally turns into eccentric behaviour. As viewers, we recognize the character's strong intention to be taken serious as a businessman. At the same time, we might appreciate the actor's nuanced performance of a funny spectacle of vanity, vulnerability and disappointed expectations.

Hamlet Goes Business presents the conflict between Hamlet and Lauri as a rather trivial and laughable matter. Kaurismäki's decision to leave out the scenes from Shakespeare's play which show Ophelia's madness and the confrontation of Hamlet and Laertes at Ophelia's funeral supports the film's shift to a light tone. The absence of emotional depth and loyal bonds in the characters' interactions neutralizes the play's tragic vision – that is, the suffering, which is inflicted on the characters by the unforeseeable outcomes of their decisions and actions. The tragedy elucidates the twofold capability of theatrical forms of enactment, which are shown as either deceptive or instructive in the play. The forceful effectiveness of the passions that a theatrical work can exert upon its audience is demonstrated by the dumbshow and the performance of *The*

Mousetrap, which the players put on stage, following Hamlet's instructions. The play-within-the-play is meant to produce proof for the truthful account of the ghost – that is, visible evidence that Claudius is guilty of poisoning Old Hamlet.

Hamlet Goes Business presents a highly condensed version of Hamlet's famous speech to the players (3.2.1–43). Hamlet and an actor are presented in a dimly lit theatre space, standing next to the stage. Hamlet slowly places banknotes, one after the other, in a neat pile on the stage. He instructs the actor how the play should be performed: 'Speak the lines nicely and softly. If you shout them as many actors do, I could just as well take them to the market place. Don't strut and wave your hands about too much or stare into distance as if you had something to say.' The actor listens attentively to Hamlet and responds, 'Sir, I believe and want to believe that we've got rid of all that.'

Hamlet commands the actors to avoid any exaggerated expressions, loud voices or overdone histrionics. For the viewers of *Hamlet Goes Business*, the appropriated scene from Shakespeare's text surely comes across as a witty comment on the film's highly distinctive approach to acting and the moderated, low-key screen performances. The stark contrasts between underplayed and ostentatious ways of delivery and gesture are overtly demonstrated by the stage performances within the film. Following Hamlet's talk with the actor, the film presents Klaus, Gertrud, Ofelia and Hamlet in a theatre space. They watch a play that invokes the form of a naturalistic drama. Three actors appear in a stage set, which sparingly indicates a garden as the scene of the action. In the actors' stylized performances, movements and words are heavily stressed. Suddenly, the stage lighting singles out a different spot on the podium. Loud instrumental music sets in, which accompanies the dumbshow presented. We see three actors, whose costumes and hairdos look nearly identical to those of Klaus, Gertrud and Old Hamlet at the film's beginning. On the left side of the stage, an actor with a Klaus-like moustache kisses the stand-in for Gertrud. While she seems carried away by passion, he secretly poisons the drink that she is carrying. She brings the drink to a man, who sits at a desk on the right side of the stage. Behind him a painted backdrop depicts the furniture from Old Hamlet's study. The actress puts the drink down on the desk and kisses the man perfunctorily on his right temple. Then she leaves slowly and approaches the villain on the left side of the stage. The treacherous couple freezes in a stationary pose.

He holds his arms around her shoulders. On the right side of the stage, the actor of Old Hamlet pours the drink, he gets up from his chair and his hands are splayed across his chest and clutch at his shirt. He bends his head backwards, tries to walk, stumbles and finally falls onto the table, where he lies stiffly. The couple has witnessed the man's agony and starts to kiss lasciviously right after his death.

Incorporating the dumbshow into the narrative film form, *Hamlet Goes Business* juxtaposes the 'exhibitionist' spectacle or 'sensational' mode of early cinema with the actors' otherwise nuanced and restrained performance style.[22] In its flaunting artificiality and its histrionic display of desire, distress and gruesome murder the dumbshow breaks strikingly with the film's predominant mode of representation.

The film elaborates the polarity of the theatrical performance, which calls attention to the means of its visibility, and the film's cool tone and unpretentious imagery to comic effect. The dumbshow's overall composition of movement and stasis is presented in a long shot. Due to the framing, the imagery presents a fixed view on the scene, as though looking onto the proscenium stage from the auditorium. In a shot-reverse-shot pattern, the images of the staged tableau are interwoven with medium shots and medium close-ups of Hamlet, Ofelia, Gertrud and Klaus, who are watching the show in the theatre space (Figure 10.1). In doing so, the montage contrasts the theatrical mode of expression with the cinematic means of visual display. On the one hand, the stage performance obviously goes against the moderate acting style which Hamlet had particularly advocated. On the other, the dumbshow's heightened emotions and its overemphasized moral antagonism seemingly provide the proper framework for the character of Klaus as he is portrayed throughout the film. Klaus, the perfidious villain with his dark moustache, appears as though he has sprung directly from the repertoire of stage and early screen melodrama.

Given the actors' plain impersonations of Klaus, Gertrud and Old Hamlet on the stage and the instrumental music – an extract from Shostakovich's symphony – the dumbshow clearly recalls the murder scene from the film's beginning for the film audience. Thus, Hamlet's staging of the play is exposed as

Figure 10.1 Hamlet (Pirkka-Pekka Petelius) and Ofelia (Kati Outinen) watching the play in *Hamlet Goes Business* (1987). © and courtesy Sputnik Ltd.

a theatrical coup for the viewers. Nevertheless, it is not until the film's ending that the full scope of Hamlet's capabilities in pretending and plotting is fully revealed.

A later scene shows an exchange between Hamlet and Simo. Hamlet is seated at the desk in the former office of Old Hamlet and Klaus. He asks Simo: 'Do you know how my father died?' Simo replies: 'Klaus poisoned him.' Hamlet corrects him 'Wrong'. First, Hamlet is presented frontally in a medium long shot. Next, a quick zoom-in to a medium close-up strongly stresses the moment of revelation: He calmly confesses to Simo: 'I did it.' Hamlet leans back in his chair and goes on to explain that Klaus had been trying to kill Old Hamlet very slowly by administering small doses of poison. Hamlet admits that he got tired of waiting. He takes a puff at his cigar and bends forward to the camera. The image appears slightly blurred by the cigar smoke. Then, an out-of-focus shot presents Hamlet's face and marks the beginning of a brief flashback scene. Filmed from a low-angle position, Hamlet is presented in the small bathroom that was introduced at the beginning of the film. While the images show him handling small flasks, Hamlet recounts in voice-over that he secretly replaced the poison Klaus used with a stronger toxin. The flashback scene ends with Hamlet sneaking out of the bathroom just before Klaus walks in.

The narrative structure and mise en scène of this sequence, which finally reveals how the murder of Old Hamlet really happened, echoes the protagonist's confession in Billy Wilder's film *Double Indemnity* (1944). Wilder's film opens with images that show the protagonist Walter Neff (Fred MacMurray) at night in his office at the insurance company. The mortally wounded Neff sits at his desk, smokes and confesses to a murder he committed into a dictaphone. Similar to Neff's confession, Hamlet's narrating voice introduces a subjective perspective on bygone events and appears as the source of the film's audiovisual discourse. Like Neff, Hamlet dies immediately after telling his version of the story, which details his involvement in the crime plot.

For the film's viewers, Hamlet's confession suddenly shifts the perspective on the presented action. Against the background of the viewers' knowledge of *Hamlet* and the persuasive presentation of the murder at the beginning of the film, this twist in the plot is more surprising than anything viewers might have imagined. The final revelation that Hamlet has also tricked us as viewers of the film allows us to reassess the virtuosity of the screen performer. Throughout the film, the cold and ironic characterization of Hamlet sustains an ambiguity. This makes the strong performance of Pirkka-Pekka Petelius still plausible when the plot pushes the character from being an avenger to being a murderer – and thus unmasks Hamlet's 'murderous theatricality'.[23] From the perspective of the film's ending, it is clear that Petelius's meticulous and masterly performance at once reveals and withholds the character's motives and self-conscious knowledge.

Resonating and displacing film noir's dark vision of modernization and alienation, Kaurismäki's reimagining of *Hamlet* muses on the intricate relationships between role playing, dissimulating and performing. The film's narrative straightforwardly – and nostalgically – restates the possibility of social relations based on solidarity, which resist capitalist treachery. By dramatizing the struggle between workers and bourgeoisie over the means of production, the film evokes a supposedly bygone era of industrial work. At the time of the film's production, Finland's traditional wood and paper industry, emblematized by the sawmill, was already obsolete. Nevertheless, the film signals the urgency to articulate class differences in times of globalized capitalism – and it demonstrates cinema's capability to create images for experiences of social reality. After all, the cinematic form of *Hamlet Goes Business* proposes a complex relationship between showing and telling, staging and exposing, seeing and believing. The film's refusal of any inherited genres strongly attests to an inventive practice of filmmaking, which repurposes the visions and representations of the industrialist mode of film production to surprising ends.

Notes

1   William Shakespeare, 'The Tragedy of Hamlet, Prince of Denmark (The First Folio, 1623)', in *The Arden Shakespeare: Hamlet: The Texts of 1603 and 1623*, ed. Ann Thompson and Neil Taylor (London: The Arden Shakespeare, 2006), 246.
2   Cf. William Shakespeare, 'The Tragical History of Hamlet, Prince of Denmark (The First Quarto, 1603)', in *The Arden Shakespeare: Hamlet: The Texts of 1603 and 1623*, ed. Ann Thompson and Neil Taylor (London: The Arden Shakespeare, 2006), 41–172; William Shakespeare, 'The Tragical History of Hamlet, Prince of Denmark (The Second Quarto, 1604–1605)', in *The Arden* Shakespeare: *Hamlet*, ed. Ann Thompson and Neil Taylor (London: The Arden *Shakespeare*, 2006), 139–464.
3   Aki Kaurismäki, quoted in Pietari Kääpä, *The National and Beyond: The Globalisation of Finnish Cinema in the Films of Aki and Mika Kaurism*äki (Oxford: Peter Lang, 2010), 112.
4   Andrew Nestingen, 'Aki Kaurismäki: From Punk to Social Democracy', in *A Companion to Nordic Cinema*, ed. Mette Hjort and Ursula Lindqvist (Chichester and Malden: Wiley-Blackwell, 2016), 294. For a more extended discussion of the 'everyday nostalgia', which Kaurismäki's films articulate and put forward for their viewers, see Andrew Nestingen, *The Cinema of Aki Kaurism*äki: *Contrarian Stories* (London: Wallflower, 2013), 96–112.
5   Nestingen, 'Aki Kaurismäki: From Punk to Social Democracy', 296.
6   Kaurismäki's only TV movie *Likaiset kädet* (1989) is a free adaptation of Sartre's play and was shot on 16 mm film.
7   In a review of Kaurismäki's *Lights in the Dust* (*Laitakaupungin valot*, 2006), Roger Ebert has summed up the distinctive formal consistency of Kaurismäki's films, which envision a world on their own terms, inhabited by peculiar types of characters: 'Like very few directors (like Tati, Fassbinder, Keaton, Fellini), he has

created a world all his own, and you can recognize it from almost every shot. His characters are dour, speak little, expect the worst, smoke too much, are ill-treated by life, are passive in the face of tragedy. Yes, and they are funny.' Roger Ebert, 'Lights in the Dust,' 17 July 2008. Available online: http://www.rogerebert.com/reviews/lights-in-the-dusk-2008 (accessed 28 December 2016).

8   While Kaurismäki privileges visual expressions over verbal exchanges in all of his films, he took the sparseness of the characters' dialogues to an extreme by using only brief intertitles in *Juha* (1998).

9   Referring to the screen history of *Hamlet*, Cynthia Baron and Sharon Marie Carnicke speak of 'at least forty-eight cinematic versions of this classic play', Cynthia Baron and Sharon Marie, *Reframing Screen Performance* (Ann Arbor: The University of Michigan Press, 2011), 128.

10 The quote is taken from a brief caption on the DVD cover of *Hamlet* (1996, Kenneth Branagh), DVD, Warner Home Video, 2007.

11 Harry Keyishian, 'Shakespeare and Movie Genre: The Case of Hamlet', in *The Cambridge Companion to Shakespeare on Film*, ed. Russell Jackson (Cambridge: Cambridge University Press, 2000), 75.

12 Kaurismäki's notes on the film's production are quoted in Sakari Toiviainen, 'The Kaurismäki Phenomenon', *Journal of Finnish Studies*, 8, no. 2 (2004): 32.

13 Kaurismäki chose excerpts from Dmitri Shostakovich's *Symphony No. 11 in G minor*, op. 103. The decision for Shostakovich's music appears to be a tribute to Grigori Kozintsev's internationally acclaimed production of *Hamlet* (1964) for which Shostakovich composed the score.

14 All quotes from the film's dialogue are from the DVD's English subtitles. *Hamlet Goes Business*, DVD, Artificial Eye, 2007.

15 All specifications of acts and scenes from Shakespeare's *Hamlet* refer to The Second Quarto.

16 Kaurismäki's droll depiction of Klaus gives a visible form to an idea, which is invoked by Shakespeare's text. After the play-within-the-play, Guildenstern informs Hamlet about Claudius's distraught state. Hamlet wittily takes Guildenstern's expression 'distempered' as meaning 'drunk'. See Shakespeare, *Hamlet*:
'GUILDENSTERN The king, sir –
HAMLET Ay, sir, what of him?
GUILDENSTERN – is in his retirement marvellous distempered.
HAMLET With drink, sir?
GUILDENSTERN No, my lord, with choler.' (3.2.291–5)

17 Stephen Heath has introduced several categories for analysing the 'presence of people' in narrative fiction films. With regard to his critical terms, the typed personage of Kaurismäki's films might be best described as a blending of 'character', 'person' and 'image'. See Stephen Heath, 'Body, Voice', in *Questions of Cinema* (Bloomington: Indiana University Press, 1981), 178–182.

18 See 'deadpan', in *The Oxford English Dictionary*. Available online: http://www.oed.com/view/Entry/47677? (accessed 4 May 2017).

19 Donna Peberdy, '"I'm just a character in your film": Acting and Performance from Autism to Zissou', *New Review of Film and Television Studies*, 10, no. 1 (2012): 56.

20 Michael Kirby, 'On Acting and Not-Acting', *The Drama Review*, 16, no. 1 (1972): 7.

21 Peberdy, "'I'm just a character in your film'", 56.
22 With 'exhibitionist' and 'sensational', I invoke the concepts that Tom Gunning and Ben Singer introduced in their discussions of early cinema. See Tom Gunning, 'The Cinema of Attraction: Early Film, Its Spectator and the Avant-Garde', *Wide Angle*, 8, no. 3/4 (1986): 63–70; Ben Singer, *Melodrama and Modernity: Early Sensational Cinema and Its Contexts* (New York: Columbia University Press, 2001).
23 Harold Bloom, *Shakespeare: The Invention of the Human* (New York: Penguin Putnam, 1998), 411.

Chapter 11

DEADPAN DOGS: AKI KAURISMÄKI'S CANINE COMEDIES

Michael Lawrence

In a particularly succinct summary, Aki Kaurismäki has been described as a 'deadpan comic visionary, Finland's number-one movie export, and champion of the underdog and other house pets'.[1] The word 'underdog' is routinely used to describe the films' central characters. As Lana Wilson suggests, Kaurismäki's protagonists are 'almost always the same character: a lonely, working-class underdog of few words in search of love and a steady job'.[2] 'Underdog' originally referred to actual dogs – dogs that usually lost fights – but is more commonly used now to describe people of little or low social standing. Kaurismäki is known for combining comedy and concern in his presentation of such characters: Dave Kehr states that Kaurismäki's 'style is defined by a deliciously deadpan irony that does not, remarkably, preclude a deep compassion for his largely working-class characters'.[3] He has made both 'the loser trilogy' and 'the underdog trilogy' (also known as the 'workers' or the 'proletariat' trilogy); however, actual dogs feature more prominently in the 'loser' trilogy.[4] Discussing his frequent collaborations with the actor Matti Pellonpää, Kaurismäki recalls how they together 'created that kind of loser, sad dog character'.[5] But Kaurismäki's underdogs (usually they are men) are repeatedly presented alongside real pet dogs: as Lloyd Hughes notes, Kaurismäki's films typically feature 'protagonists who glumly eke out a living on the margins of society (and are often accompanied by a dog)'.[6] If the characters in Kaurismäki's films are almost always recognized as underdogs, the human actors' physical appearance and performances, specifically their faces and expressions, are very often described in ways that develop further the characters' association with dogs. Dogs are routinely invoked when critics refer to the social status of the typical Kaurismäki protagonist but also when physical dimensions of the actors and their performances are described.

Discussing Janne Hyytiäinen from *Laitakaupungin valot* (Lights in the Dusk, 2006), for example, Ian Johnston refers to the 'mute hangdog look on his face, his eyes slowly flicking down and rising up again in a mournful expression of misery and resignation'.[7] Similarly, Bert Cardullo refers to

Markku Peltola from *Mies vailla menneisyyttä* (The Man Without a Past, 2002) as 'a sad-looking, hangdog, even canine-featured type of character'.[8] The term 'hangdog', originally referring to the expression on a hanged dog's face, now more commonly connotes a downcast, woebegone and defeated expression. Critics discuss Kaurismäki's actors in zoomorphic terms, and detect a doggish dimension in their demeanour, as if literalizing the animal origins of their hangdog expressions and underdog status. But in such responses, the actors' largely expressionless faces are described in ways that collapse the canine with the saturnine: the deadpan performances of the actors playing these underdogs produce apprehensions of dejection which is then equated with the apparent sadness of real dogs. Describing Pellonpää in *La Vie de Bohème* (1992), Richard Porton, for example, suggests he 'resembles a particularly melancholic basset hound', while Luc Sante describes him as 'doglike', '[giving] the impression of a stately but wounded hound'.[9] Confronted with the comedy of expressionlessness, the critics discern a non-human unhappiness. But why should deadpan faces evoke miserable dogs?

In *The Expression of the Emotions in Man and Animals* (1872), Charles Darwin provides an anecdote about walking his dog. Whenever he turned to take a path towards a hothouse, where he sometimes worked, Darwin writes, the dog

> did not know whether I should continue my walk; and the instantaneous and complete change of expression which came over him, as soon as my body swerved in the least towards the path (and I sometimes tried this as an experiment) was laughable. His look of dejection was known to every member of the family, and was called his *hot-house face* … His aspect was that of piteous, hopeless dejection; and it was, as I have said, laughable, as the cause was so slight. [10]

Darwin and his family found their dog's face funny because the dejection perceived therein was understood as an overreaction. Deadpan performances by humans are deemed funny due to the actor's apparent inability to react appropriately. As Chris Norris suggests, the 'exact mechanics' of deadpan 'remain mysterious. As an emotive gesture, it's uniquely contextual … a non-reaction to a reaction-begging event'.[11] Donna Peberdy notes that 'deadpan is commonly used to refer to a lack of expression (facial, vocal, bodily) or immobility' but suggests that 'behind the deadpan, or monotone voice or lifeless body, are emotions that the character struggles to express'.[12] This discrepancy between deadpan performance (the outward signs) and actual feeling (the interior emotions) has been invoked to describe Kaurismäki's cinema: Philip Kemp suggests that '[behind] the dour, unsmiling Nordic face of Aki Kaurismäki's films, it's becoming increasingly evident, beats a heart of pure mush'.[13] This chapter considers the relationship between Kaurismäki's deadpan comedy and his films' simultaneous championing of the underdog and privileging of real dogs by exploring the roles played by dogs in the films and by attending to the question of the canine actor's facial expressivity. In *Laughter: An Essay on the Meaning of the Comic* (1911), Henri Bergson suggests: 'You may laugh at an animal, but only because you have detected in it some human attitude or expression.'[14] Domesticated dogs, however, are perhaps a special kind of animal: as Erica Fudge has argued, pets are 'both human and animal; they live with us, but are not us; they have names like us, but cannot call us by our names.'[15] How and why do we laugh or smile when confronted by Kaurismäki's dogs, and what kind of comedy is produced by the performances of Kaurismäki's canine actors?

The routine appearance of dogs in Kaurismäki's films is regularly noted by critics, but it is rarely discussed at any length. In his review of *Toivon tuolla puolen* (The Other Side of Hope, 2017), for example, David Rooney writes: 'it wouldn't be a Kaurismäki film without an irresistible screen dog.'[16] Luc Sante, writing about *La Vie de Bohème*, goes so far as to suggest 'no director in the entire history of motion pictures has understood and showcased dogs as effectively': 'Dogs appear in nearly all of his films, and they are never there for merely decorative purposes.'[17] But Sante only briefly considers one canine actor, Laika, and only to suggest that 'with her soulful demeanor and her silken black Belgian shepherd looks', she is 'perfectly cast' in the film as Baudelaire, 'the long-suffering bohemian conscript.'[18] Likewise, Sylvia Blum-Reid, in a discussion of *Le Havre* (2012), states that dogs 'are omnipresent meaningful presences in Kaurismäki's films' but then barely mentions that film's canine character/actor (also called Laika) and provides no further explanation or elaboration of her initial claim.[19] Some critics, however, have described the dogs in more productive ways. In a review of *Kauas pilvet karkaavat* (Drifting Clouds, 1996), Peter Matthews refers to the canine character Pietari as 'eerily silent' and 'a great Kaurismäki character in its own right.'[20] And Jonathan Romney, discussing a scene from that film, describes Pietari as a 'rigid, eloquently impassive terrier.'[21] For both these critics, then, Pietari's presence or performance is notable precisely for its uncommunicative or inexpressive qualities; and for Matthews, this seems to accord with the director's more general approach to representing 'character' as such. As Philip Kemp has suggested: 'No one in a Kaurismäki movie ever looks scared, happy or furious.'[22] This chapter considers the 'meaningful presences' of the dogs in Kaurismäki's cinema, and the 'purposes' that they serve, by examining: the ways the dogs are presented in promotion for the films, positioned in the film's paratexts, and discussed by the director; the presence of the dogs in the films' representations of human underdogs; and the relationship between the canine actors' performances and the comic representation of inexpressive and uncommunicative human characters.

In Kaurismäki's short film *Valimo* (The Foundry, 2007), a group of men down tools to solemnly attend a film screening at a tiny cinema lodged somewhat inexplicably inside the foundry in which they work. The film that is projected in *The Foundry*'s final minutes is the second version of Louis Lumière's *La Sortie de l'Usine Lumière à Lyon* (Workers Leaving the Lumière Factory in Lyon, 1895). Kaurismäki's film includes two 5-second excerpts from the Lumière actuality, which lasts just over 30 seconds. In the first excerpt, a dog bounds out of the factory door chasing after a man riding his bicycle and then exits bottom right, and in the second excerpt a dog (perhaps the same dog) runs from right to left across the bottom of the screen. However, while more than 20 seconds separate these moments in the original film (they occur at the start and at the very end), only 8 seconds separate them in *The Foundry*, when the film shows the workers eating their sandwiches and gazing up without expression at the screen. In Kaurismäki's film, then, the Lumière film projected at the foundry has been surreptitiously and scrupulously edited: the elision functions here to prioritize the brief moments in which dogs appear alongside the factory workers. In a discussion of dogs as 'distractions' in early cinema, Pao-chen Tang suggests that while the human workers in all three versions of Lumière's film are shown flowing obediently to either the left or the right of the camera, the dogs (who also appear in each version) move with a 'natural randomness' that 'tempers' the 'compositional geometry' of the films' 'scenography of display'.[23] The spontaneity and contingency of the dogs' movements 'distract us from being fully absorbed into the clearly staged attractions' and 'serve as a kind of resistance to pre-established systematicity'.[24] If Lumière's dogs embody for Tang 'the unpredictability of the instant', their being privileged in Kaurismäki's film reflects the predictability of this auteur (specifically, his penchant for dogs); paradoxically, however, by purposely rearranging the random appearances of dogs in his edited version of Lumière's film, Kaurismäki subjects the original footage (and the dogs that feature therein) to his own 'pre-established systematicity', in which dogs are always accorded special attention but rarely temper the precise 'compositional geometry' of the films in which they appear.[25] In Kaurismäki's films, the dogs certainly demand and deserve our attention, but they do not often distract us (as do Lumière's dogs) from the 'clearly staged' dimensions of the films' meticulous design, and instead they reinforce (rather than resist) the systematic rigour and rigidity that characterizes the films' presentation of human performances.

Only very occasionally do Kaurismäki's films show dogs moving in unpredictable ways, disappearing and reappearing by their own volition. Towards the end of *Le Havre*, the young Gabonese refugee Idrissa (Blondin Miguel), who is being sheltered by Marcel (André Wilms), plays a record in the parlour and then stands perfectly still, listening to the music. The next scene shows Laika the dog sat quietly watching Marcel and Idrissa who are talking in the backyard. A subsequent cut to a close-up of the record spinning around clearly shows the label at the record's centre: it is the His Master's Voice label, with its distinctive image of a small dog listening to a gramophone, originally painted by Francis Barraud in 1895. Fudge has suggested that this is 'one of the most famous animal paintings in the world', one which, moreover, presents 'a dog with the capacity to listen, not just to hear … an active rather than a passive participant in its world … listening as we might listen: with pleasure, with attentiveness'.[26] Laika, like so many of the dogs that feature in Kaurismäki's films, is presented for the most part as attentive, engaged by her surroundings, suggesting an 'active rather than a passive' participation in the story (at one point she leads Marcel to a cupboard in which Idrissa is hiding). But ironically, in her very last scene, Laika is momentarily distracted by something outside the frame and disappears for a few seconds before returning to her original position, looking up at Marcel and Idrissa where they are sat at the table in the backyard. On the whole, dogs rarely embody 'the unpredictability of the instant'. Only very occasionally are dogs shown displaying much vigour or expending much energy (though Rodolfo and Lauri are briefly shown playing with their dogs in *La Vie de Boheme* and *Drifting Clouds*, and in *Juha* the dog runs after a bus in pursuit of its master), and instead they tend to appear more like Barraud's painted dog, sitting extremely still (either on the floor, on the end of a bed or even balanced on an ironing board) and looking at the human characters (Figure 11.1).

Sometimes dogs feature only very briefly in Kaurismäki's films. The dog's appearance rarely seems contingent, but in *Calamari Union* (1985), for example, when the men travelling to Eria stop to eat some food they have stolen from a supermarket, a little black dog (uncredited) runs across the beach and sits

Figure 11.1 Ilona (Kati Outinen), Lauri (Kari Väänänen) and their dog Pietari in *Drifting Clouds* (1996). © and courtesy Sputnik Ltd.

beside them, and one pets its head while another (Matti Pellonpää) recites 'Lazy Morning' (in Finnish) by the French poet Jacques Prévert. When the man stops stroking the dog to light a cigarette it promptly trots away and is never seen again. The dog's appearance more often seems deliberate but can be ambiguous, inexplicable, even uncanny; at the beginning of *Varjoja paratiisissa* (Shadows in Paradise, 1986), following the sudden death of the older garbage collector, the film cuts abruptly to a shot of a large black dog (uncredited) running through an urban wasteland, evoking the dog from Andrei Tarkovsky's *Stalker* (1979). Only rarely are dogs presented for explicitly comic effect, at the beginning of *Leningrad Cowboys Go America* (1989), a large black dog (called simply 'Siberian Dog' in the credits and played by Laika) is shown in a medium close-up looking up at the old farmer who has turned impassively to face his dog, having just been presented with the frozen body of his son; while the shot-reverse-shot implies the significance of the relationship between the farmer and his dog, the dog, like everybody else in the scene, and in accordance with the film's central gimmick, sports a gigantic rockabilly quiff.[27] In *La Vie de bohème*, Rodolfo surreptitiously takes the bone his dog Baudelaire is chewing in order to make some soup for Mimi (Evelyne Didi), who has come to his flat for dinner; the character's deft but desperate actions here evoke Chaplin. But Baudelaire quietly accepts Rodolfo's affections for Mimi, just as Laika (in *Le Havre*) admits without complaint Idrissa the refugee boy into the house she shares with Marcel and Arletty.

Indeed, dogs most frequently appear as placid, patient and watchful members of domestic households, living with their single or married owners (*La Vie de Bohème, Drifting Clouds, Juha* (1999), *Le Havre*) sometimes, characters assume responsibility for dogs with unsuitable owners (*Lights in the Dusk* (2006), *The Man Without a Past* (2002)) or take in strays (*The Other Side of Hope*). In Kaurismäki's films, dogs appear as ordinary rather than heroic companions; an impression of their attentive involvement in their surroundings, and specifically their watchful apprehension of the human dramas that unfold around them, is produced by their being included, in an apparently non-ironic and admirably equitable manner, in the films' rigorous organization of continuity, and specifically through the films' scrupulous eyeline matching.

The pivotal status of Kaurismäki's dogs, as either (or both) actors and props, is suggested by their placement on the Curzon Artificial Eye posters for the UK releases of both *Le Havre* and *The Other Side of Hope* (2017): on the former, the dog Laika (Laika) stands at the feet of the two main characters Marcel and Idrissa beside the shoeshine stool and the pineapple, and on the latter, the dog Koistinen (Valpu) is positioned to the right of the two main characters Khaled (Sherwan Haji) and Wikström (Sakari Kuosmanen), while a suitcase and a large potted cactus are arranged on their left. The dogs therefore on the one hand appear to be central characters (they are important enough to feature on the posters alongside their human counterparts, even if they feature only briefly in the film, like Koistinen/ Valpu), but on the other hand, due partly to the size of the dogs but also to the design of the posters, they might simply belong to the films' whimsically surreal mise en scène (they are merely 'decorative' tokens of the films' quirkiness, foregrounded here like the pineapple or the cactus).

Kaurismäki's canine actors are usually included alongside the human actors in the films' closing credits, a conventional acknowledgement of the non-human animal's participation in a film, but in his more recent features their names also appear in the *opening credits*, a far less common practice, reflecting a more equitable recognition of their contribution, an idiosyncratic inclusivity that is subversive precisely due to its straightforward (its 'straightfaced') presentation or performance of a rather radical non-anthropocentric stance. For example, whereas in *Leningrad Cowboys Go America*, *Drifting Clouds* and *Juha* the dogs (Laika, Pietari and Piitu) are named only in the closing credits, in sixteenth, eighth and twelfth place respectively, and the opening credits for *La Vie de Bohème* conclude with a special mention for 'Laika dans le rôle de Baudelaire', those for *The Man Without a Past* and *Lights in the Dusk* include the dogs (Tähti and Paju) among the film's supporting actors (both appear in sixth place) and in *Le Havre*, the dog (Laika) is presented as a leading actor: hers is the eighth and final name presented on its own, with the names of supporting actors, such as Jean-Pierre Leaud, appearing afterwards, and presented in groups. Across his career, in other words, Kaurismäki has demonstrated an increasingly non-anthropocentric (because non-hierarchical) approach to listing his films' human and non-human actors (or 'stars') as his audiences have become increasingly familiar with his films' distinctive presentation of the relationship between humans and dogs.[28]

Promotion for Kaurismäki's recent films likewise privileges the dogs as important members of the cast and, moreover, integral presences in the director's oeuvre, and with a more pronouncedly deadpan approach, an apparently non-ironic presentation of these dogs as members of an acting 'dynasty' whose exclusive involvement in Kaurismäki's films is unrelated to, because not explicitly explained with reference to, their actually being his own pet dogs. A press kit for *Le Havre*, for example, includes full-page portraits of the film's five stars, including Laika, who is described as 'a canine actress of fifth-generation', and a press kit for *The Man Without a Past* describes Tähti as 'a descendant of a famous dog-actress family; her grandmother Laika had the unforgettable role of Baudelaire in the film *La Vie de Bohème* by Aki Kaurismäki and her mother, Pittu, performed one of the principle roles in Kaurismäki's *Juha*'.[29]

The Optimum DVD cover for *The Man Without a Past* includes an image of Tähti as Hannibal in the bottom right corner beside a familiar film festival symbol: the award represented by this symbol is the Cannes Film Festival

Palm Dog Award, which Tähti won in 2012. The same symbol appears at the top of the DVD cover, where the film's other and perhaps more prestigious prizes are listed: Cannes Winner Best Actress, Cannes Winner Ecumenical Jury Award and Cannes Winner Grand Prix. To my knowledge, *The Man Without a Past* is the only film to have won the Palm Dog and then prominently advertised the fact on its DVD packaging: Tähti's recognition by Cannes is presented here with apparent seriousness and as being of equal importance as the festival's recognition of the film's lead human actress, in keeping with the press kit's description of her as 'a descendant of a famous dog-actress family'.[30]

Kaurismäki's own comments concerning his dogs are consistently deadpan: he apparently refuses to expound the equitable regard for his canine actors indicated by his films' credits and promotional materials. He instead offers terse-sounding and evasive explanations that suggest an exploitative or instrumental relation with his pet dogs. In one interview from 2002, for example, he explains: 'I have three dogs and they have to act for their food'.[31] In another interview, from 2012, he says 'since I am the producer, I always use my own dogs. They're cheap. I have to feed them anyway'.[32] He avoids discussing with any seriousness or in any detail the practicalities of working with canine actors: asked about directing the cast of *Le Havre*, Kaurismäki concludes his remarks with a throwaway comment: 'and my wife takes care of the dog'.[33] Kaurismäki's wife, Paula Oinonen, is indeed credited as the dog trainer on that film, as well as for *The Man Without a Past* and *La Vie de Bohème*. But accounts that purportedly offer an honest insight into the domestic provenance of his films' repeated presentation of canine characters imply he only begrudgingly complies with, or is beleaguered by, his wife's suggestions and demands. In a 2003 interview, for example, he refers in passing to his wife as 'the one who lately always insists that I write a part for my dog, Tähti, in each of my films'.[34] In 2011, however, he offers an elaboration of this situation and suggests that his wife pleadingly pesters him until he submits and that he does so simply in order to work in peace:

> whenever I close my door and start to write, on the third day, she knocks. "Sorry, can I come in?" And I know what she's going to say: "What about if you have a dog in your film? Wouldn't it be interesting if there was a little dog who's chasing ...." I say: "Yeah, yeah, close the door. I'll write the dog in'".[35]

In another interview, Kaurismäki describes his wife as the dogs' 'agent' and adapts his account of the marital negotiations accordingly: 'When I start to write the screenplay, always on the third days my wife comes and says: "Is there any part for a dog?" She's a good manager.[36]Such utterances suggest a self-consciously deadpan discrepancy between the evidence offered (here, his words, and the lack of feeling implied by them) and what we might reasonably assume these words obscure (his genuine fondness for dogs).

Adrienne L. McLean reminds us that

[dogs] can be trained, by shaping their behaviours with rewards of play or treats or, unfortunately, punishment or the threat of it, to do lots of things: to nod, wave, tilt their heads, bow, lick their lips, growl, bark, cover their eyes, pick up or fetch any number of objects, limp, run in certain directions, stop, back up, sit, lie down, roll over, crawl, tug, play dead, and combinations of all of these – the range of trainable dog actions is astonishing – in response to voice or hand signals. [37]

If Kaurismäki's human actors display few conventional signs of 'acting' due to their largely expressionless faces, then Kaurismäki's canine actors likewise display little evidence of the 'training' that typically produces performances by dogs in more conventional (and commercial) cinema. In *The Man Without a Past*, a dog's apparent unresponsiveness (its owner's inability to shape its behaviour in the fiction) embodies the non-demonstrative performance style of Kaurismäki's canine actors (and illustrates, paradoxically, the ability of Kaurismäki, the dog's real owner, to shape its appearance on screen). The protagonist, M (Markku Peltola), is living in a shipping container rented to him by a security guard (Sakari Kuosmanen) who at one point visits him accompanied by his dog. The security guard is demanding his rent, and when M explains that he can't pay until the end of the week, the guard drops the dog's leash and orders the dog to 'attack' but the dog doesn't move and simply stands there, looking across at M. Despite the dog's failure to attack, the guard insists that M was lucky and that 'usually people end up dead'. When the guard threateningly grabs hold of M, there is a shot of the dog sat on the floor looking up, rather than assisting his owner. The guard asks M to care for his dog for a week but advises him not to pet it, and to feed it only raw meat; when M asks the guard for his dog's name, there is a shot of the dog sat down resting its chin on the ground, no longer looking towards them, as the guard answers: 'Hannibal'. In the subsequent shot of the dog, it is sat placidly on the bed beside the sleeping M. Later, when M attempts to return the dog to the security guard, it remains utterly unresponsive when the guard calls its name; instead, it sits down beside M, suggesting a new allegiance has been made. The comedy of these sequences derives from the guard presenting his 'killer' dog with such confidence and the dog's actual behaviour when the guard orders it to attack. Kemp's suggestion that in Kaurismäki's films 'no one ever looks scared, happy or furious' extends to the canine characters/actors as well; the dog's performance here (in the fiction) thus resonates with Norris's description of deadpan, a 'non-reaction to a reaction-begging event', and illustrates Kaurismäki's more general approach to performance.

In *The Other Side of Hope*, deadpan performances are presented in narrative situations in which the lack of expression on the characters' faces is motivated and justified in specific ways. During the all-night card game, for instance, Wikström and his opponent are appropriately and tactically 'poker-faced' throughout, and during his interviews with the immigration officer, Khaled is almost as expressionless recounting his experiences in Allepo as the immigration officer is while listening to and assessing his story. While the poker game sequence suggests a self-consciously ostentatious presentation of the actors'/characters' immobile and inscrutable faces, in which suspense concerning the outcome (will Wikström win the game and buy the restaurant?) is generated as comedy, the interview scenes present the actors'/characters' faces in relation to the official assessment of the asylum seeker's case, whereby facial expressions on the one hand provide or perform evidence of trauma and on the other hand present and maintain bureaucratic imperviousness, and in which suspense concerning the outcome (will Khaled be granted asylum?) is central to the film's critique of Europe's response to refugees. At the beginning of the film, when Khaled arrives at the port in a coal container, he easily sneaks past the security guard, who is watching television; Finnish audiences would certainly recognize the dog on the television screen as Ransu (Karvakuono), a popular puppet character from the long-running children's show *Pikku Kakkonen* (1978–). The film then appears to align the Syrian refugee character with the real dog that belatedly but inevitably appears. When Wikström first discovers the dog, Koistinen, in the restaurant kitchen, the film cuts from a medium close-up showing his expressionless face looking down at the dog to a shot of the dog looking up at Wikström, before Wikström tells the waitress they cannot keep the dog. This brief scene resonates with the interview sequences in which the face-to-face encounter nevertheless results in Khaled being denied asylum (however, both Khaled and Koistinen are offered sanctuary at the restaurant and are hidden together in the women's toilet, Khaled holding Koistinen, when health inspectors visit).

One of the more notable encounters between an underdog and a real dog in Kaurismäki's cinema takes place towards the beginning of *Lights in the Dusk*. The lonely security guard Koistinen (Janne Hyytiänen) walks past a dog tied to a railing outside a pub. The dog looks up at Koistinen as he passes and Koistinen looks back at the dog; the camera stays on the dog, looking in Koistinen's direction, after Koistinen has left. A little later, Koistinen sees that the dog is still tied to the railing, and a young boy tells him the dog's owners are inside the pub; he looks across and down at the dog, and the following shot shows the dog looking up at him. Koistinen goes inside the pub and explains to three burly men that their dog has been left outside for a week without any water. The four men troop off towards the back of the pub; the camera stays on the table until the three men return to their drinks, laughing. Outside, Koistinen, badly beaten up, emerges from behind the corner of the pub and looks over at the boy and the dog, and in the following reverse shot, the boy and the dog both look back at him from where they sit on the left and in the middle of the frame, their heads turned to the right to face Koistinen.

The French DVD box set *Tout Aki Kaurismäki, 25 ans de cinema* (Pryamide, 2008) has on its cover an image of the canine actor Paju, who features in the sequence described earlier. The choice of this image as an evocative emblem for Kaurismäki's oeuvre suggests not only that the figure of the dog functions metonymically for Kaurismäki's cinema, but that to understand this particular body of work requires us to consider the significance of the dogs that appear so regularly in his films or, more specifically, the significance of the dog's look.[38] This moment epitomizes Kaurismäki's comedy, which Jonathan Romney has described as 'deadpan in the extreme': audiences might smile or even laugh, but the characters' faces evince no emotion whatsoever.[39] Moreover, the looks exchanged between Koistinen and the dog in this sequence invite a consideration of the relationship between deadpan and non-human performance.

Alexandra Horowitz has discussed what she calls 'dissonant dogness' in films, when dogs 'behave incongruously with their context or assigned roles in discernible ways', and focuses in particular on those moments in which dogs appear distracted by something off-screen and in which dogs fail to demonstrate the attention that would be appropriate to the scene: 'Attention', she writes, 'as represented visually in direction of gaze and bodily stance … is indicative of the perception, understanding, and interest an animal has in its environment … Dogs attend to us: they look at people, especially familiar people, in the eyes, a behaviour not typical of any other nonhuman animal.'[40] A common 'incongruity', Horowitz notes, 'is a cinematic dog's lack of eye contact, gaze holding, or facial bearing consistent with listening to someone speaking to it.'[41] Kaurismäki's dogs are almost always presented so as to emphasize their attentive interest in the action of the scene and are usually shown looking directly at characters either within the frame or else this is suggested with shot-reverse-shot editing, implying the dog is actively listening and watching (Laika's momentary distraction in *The Man Without a Past* notwithstanding). As Jarmo Valkola has argued, '[the] looks and glances of the characters have a special meaning in Kaurismäki's cinematic language. While many other facial features are made immobile, the light from the eyes of the characters pierces through the space and silence around them.'[42] Eyeline matching, 'a central structural element of the film art as such … has a special importance' in Kaurismäki's cinema; indeed, he is 'devoted' to the rigorous representation of such 'looks' and they are 'crucial effects of his filmmaking style'.[43] However, when dogs are sutured into such a system, while such 'facial bearing consistent with listening' can imply interested attention, we are nevertheless confronted with the obligation to interpret their faces for signs or evidence of their 'understanding'. For example, in *Juha* there is a shot of the unnamed dog (played by Pittu, who appeared briefly in *La Vie de Bohème* as Baudelaire's 'friend') sitting on the bed beside the fitfully sleeping Juha (Sakari Kuosmanen), following the departure of Juha's wife Marja (Kati Outinen) with the flash gentleman Shemeikka (André Wilms). Juha reaches his hand out to the empty space on his left; after a close-up of Juha's hand gripping and then stroking the empty mattress, there is a medium close-up of the dog apparently looking directly at Juha's hand and then turning its head away. While the expression on the dog's face is ultimately impossible to read for evidence of its emotional state, the situation in which the dog is placed, and the editing with which the impression of the dog's attention is achieved, invite us to imagine the dog's sympathetic comprehension (rather than its mere observation) of Juha's loneliness. When the dog turns its head away, we might imagine that Juha's suffering is more than the dog can bear, even though we are simply watching Pittu's attention dispersed around the set.

McLean proposes that 'just like human actors, dogs … can be analysed through their facial expressiveness … their movements, and the way they are staged … their relation to and interaction with setting and props, as well as other actors, human or animal', but she notes that manipulative editing can be deployed to 'suggest cause and effect through the juxtaposition of shots'.[44] As such, 'the expressiveness of dogs in film … is often assumed to be the result of "trickery", either by the dog at the behest of its trainer or by the formal techniques of film itself'.[45] But compared with a dog's physical interactions with setting, props and other actors, 'facial expressiveness' seems particularly difficult to analyse when considering the ways a canine character is constructed for and presented on screen. In her discussion of Uggie, who won the Cannes Film Festival Palm Dog award for his role as Jack in *The Artist* (Michel Hazanavicius, 2011), Stella Hockenhull suggests he 'has certain performance abilities and proficiencies', 'an idiosyncratic set of gestures, movements and postures, along with a gamut of individual behavioural patterns, facial nuances and tricks which constitute his technical capabilities and contribute to his performance'.[46] A 'repertoire of performance signs' (such as 'playing dead') is deployed in the film so that Uggie's character is 'perceived as loyal, heroic and endearing'.[47] However, Hockenhull's repeated use of the phrase 'as though' when describing 'the ways [Uggie's] actions create significance in the narrative' ('as though realising the danger', 'as though listening', 'as though to revive his master') reveals the extent to which the audience's perceptions (of the dog's endearing heroism) depend on the repeated disavowal of the 'as though' each time a 'performance sign' is presented in the fiction.[48] And Hockenhull's description of Uggie's 'facial nuances', moreover, is limited to a single reference to a shot showing 'the dog's eyes … bright and inquiring', suggesting the difficulty of discerning legible 'performance signs' (even or especially of the 'as though' variety) in even award-winning canine actors' facial expressions. As Erica Fudge has argued, 'anthropomorphic interpretations, such as the one that assumes that when a dog's mouth forms a shape that resembles a human smile it too is smiling, blank out difference and transform the world into the human'.[49] In *Lights in the Dusk*, while Koistinen's actions suggest concern for the dog, there aren't any obvious signs of sympathy on his face when he looks down at the dog before entering the pub; correspondingly, there are no signs of surprise on the boy's face upon Koistinen's return. Moreover, there is no ostensible evidence of the dog's feeling any specific emotion at all; it simply stands still and stares, just as the human characters do; the immobility and inscrutability of the dog's face and carriage is no different to the humans' expressionless faces and motionless bodies. Due to their proximity, the human actors' emotionless faces might encourage us to apprehend on or in the dog's face a similar blankness, but perhaps it is the other way around: while we could regard the dog's apparent lack of expression as corresponding to and even mirroring the human actors' performances (whereby the dog appears to be just like the humans – an anthropomorphic interpretation of the non-human performance), we might also consider the human actors' apparent lack of emotion as corresponding to and even mirroring the dog's 'performance' (whereby the humans appear to be just like the dog – a zoomorphic interpretation of the human performances).

In *Paris Spleen* (1869), Charles Baudelaire celebrates 'The Faithful Dog', 'the pitiful dog, the dog everybody kicks around because he is dirty and covered with fleas, except the poor man whose companion he is, and the poet who looks upon him with a brotherly eye'.[50] These dogs, moreover, can return the looks bestowed upon them. Baudelaire continues: 'I sing the luckless dog who wanders alone through the winding ravines of huge cities, or the one who blinks up at some poor outcast of society with its soulful eyes, as much as to say, "take me with you, and out of our joint misery we will make a kind of happiness"'.[51] However, the dog's expression is made to say what the poet wants it to say: the 'as much as to say' here perhaps anticipates Hockenhull's 'as though'; and as McLean notes, 'a film can be edited to make a dog's expression appear to be "soulful" or "yearning" in a close-up when he or she is actually reacting to a plate of off-screen food'.[52]

Murray Smith, discussing 'the foundational significance of facial expression in film', suggests film 'depends to a greater extent than any preceding art form on the interplay among emotions as these are expressed in the human face and voice (as well as in posture and gesture)'.[53] Certain directors, Smith avers, 'have developed styles in which oblique or ambiguous facial expression plays a key role': the 'attenuation of emotional expression' in the films of Robert Bresson and Takeshi Kitano, for example, produced by the blank and expressionless faces of the actors, provides a kind of 'negative evidence' in support of the evolutionary theories that, since Darwin, have proposed the existence of a range of quickly, easily legible expressions corresponding to basic emotions, and suggests that 'understanding how facial expression ordinarily functions sharpens our appreciation of the aesthetic sculpting of expression by particular artists'.[54] Jonathan Romney, discussing *The Man Without a Past*, suggests: 'Few recent films have depended so much on their stars' facial architecture ... When the hero and his Salvation Army inamorata exchange their first glance, barely a glimmer registers on Kati Outinen's face, yet her blankness and her delicate timing announce unmistakably that it's love at first sight'.[55] Kaurismäki has described Outinen as 'a very/intelligent actress who knows how to create an inner life behind an impassive face. She's the opposite of those actors whose impassiveness hides emptiness'.[56] If Kaurismäki's cinema is characterized by an 'attenuation of emotional expression' in which the actors' faces are rarely 'quickly' or 'easily legible' and are much more often 'oblique' or 'ambiguous', then the performances by dogs contribute in important ways to the comedy generated by facial inexpressivity. Because of our belief in the dog's emotional inner life, the dog's face confronts us with the same challenge as the face of a deadpan performer, or, in other words, the deadpan performer presents us with a challenge similar to that with which we contend when we face a dog. Kaurismäki's actors, both human and canine, reveal the zoomorphic principles of blankness as a mode of facial acting. When a human actor performs deadpan they present a mask that obscures the emotions we assume to be there, just as the dogs in Kaurismäki's films are shown in ways that invite us to wonder at the thoughts their faces cannot show; deadpan is thus a zoomorphic mode in which the human face, now becoming a riddle like the animal's face, functions as a barrier preventing the identification of those 'quickly, easily legible expressions corresponding to basic emotions'.

Notes

1   *Film Comment* 39, no. 2 (March–April 2003), 4.
2   Lana Wilson, 'Aki Kaurismäki'. *Senses of Cinema* 51 (July 2009). Available online: http://sensesofcinema.com/2009/great-directors/aki-kaurismaki/ (accessed 17 May 2017).
3   Dave Kehr, 'Amnesia, Without the Melodrama', *New York Times*, 6 April 2003. Available online: http://www.nytimes.com/2003/04/06/movies/film-amnesia-withoutthemelodrama.html (accessed 17 May 2017).
4   Artificial Eye (The AK Collection: Vol. 1) calls these films the underdog trilogy while Eclipse calls them the proletariat trilogy.
5   Kehr, 'Amnesia, Without the Melodrama'.
6   Lloyd Hughes, 'Aki Kaurismäki', in *The Rough Guide to Film: An A-Z of Directors and Their Movies*, ed. Richard Armstrong, Tom Charity, Lloyd Hughes and Jessica Winter (London: Penguin, 2007), 267.
7   Ian Johnston, 'Blow the Man Down: Aki Kaurismäki's *Lights in the Dusk*', *Bright Lights Film Journal*, 1 August 2007. Available online: http://brightlightsfilm.com/blow-manakikaurismakis-lights-dusk/#.WQCoXBSp2n0 (accessed 17 May 2017).
8   Bert Cardullo, 'Lonely People, Living in the World: The Films of Aki Kaurismäki', *Soundings on Cinema: Speaking to Films and Film Artists* (Albany: State University of New York Press, 2008), 170.
9   Richard Porton, *Film and the Anarchist Imagination* (London and New York: Verso, 1999), 235; Luc Sante, '*La* Vie *de bohème*: The Seacoast of Bohemia: The Seacoast of Bohemia', Essay included in the Criterion DVD of *La* Vie *de bohème*, 20 January 2014. Available online: https://www.criterion.com/current/posts/3025-la-vie-de-boheme-the-seacoast-of-bohemia (accessed 17 May 2017).
10   Charles Darwin, *The Expression of the Emotions in Man and Animals*, 3rd Edition (London: HarperCollins, [1872] 1998), 62.

11 Chris Norris, 'In Bloom: The Inscrutable Jim Jarmusch Directs the Poker-faced Bill Murray in *Broken Flowers*', *Film Comment*, 41, no. 4 (July–August 2005): 35.

12 Donna Peberdy, '"I'm Just a Character in Your Film": Acting and Performance from Autism to Zissou', *New Review of Film and Television Studies*, 10, no. 1 (2012): 59.

13 Philip Kemp, '*The Man Without a Past*', *Sight and Sound*, 13, no. 2 (February 2003): 53.

14 Henri Bergson, *Laughter: An Essay on the Meaning of the Comic*, translated by Cloudesley Brereton and Fred Rothwell (New York: Dover Publications, [1911] 2005), 1, 2.

15 Erica Fudge, *Animal* (London: Reaktion Books, 2002), 27–28.

16 David Rooney, '*The Other Side of Hope*', *Hollywood Reporter*, 14 February 2017. Available online: http://www.hollywoodreporter.com/review/other-side-of-hope-berlin2017975923 (accessed 17 May 2017).

17 Luc Sante, '*La* Vie de Bohème: The Seacoast of Bohemia'.

18 Ibid.

19 Sylvia Blum-Reid, *Traveling in French Cinema* (Basingstoke and New York: Palgrave Macmillan, 2016), 118.

20 Peter Matthews, '*Drifting Clouds*', *Sight and Sound*, 7, no. 6 (June 1997): 51.

21 Jonathan Romney, 'The Kaurismäki Effect', *Sight and Sound*, 7, no. 6 (June 1997): 11.

22 Philip Kemp, '*The Man Without a Past*', *Sight and Sound*, 13, no. 2 (February 2003): 53.

23 Pao-chen Tang, 'Of Dogs and Hot Dogs: Distractions in Early Cinema', *Early Popular Visual Culture*, 15, no. 1 (2017): 3, 4.

24 Ibid., 5, 6.

25 Ibid., 5.

26 Fudge, *Animal*, 67, 68.

27 A similar dog appears in *Leningrad Cowboys: Those Were the Days* (1991), a 6-minute short about a man (Silu Seppälä) and his donkey roaming the streets in 'Paris, 1994'. He feeds the donkey outside a bar where the Cowboys play, and there is a brief shot of the dog (presumably played again by Laika) apparently watching the singer as she approaches the stranger and then apparently turning to look at the barman, who watches as the singer leaves hand in hand with the stranger. The film concludes with a shot of the barman drowning his sorrows and petting the similarly abandoned donkey.

28 This approach was perhaps anticipated by the closing credits for *Leningrad*: Laika is listed before Jim Jarmusch, who has a cameo as a mechanic. However, Valpu, the canine actor who features in *The Other Side of Hope*, is not listed in the film's opening credits, despite appearing in several sequences (and for roughly the same time as does Paju in *Lights in the Dusk*).

29 Press kits available online: http://www.the-matchfactory.com/films/items/lehavre.html?file … /l/le … /pressbook … pdf and http://www.sonyclassics.com/manwithoutapast/_media/man_presskit.pdf (accessed 17 May 2017).

30 Laika won a Special Jury Prize for her performance in *Le Havre* in 2011. Kaurismäki is the only director whose films have twice won Palm Dog awards.

31 Gordon Sander, 'Romantic as a Caterpillar: The Arts Interview', *Financial Times: FT Weekend*, 28 December 2002, 7.

32 Michael Brooke, 'Minor Quay', *Sight and Sound*, 22, no. 5 (May 2012): 18.
33 Annika Pham, 'Aki Kaurismäki: "I feel better if the audience gets one or two laughs for their ticket"', Nordisk Film & TV Fond, 9 September 2011. Available online: http://www.nordiskfilmogtvfond.com/news/stories/aki-kaurismaeki-i-feel-better-if-theaudiencegets-one-or-two-laughs-for-their-ticket/ (accessed 17 May 2017).
34 Bert Cardullo, 'An Interview with Aki Kaurismäki', *Soundings on Cinema: Speaking to Films and Film Artists* (Albany: State University of New York Press, 2008), 175.
35 Giovanni Marchini Camia, 'The Good Thing about Problems Is That They Are Timeless', *Exberliner*, 7 September 2011. Available online: http://www.exberliner.com/culture/film/'thegood-thing-about-problems-is-that-they-aretimeless'/ (accessed 17 May 2017).
36 Michael Brooke, 'Minor Quay', *Sight and Sound*, 22, no. 5 (May 2012): 18.
37 Adrienne L. McLean, 'Introduction: Wonder Dogs', in *Cinematic Canines: Dogs and Their Work in the Fiction Film*, ed. Adrienne L. McLean (New Brunswick, nl and London: Rutgers University Press, 2014), 4.
38 Similarly, a recent monograph on Kaurismäki's films has on its cover an image of the canine actor Tähti from *The Man Without a Past*. See Pilar Carrera, *Aki Kaurismäki* (Madrid: Cátedra, 2012).
39 Romney, 'The Kaurismäki Effect', 11.
40 Alexandra Horowitz, 'The Dog at the Side of the Shot: Incongruous Dog (*Canis familiaris*) Behaviour in Film', in *Cinematic Canines: Dogs and Their Work in the Fiction Film*, ed. Adrienne L. McLean (New Brunswick, NJ and London: Rutgers University Press, 2014), 223, 226.
41 Horowitz, 'The Dog at the Side of the Shot', 229.
42 Jarmo Valkola, *Landscapes of the Mind: Emotion and Style in the Aki Kaurismäki's Films* (Saarbrücken: LAP Lambert Academic Publishing, 2012), 215.
43 Valkola, *Landscapes of the Mind*, 157.
44 McLean, 'Introduction: Wonder Dogs', 15–16.
45 Ibid., 4.
46 Stella Hockenhull, 'Celebrity Creatures: The "Starification" of the Cinematic Animal', in *Revisiting Star Studies: Cultures, Themes and Methods*, ed. Sabrina Qiong Yu and Guy Austin (Edinburgh: Edinburgh University Press, 2017), 288–289.
47 Hockenhull, 'Celebrity Creatures', 290–291.
48 Ibid., 286, 287, 288.
49 Erica Fudge, *Pets* (London: Acumen, 2008), 56.
50 Charles Baudelaire, *Paris Spleen*, translated by Louise Varèse (New York: New Directions, [1869] 1947), 104.
51 Baudelaire, *Paris Spleen*, 105. In his review of *La Vie de Bohème*, Terrence Rafferty suggests 'Marcel, Rodolfo, and Schaunard are the human counterparts of the "good dogs" eulogized by Baudelaire in the final pages of *Le Spleen de Paris*'. See 'A Dog's Life', *New Yorker*, 69, no. 25 (9 August 1993): 93.
52 McLean, 'Introduction: Wonder Dogs', 4.
53 Murray Smith, 'Darwin and the Directors: Film, Emotion and the Face in the Age of Evolution', in *Evolution, Literature and Film: A Reader*, ed. Brian Boyd, Joseph Carroll and Jonathan Gottschall (New York: Columbia University Press, 2010), 260.

54 Smith, 'Darwin and the Directors', 264, 268.
55 Jonathan Romney, 'Last Exit to Helsinki: The Bleak Comedic Genius of Aki Kaurismäki, Finland's Finest', *Film Comment*, 39, no. 2 (March/April 2003): 47.
56 Michel Ciment, 'Aki Kaurismäki', *Film World: Interviews with Cinema's Leading Directors*, translated by Julie Rose (Oxford and New York: Berg, 2009), 202.

FILMOGRAPHY

Films by Aki Kaurismäki

Saimaa-ilmiö (The Saimaa Gesture, co-directed with Mika Käurismaki, 1981)
Rikos ja rangaistus (Crime and Punishment, 1983)
Calamari Union (1985)
Varjoja paratiisissa (Shadows in Paradise, 1986)
Rocky VI (short) (1986)
L.A. Woman (short) (1987)
Hamlet liikemaailmassa (Hamlet Goes Business, 1987)
Thru the Wire (short) (1987)
Rich Little Bitch (short) (1987)
Ariel (1988)
Leningrad Cowboys Go America (1989)
Likaiset kädet (Les Mains Sales, 1989)
Tulitikkutehtaan tyttö (The Match Factory Girl, 1990)
I Hired a Contract Killer (1990)
Leningrad Cowboys: Those Were the Days (short) (1991)
Leningrad Cowboys: These Boots (short) (1992)
La Vie de Bohème (1992)
Pidä huivista kiini, Tatjana (Take Care of Your Scarf, Tatiana, 1994)
Total Balalaika Show (1994)
Leningrad Cowboys Meet Moses (1994)
Kauas pilvet karkaavat (Drifting Clouds, 1996)
Oo aina ihminen (Always Be a Human) (short) (1996)
Välittäjä (The Employment Agent) (short) (1996)
Juha (1999)
Dogs Have No Hell (short) (2002)
Mies vailla menneisyyttä (The Man Without a Past, 2002)
Bico (short) (2004)
Laitakaupungin valot (Lights in the Dusk, 2006)
Valimo (The Foundry) (short) (2007)
Le Havre (2011)
Tavern Man (short) (2012)
Juice Leskinen & Grand Slam: Bluesia Pieksämäen asemalla (short) (2013)
Toivon tuolla puolen (The Other Side of Hope, 2017)

BIBLIOGRAPHY

Adorno, Theodor. *Minima Moralia: Reflections on a Damaged Life*. London: Verso, 2005.

Affron, Charles. *Cinema and Sentiment*. Chicago: University of Chicago Press, 1982.

Agamben, Giorgio. 'Notes on Gesture'. In *Infancy and History: The Destruction of Experience*, translated by Liz Heron, 133–140. London and New York: Verso, 1978.

Altman, Rick. 'The American Film Musical: Paradigmatic Structure and Mediatory Function'. In *Genre: The Musical: A Reader*, edited by Altman, 197–207. London: British Film Institute, 1981.

Altman, Rick. *The American Film Musical*. Bloomington, IN: Indiana University Press, 1987.

Anonymous. 'Kaurismäen Arielille kiitosta New York Timesissa' *Uusi Suomi*, 26 September 1989. A clipping held in Ariel file at the National Audiovisual Institute, Helsinki.

Arnheim, Rudolf. *Film as Art*. Berkeley, LA, London: University of California Press, 1957.

Bacon, Henry. 'Aki Kaurismäen sijoiltaan olon poetiikka'. In *Taju kankaalle: Uutta suomalaista elokuvaa paikantamassa*, edited by Kimmo Ahonen, Juha Rosenqvist, Janne Rosenqvist and Päivi Valotie, 89–97. Turku: Kirja-Aurora, 2003.

Bacon, Henry. 'Aki Kaurismäen sijoiltaan olon poetiikka'. In *Taju kankaalle*, edited by K. Ahonen et al., 88–97. Turku: Kirja-Aurora, 2003.

Bacon, Henry. 'Deforming Helsinki on Film'. *Datutop 29 – City + Cinema – Essays on the Specificity of Location in Film*, Tampere University of Technology, Department of Architecture, Autumn 2007.

Bacon, Henry. *The Fascination of Film Violence*. Basingstoke: Palgrave Macmillan, 2015.

Bacon, Henry and Jaakko Seppälä. 'Two Modes of Transnational Filmmaking'. In *Finnish Cinema: A Transnational Enterprise*, edited by Henry Bacon, 211–222. London: Palgrave Macmillan, 2016.

Badiou, Alain. *Ethics: An Essay on the Understanding of Evil*. London and New York: Verso, 2002.

Badley, Linda. *Lars von Trier*. Champaign, IL: University of Illinois Press, 2011.

Balázs, Béla. *Theory of the Film: Character and Growth of a New Art*. London: Dennis Dobson Ltd, [1952] 1970.

Baron, Cynthia and Sharon Marie. *Reframing Screen Performance*. Ann Arbor: University of Michigan Press, 2011, 128.

Barthes, Roland. 'Diderot, Brecht, Eisenstein'. In *Image Music Text*, trans. by Stephen Heath, 69–78. London: Fontana, 1977.

Baudelaire, Charles. *Paris Spleen*. 1869. Trans. Louise Varèse. New York: New Directions, 1947.

Bazin, André. *What Is Cinema*, trans. Hugh Gray, vol. 1. Berkeley: University of California Press, [1967] 2005.

Benjamin, Walter. 'The Formula in Which the Dialectical Structure of Film Finds Expression'. In *The Work of Art in the Age of Its Technological* Reproducibility, *and Other Writings on Media*, edited by Michael W. Jennings, Brigid Doherty, and Thomas Y. Levin , trans. Edmund Jephcott et al., 340–352. Cambridge, MA, London: Harvard University Press, [1935] 2008.

Berger, John. *And Our Faces, My Heart, Brief as Photos*. London: Bloomsbury, 2005.

Bergson, Henri. *Laughter: An Essay on the Meaning of the Comic*. Trans. Cloudesley Brereton and Fred Rothwell. New York: Dover Publications, [1911] 2005.

Berlant, Lauren. *Cruel Optimism*. Durham and London: Duke University Press, 2011.

Bloom, Harold. *Shakespeare: The Invention of the Human*. London: Fourth Estate, 1999.

Blum-Reid, Sylvia. *Traveling in French Cinema*. Basingstoke and New York: Palgrave Macmillan, 2016.

Booth, Wayne C. *A Rhetoric of Irony*. Chicago and London: University of Chicago Press, 1975.

Bordwell, David. *Ozu and the Poetics of Cinema*. Ann Arbor, MI: Michigan Publishing, University of Michigan Library, 1988.

Bordwell, David and Kristin Thompson. *Film Art – An Introduction*. International edition. New York: McGraw-Hill, [1979] 1993.

Bourdieu, Pierre. *Distinction: A Social Critique of the Judgement of Taste*. Trans. Richard Nice. London: Routledge, [1984], 2010.

Branigan, Edward. 'The Space of Equinox Flower'. In *Close Viewings: An Anthology of New Film Criticism*, edited by P. Lehman, 73–108. Florida State University Press, 1990.

Branigan, Edward. 'The Articulation of Colour in a Filmic System: *Deux ou trois Choses Que Je Sais d'elle*', *Wide Angle* 1, no. 3 (1976), 20–31, revised and reprinted. In *Color: The Film Reader*, edited by Angela Dalle Vache and Brian Price, 170–182. London: Routledge, 2006.

Brassier, Ray. 'Prometheanism and Its Critics'. In *Accelerate: The Accelerationist Reader*, edited by Robin Mckay and Armen Avanessian, 486–487. Berlin: Urbanomic, 2014.

Braudy, Leo. *The World in a Frame: What We See in Films*. Chicago and London: The University of Chicago Press, [1976] 2002.

Brecht, Bertolt. 'Two Essay Fragments on Non-professional Acting'. In *Brecht on Theatre*, 3rd Edition edited by Marc Silberman, Steve Giles, and Tom Kuhn, 206–211. London and New York: Bloomsbury, [1939] 2014.

Bresson, Robert. *Notes on Cinematography*. Trans. by Jonathan Griffin. New York: Urizen Books, 1975.

Brinkema, Eugenie. *The Forms of the Affects*. Durham: Duke University Press, 2014.

Brooke, Michael. 'Minor Quay'. *Sight & Sound* 22, no. 5 (2012): 16–20.

Bruner, Jerome. *Acts of Meaning*. Cambridge, MA: Harvard University Press, 1990.

Butler, Judith. 'Un populisme de gauche doit conduire à une démocratie radicale', *Liberation*, January 2017. Available online: http://www.liberation.fr/ debats/2017/01/20/judithbutler-un-populisme-degauche-doit-conduire-a-une-democratieradicale_1542916 (accessed 11 May 2017).

Camia, Giovanni Marchini. 'The Good Thing about Problems Is That They Are Timeless', *Exberliner*, 7 September 2011. Available online: http://www.exberliner. com/culture/film/"the-good-thing-about-problemsis-that-they-are-timeless"/ (accessed 17 May 2017).

Cardullo, Bert. 'Finnish Character: An Interview with Aki Kaurismäki', *Film Quarterly* 59, no. 4 (2006): 8–9.

Cardullo, Bert. 'An Interview with Aki Kaurismäki'. *Soundings on Cinema: Speaking to Films and Film Artists*, 175–182. Albany: State University of New York Press, 2009.

Cardullo, Bert. 'Lonely People, Living in the World: The Films of Aki Kaurismäki'. *Soundings on Cinema: Speaking to Films and Film Artists*, 159–175. Albany: State University of New York Press, 2009.

Carrera, Pilar. *Aki Kaurismäki*. Madrid: Cátedra, 2012.

Carrol, Nöel. 'Notes on the Sight Gag'. In *Comedy/Cinema/Theory*, edited by Andrew Horton, 25–42. Berkeley, LA and London: University of California Press, 1991.

Cavell, Stanley. *The World Viewed: Reflections on the Ontology of Film*. Cambridge, MA and London: Harvard University Press, 1979.

Caws, Mary Ann. *Surrealism*. London: Phaidon Press Limited, 2004.

Ciment, Michel. 'Aki Kaurismäki'. In *Film World: Interviews with Cinema's Leading Directors*, trans. by Julie Rose, 199–206. Oxford and New York: Berg, 2009.

Colebrook, Claire. *Irony*. London and New York: Routledge, 2004.

Connah, Roger. *K/K A Couple of Finns and Some Donald Ducks*. Helsinki: VAPK, 1991.

Crary, Jonathan. *24/7: Late Capitalism and the Ends of Sleep*. London: Verso, 2012.

Critchley, Simon. *Infinitely Demanding: Ethics of Commitment, Politics of Resistance*. London and New York: Verso, 2014.

Currie, Gregory. *Narratives & Narrators: A Philosophy of Stories*. Oxford: Oxford University Press, 2010.

Darwin, Charles. *The Expression of the Emotions in Man and Animals*. 3rd Edition. London: HarperCollins, [1872], 1998.

Davis, Mike. *Ecology of Fear*. New York: Metropolitan Books, 1998.

Deleuze, Giles. *Cinema 1: The Movement-Image*. Habberjam, MN: University of Minnesota Press, 1986.

Doane, Mary Ann. 'The Close-up: Scale and Detail in the Cinema', *Differences*, 14, no. 3 (2003): 89–111.

Doherty, Thomas. *Hollywood's Censor: Joseph I. Breen & the Production Code Administration*. New York, NY: Columbia University Press, 2007.

Dyer, Richard. 'Entertainment and Utopia'. In *Genre: The Musical: A Reader*, edited by Rick Altman, 175–189. London: British Film Institute, 1981.

Dyer-Witheford, Nick. 'Red Plenty Platforms', *Culture Machine*, 14 (2013): 1–27.

Ebert, Roger. 'Lights in the Dusk', 17 July 2008. Available online: http://www.rogerebert.com/reviews/lights-in-the-dusk-2008 (accessed 28 December 2016).

Elsaesser, Thomas. 'The Global Author: Control, Creative Constraints and Performative Self-contradiction'. In *The Global Auteur: The Politics of Authorship in 21st Century Cinema*, edited by Seung-hoon Jeong and Jeremi Szaniawski, 21–42. New York: Bloomsbury, 2016.

Epstein, Jean. 'Cinema and Modern Literature'. In *Jean Epstein: Critical Essays and New Translations*, edited by Sarah Keller and Jason N. Paul, 271–276. Amsterdam: Amsterdam University Press, [1921] 2012.

Everett, Wendy. 'Through a Fractal Lens: New Perspectives on the Narratives of Luis Buñuel'. In *A Companion to Luis Buñuel*, edited by Rob Stone and Julián Daniel Gutiérrez-Albilla, 518–534. Malden et al.: Wiley-Blackwell, 2013.

Farber, Manny. 'Introduction to Negative Space'. In *Farber on Film: The Complete Film Writings of Manny Farber*, edited by R. Polito, 691–697. New York, NY: Library of America, 2009.

Feuer, Jane. *The Hollywood Musical*. Bloomington, IN: Indiana University Press, 1982.

Feuer, Jane. 'The Self-reflexive Musical and the Myth of Entertainment'. In *Film Genre Reader II*, edited by Barry Keith Grant, 441–455. Austin: University of Texas Press, 1995.

Feuer, Jane. 'Is Dirty Dancing a Musical'. In *The Times of Our Lives: Dirty Dancing and Popular Culture*, edited by Yannis Tzioumakis and Siân Lincoln, 59–72. Detroit: Wayne State University Press, 2013.

Ford, Hamish. 'Antonioni's *L'Avventura* and Deleuze's Time-Image', *Senses of Cinema*, 28 October 2003. Available online: http://sensesofcinema.com/2003/feature-articles/l_avventura_deleuze/ (accessed 11 January 2017).

Foucault, Michel. *The History of Sexuality*. New York: Random House, 1978.

Flusser, Vilém. *Gestures*. Trans. by Nancy Ann Roth. Minneapolis and London: University of Minnesota Press, 2014.

Fuchs, Christian. 'Donald Trump: A Critical Theory-Perspective on Authoritarian Capitalism', *tripleC: Communication, Capitalism & Critique*, 15, no. 1 (2017): 1–72.

Fudge, Erica. *Animal*. London: Reaktion Books, 2002.

Fudge, Erica. *Pets*. London: Acumen, 2008.

Gee, Felicity. 'Surrealist Legacies: The Influence of Luis Buñuel's "irrationality" on Hiroshi Teshigahara's "documentary fantasy"'. In *A Companion to Luis Buñuel*, edited by Rob Stone and Julián Daniel Gutiérrez-Albilla, 572–589. Malden et al.: Wiley-Blackwell, 2013.

Gottlieb, Sidney. 'Hitchcock and the Art of the Kiss: A Preliminary Survey'. In *Framing Hitchcock: Selected Essays from the Hitchcock Annual*, edited by Sidney Gottlieb and Christopher Brookhouse, 132–146. Detroit, MI: Wayne State University Press, 2002.

Guattari, Felix. *The Three Ecologies*. New York: Bloomsbury, 2000.

Gunning, Tom. 'The Cinema of Attraction: Early Film, Its Spectator and the Avant-Garde'. *Wide Angle*, 8, no. 3/4 (1986): 63–70.

Haas, Christine. 'Sanoitteko Kaurismäki?' *La Strada* 4/1988. A clipping held in Aki Kaurismäki file at the National Audiovisual Institute, Helsinki.

Hardt, Michael and Antonio Negri. *Multitude: War and Democracy in the Age of Empire*. New York: Penguin, 2005.

Hattenstone, Simon. 'Seven Rounds with Aki Kaurismäki', *The Guardian*, 4 April 2012. Available online: https://www.theguardian.com/film/2012/apr/04/akikaurismakile-havre-interview

Heath, Stephen. 'Body, Voice'. In *Questions of Cinema*, 176–193. Bloomington: Indiana University Press, 1981.

Hegel, G. W. F. *Aesthetics: Notes on Fine Art*, Vol. 2, trans. T. M. Knox. Oxford: Oxford University Press, [1935] 1975.

Hermerén, Göran. *Influence in Art and Literature*. Princeton: Princeton University Press, 1975.

Herzog, Amy. *Dreams of Difference, Songs of the Same: The Musical Moment in Film*. Minneapolis, MN: University of Minnesota Press, 2009.

Hoberman, J. 'Dream Act: Town Rallies to Help an Immigrant in Utopian Le Havre', *Village Voice* (2011): np. Available online: http://www.villagevoice.com/2011-1019/film/dream-act-town-rallies-to-help-an-immigrant-in-utopian-le-havre/full/

Hockenhull, Stella. 'Celebrity Creatures: The "Starification" of the Cinematic Animal'. In *Revisiting Star Studies: Cultures, Themes and Methods*, edited by Sabrina Qiong Yu and Guy Austin, 279–294. Edinburgh: Edinburgh University Press, 2017.

Holmes, Brian. *Unleashing the Collective Phantoms: Essays in Reverse Imagineering.* New York: Autonomedia, 2008.

Horowitz, Alexandra. 'The Dog at the Side of the Shot: Incongruous Dog (*Canis familiaris*) Behaviour in Film'. In *Cinematic Canines: Dogs and Their Work in the Fiction Film*, edited by Adrienne L. McLean, 219–234. New Brunswick, NJ and London: Rutgers University Press, 2014.

Hughes, Lloyd. 'Aki Kaurismäki'. In *The Rough Guide to Film: An A-Z of Directors and Their Movies*, edited by Richard Armstrong, Tom Charity, Lloyd Hughes and Jessica Winter, 267–268. London: Penguin, 2007.

Hutcheon, Linda. *The Politics of Postmodern.* London and New York: Routledge, [1989] 2002.

Hutcheon, Linda. *Irony's Edge: The Theory and Politics of Irony.* 1995. London and New York: Routledge, 2005.

Iampolski, Mikhail. *The Memory of Tiresias: Intertextuality and Film.* Berkeley, CA: University of California Press, 1998.

Iovino, Serenella and Serpil Opperman. 'Material Ecocriticism, Materiality, Agency and Models of Narrativity'. *Ecozone*, 3, no. 1 (2012): 75–91.

Jameson, Frederic. 'The Existence of Italy', in *Signatures of the Visible*. New York and London: Routledge, 1992.

Johnston, Ian. 'Blow the Man Down: Aki Kaurismäki's *Lights in the Dusk*', *Bright Lights Film Journal*, 1 August 2007. Available online: http://brightlightsfilm.com/blow-man-aki-kaurismakislightsdusk/#.WQCoXBSp2n0 (accessed 17 May 2017).

Jones, Owen. 'The Left Needs a New Populism Fast. It's Clear What Happens If We Fail', *Guardian*, November 2016. Available online: https://www.theguardian.com/commentisfree/2016/nov/10/the-leftneedsa-new-populism-fast

Kääpä, Pietari. 'The Working Class Has No Fatherland: Aki Kaurismäki's Films and the Transcending of National Specificity', *Journal of Finnish Studies*, 8, no. 2 (2004): 77–95.

Kääpä, Pietari. 'Displaced Souls Lost in Finland: The Kaurismäkis' Films as the Cinema of the Marginalised', *Wider Screen*, 16 October 2006: np. Available online: http://widerscreen.fi/2006/2/displaced_souls_lost_in_finland.htm

Kääpä, Pietari. 'The National and Beyond: The Globalisation of Finnish Cinema in the Films of Aki and Mika Kaurismäki, 1981–1995', unpublished PhD dissertation, School of Film and Television Studies, University of East Anglia, 2008.

Kääpä, Pietari. *The National and Beyond: The Globalisation of Finnish Cinema in the Films of Aki and Mika Kaurismäki.* Oxford: Peter Lang, 2010.

Kääpä, Pietari. *The Cinema of Mika Kaurismäki: Transvergent Cinescapes, Emergent Identities.* Bristol: Intellect, 2011.

Kääpä, Pietari. *Ecology and Contemporary Nordic Cinema.* London: Bloomsbury, 2014.

Kant, Imanuel. *Critique of Judgement*, Oxford: Oxford University Press, 2007.

Kehr, Dave. 'Amnesia, Without the Melodrama', *New York Times*, 6 April 2003. Available online: http://www.nytimes.com/2003/04/06/movies/filmamnesia-without-themelodrama.html (accessed 17 May 2017).

Kember, Sarah and Zylinska, Joanna Zylinska. *Life after New Media: Mediation as a Vital Process.* Cambridge, MA and London: MIT Press, 2012.

Kemp, Philip. 'The Man Without a Past', Sight and Sound, 13, no. 2 (February 2003): 53.

Keyishian, Harry. 'Shakespeare and Movie Genre: The Case of Hamlet'. In The Cambridge Companion to Shakespeare on Film, edited by Russell Jackson, 72–81. Cambridge: Cambridge University Press, 2000.

King, Geoff. Indie 2.0: Change and Continuity in Contemporary American Indie Film. London and New York: I. B. Tauris, 2014.

Kioupkiolis, Alexandros. 'Podemos: The Ambiguous Promises of Left-wing Populism in Contemporary Spain', Journal of Political Ideologies, 21, no. 2 (2016): 99–120.

Kirby, Michael. 'On Acting and Not-Acting', The Drama Review, 16, no. 1 (1972): 7.

Kivimäki, Sanna. 'Working-class Girls in a Welfare State: Finnishness, Social Class and Gender in Aki Kaurismäki's Workers' Trilogy (1986–1990)', Journal of Scandinavian Cinema, 2, no. 1 (2012): 73–88.

Klevan, Andrew. Disclosure of the Everyday: Undramatic Achievement in Narrative Film. Trowbridge: Flicks Books, 2000.

Koivunen, Anu. 'Do You Remember Monrépos? Melancholia, Modernity and Working-class Masculinity in The Man Without a Past'. In Northern Constellations: New Readings in Nordic Cinema, edited by C. Claire Thompson, 133–148. Norwich: Norvik Press, 2006.

Kracauer, Siegfried. Theory of Film: The Redemption of Physical Reality. Princeton, NJ: Princeton University Press, 1997.

Krämer, Sybille and Horst Bredekamp. 'Culture, Technology, Cultural Techniques – Moving beyond Text', Theory, Culture and Society, 30, no. 6 (2013): 20–29.

Kyösola, Satu. 'The Archivist's Nostalgia', Journal of Finnish Studies, 8, no. 2 (2004): 46–62.

Laclau, Ernesto. On Populist Reason. New York and London: Verso, 2005.

Lavery, Jason. The History of Finland. Westport, CT, London: Greenwood Press, 2006.

Linares, Thomas. 'The "Lost" but Never Defeated Heroes of Aki Kaurismäki'. In Aki Kaurismäki, edited by Elena Christopoulou, 62–65. Athens: 53rd Thessaloniki International Film Festival, 2012.

Loader, Jayne. 'Jeanne Dielman. Death in Installments', Jump Cut, 16, no. 1012, 1977. Available online: https://www.ejumpcut.org/archive/onlinessays/JC16folder/JeanneDielman.html (accessed 12 March 2017).

Longfellow, Brenda. 'Love Letters to the Mother: The Works of Chantal Akerman', CTheory, 13 no. 1–2 (1989): 73–90.

Lordon, Frédéric. Willing Slaves of Capital: Spinoza and Marx on Desire. Transl. by Gabriel Ash. London: Verso, 2014.

Lukács, Georg. Studies in European Realism. A Sociological Survey of the Writings of Balzac, Stendhal, Zola, Tolstoy, Gorki and Others. London: The Merlin Press, [1950] 1972.

MacDowell, James. 'Notes on Quirky', Movie: A Journal of Film Criticism, 1, no. 1 (2010), 1–16.

Macnab, Geoffrey. Screen Epiphanies: Filmmakers on the Films that Inspired Them. London: BFI, 2010.

Margulies, Ivone. Nothing Happens: Chantal Akerman's Hyperrealist Everyday. Durham: Duke University Press, 1996.

Martin, Adrian. 'Intimate Metamorphosis: Film & Architectural Space', Architectural Review Asia-Pacific, 128 (2013). Available online: http://www.

australiandesignreview.com/features/28050-intimatemetamorphosisfilm-architectural-space (accessed 12 March 2017).

Marx, Karl. *Capital: Volume 1*. London: Penguin, 1976.

Marx, Karl. *Early Writings*. Trans. by Rodney Livingstone. London: Penguin, [1844] 2014.

Maskulin, Sanna. "'Kinkkua, anna minä' – "Ham, let me" – kaurismäkeläisen dialogin erityispiirteitä', *Lähikuva*, 4 (1999): 32–43.

Matthews, Peter. '*Drifting Clouds*', *Sight and Sound*, 7, no. 6 (June 1997): 51.

Mauss, Marcel. 'Techniques of the Body', *Economy and Society*, 2, no. 1 (1973): 70–88.

Mazierska, Ewa and Laura Rascaroli. *Crossing New Europe: Postmodern Travel and the European Road Movie*. London: Wallflower Press, 2006.

McLean, Adrienne L. 'Introduction: Wonder Dogs.' In *Cinematic Canines: Dogs and Their Work in the Fiction Film*, edited by Adrienne L. McLean, 1–30. New Brunswick, NJ and London: Rutgers University Press, 2014.

Mercado, Gustavo. *The Filmmaker's Eye: Learning (and Breaking) the Rules of Cinematic Composition*. Amsterdam et al.: Focal Press, 2001.

Mouffe, Chantal. 'In Defence of Left-wing Populism', *The Conversation*, April 2016. Available online: http://theconversation.com/in-defence-of-left-wing-populism-55869

Naney, Bence. 'Two-dimensional versus Three-dimensional Pictorial Organization in Film'. A Presentation in the The Society for Cognitive Studies of the Moving Image 2015 conference. London: 18 June 2015.

Nestingen, Andrew. 'Leaving Home: Global Circulation and Aki Kaurismäki's Ariel'. In *In Search of Aki Kaurismäki*, edited by Andrew Nestingen, 96–115. Ontario: Aspasia books, 2004.

Nestingen, Andrew. 'Aki Kaurismäki's Crossroads: National Cinema and the Road Movie'. In *Transnational Cinema in a Global North: Nordic Cinema in Transition*, edited by Andrew Nestingen and Trevor G. Elkington, 279–305. Detroit: Wayne State University Press, 2005.

Nestingen, Andrew. *Crime and Fantasy in Scandinavia*. Detroit: University of Washington Press, 2008.

Nestingen, Andrew. *The Cinema of Aki Kaurismäki: Contrarian Stories*. New York: Wallflower Press, 2013.

Nestingen, Andrew. 'Aki Kaurismäki – From Punk to Social Democracy'. In *A Companion to Nordic Cinema*, edited by Mette Hjort and Ursula Lindqvist, 291–312. London: John Wiley & Sons, 2016.

Niskanen, Eija. Interview with Hojo, Masato. Eurospace office, Shibuya, Tokyo, March, 2017.

Niskanen, Eija. Interview with Watanabe, Hirobumi. Ikebukuro, Tokyo, March 10, 2017.

Niskanen, Eija. Interview with Yamashita, Nobuhiro. Udine Far East Film Festival, April 28, 2017.

Norris, Chris. 'In Bloom: The Inscrutable Jim Jarmusch Directs the Poker-faced Bill Murray in *Broken Flowers*' *Film Comment*, 41, no. 4 (July–August 2005), 34–36.

O'Hagan, Sean. 'Wandering Star', *The Observer*, 2 October 2005. Available online: http://www.theguardian.com/film/2005/oct/02/features.magazine (accessed 29 September 2015).

Pao-chen Tang. 'Of Dogs and Hot Dogs: Distractions in Early Cinema', *Early Popular Visual Culture*, 15, no. 1 (2017): 1–15.

Pauly, Tzvetomila. 'Take Care of Your Scar(f), Lilya! De-stigmatizing the Image of the Post-Soviet Other in Nordic Cinema', *Baltic Screen Media Review*, 2 (2015): 36–53.

Peberdy, Donna. '"I'm Just a Character in Your Film": Acting and Performance from Autism to Zissou', *New Review of Film and Television Studies*, 10, no. 1 (2012): 46–67.

Pechter, W. S. *Twenty-Four Times a Second: Films and Film-Makers* New York: Harper & Row, 1971.

Peden, Sanna. 'Soup, Soap and National Reawakening – the Ambiguous Role of the Salvation Army in The Man Without a Past', *Wider Screen*, 8, no. 2 (2007).

Peden, Sanna. 'Crossing Over: On Becoming European in Aki Kaurismäki's Cinema'. In *Frontiers of Screen History: Imagining European Borders in Cinema, 1945–2010*, edited by Raita Merivirta, Kimmo Ahonen, Heta Mulari and Rami Mähkä, 113–131. Bristol: Intellect, 2013.

Perez, Gilberto. *The Material Ghost: Films and Their Medium*. Baltimore: Johns Hopkins University Press, 1998.

Perez, Gilberto. 'The Priest and the Pineapple. Buñuel's *Nazarin*'. *La Furia Umana*, 6. Available online: http://www.lafuriaumana.it/index.php/archives/36-lfu-6/316-gilberto-perez-thepriestand-the-pineapple-bunuel-s-nazarin (accessed 17 December 2015).

Perkins, Victor. 'Where Is the World? The Horizon of Events in Movie Fiction'. In *Style and Meaning: Studies in the Detailed Analysis of Film*, edited by John Gibbs and Douglas Pye, 16–41. Manchester: Manchester University Press, 2005.

Perkins, Victor. 'Moments of Choice', *Rogue* 9 (2006). Available online: http://www.rouge.com.au/9/moments_choice.html (accessed 8 March 2017).

Peucker, Brigitte. 'Filmic Tableau Vivant: Vermeer, Intermediality and the Real.' In *Rites of Realism: Essays on Corporeal Cinema*, edited by Ivone Margulies, 294–314. Durham and London: Duke University Press, 2003.

Pham, Annika. 'Aki Kaurismäki: "I feel better if the audience gets one or two laughs for their ticket"'. Nordisk Film & TV Fond, 9 September 2011. Available online: http://www.nordiskfilmogtvfond.com/news/stories/aki-kaurismaeki-ifeel-betterif-the-audience-gets-one-or-two-laughs-for-their-ticket/ (accessed 17 May 2017).

Piela, Mikko. '"En ole löytänyt vielä omaa tyyliäni"', *KU-Viikkolehti*, 24 December 1983. A clipping held in Aki Kaurismäki file at the National Audiovisual Institute, Helsinki.

Porton, Richard. *Film and the Anarchist Imagination*. London and New York: Verso, 1999.

Rafferty, Terrence. 'The New Cinema: A Dog's Life'. *New Yorker*, 69, no. 25 (9 August 1993): 93–94.

Rascaroli, Laura. 'Becoming-minor in a Sustainable Europe: The Contemporary European Art Film and Aki Kaurismäki's *Le Havre*', *Screen*, 54, no. 3 (2013): 323–340.

Ray, Robert B. *The ABCs of Classic Hollywood*. Oxford: Oxford University Press, 2008.

Rees, Elle. 'The Nordic "Quirky Feel-Good"'. In *Nordic Genre Film: Small Nation Film Cultures in the Global Marketplace*, edited by Tommy Gustafsson and Pietari Kääpä, 147–158. Edinburgh: Edinburgh University Press, 2015.

Ricoeur, Paul. *The Rule of Metaphor – Multi-disciplinary Studies of the Creation of Meaning in Language*. Trans. Robert Czerny with Kathleen McLaughlin and John Costello. London and Henley: University of Toronto Press, 1978.

Romney, Jonathan. 'The Kaurismäki Effect', *Sight and Sound* 7, no. 6 (June 1997): 10–14.

Romney, Jonathan. 'Last Exit to Helsinki: The Bleak Comedic Genius of Aki Kaurismäki, Finland's Finest', *Film Comment*, 39, no. 2 (March/April 2003): 43–47.

Römpötti, T. *Vieraana omassa maassa: suomalaiset road-elokuvat vapauden ja vastustuksen kertomuksina 1950-luvun lopusta 2000-luvulle*. Jyväskylä: University of Jyväskylä Press, 2012.

Rooney, David. 'The Other Side of Hope', *Hollywood Reporter*, 14 February 2017, Available online : http://www.hollywoodreporter.com/review/other-side-of-hope-berlin2017975923 (accessed 17 May 2017).

Rosenbaum, Jonathan. 'Wallflower's Revenge', *Chicago Reader*, 19 February 1993. Available online : http://www.jonathanrosenbaum.net/1993/02/wallflower-s-revenge/ (last accessed 31 March 2016).

Ross, Sara and James Castonguay. 'Asta the Screwball Dog: Hollywood's Canine Sidekick'. In *Cinematic Canines: Dogs and Their Work in the Fiction Film*, edited by Adrienne L. McLean, 78–103. New Brunswick, NJ and London: Rutgers University Press, 2014.

Saint-Cyr, Marx. 'Aki Kaurismäki and the Art of Getting by', *Cineaction*, 92 (2014): 17–23.

Sander, Gordon. 'Romantic as a Caterpillar: The Arts Interview', *Financial Times: FT Weekend*, 28 December 2002: 7.

Santé, Luc. '*La* Vie de Bohème: The Seacoast of Bohemia'. Essay included in the Criterion DVD of *La* Vie de Bohème, 20 January 2014. Available online: https://www.criterion.com/current/posts/3025-la-vie-de-bohemetheseacoast-of-bohemia (accessed 17 May 2017).

Saxton, Libby. 'Secrets and Revelations: Off-screen Space in Michael Haneke's *Caché* (2005)', *Studies in French Cinema*, 7, no. 1 (2007): 5–17.

Schepelern, Peter. 'The Element of Crime and Punishment: Aki Kaurismäki, Lars von Trier and the Traditions of Nordic Cinema', *Journal of Scandinavian Cinema*, 1, no. 1 (2010): 87–103.

Schumacher, Ernst. 'The Dialectics of Galileo'. In *Brecht Sourcebook*, edited by Carol Martin and Henry Bial, 113–123. London: Routledge, 2000.

Schumpeter, Joseph Alois. *Capitalism, Socialism and Democracy*. London: Allen and Unwin, 1954.

Sennett, Richard. *The Craftsman*. New Haven: Yale University Press, 2008.

Seppälä, Jaakko. 'On the Heterogeneity of Cinematography in the Films of Aki Kaurismäki', *Projections*, 9, no. 2 (2015): 20–39.

Seppälä, Jaakko. 'Doing a Lot with Little: The Camera's Minimalist Point of View in the Films of Aki Kaurismäki', *Journal of Scandinavian Cinema*, 6, no. 1 (2016): 5–23.

Seremetakis, C. Nadia. 'The Memory of the Senses, Part 1: Marks of the Transitory'. In *The Senses Still*, edited by Seremetakis, 1–18. Chicago: University of Chicago Press, 1994.

Shakespeare, William. 'The Tragical History of Hamlet, Prince of Denmark (The First Quarto, 1603)'. In *The Arden Shakespeare: Hamlet: The Texts of 1603 and 1623*, edited by Ann Thompson and Neil Taylor, 41–172. London: The Arden Shakespeare, 2006.

Shakespeare, William. 'The Tragical History of Hamlet, Prince of Denmark (The Second Quarto, 1604–5)'. In *The Arden Shakespeare: Hamlet*, edited by Ann Thompson and Neil Taylor, 139–464. London: The Arden Shakespeare, 2006.

Shakespeare, William. 'The Tragedy of Hamlet, Prince of Denmark (The First Folio, 1623)'. In *The Arden Shakespeare: Hamlet: The Texts of 1603 and 1623*, edited by Ann Thompson and Neil Taylor, 173–360. London: The Arden Shakespeare, 2006.

Shaviro, Steven. *Post Cinematic Affect*. London: John Hunt Publishing, 2010.

Shumway, David R. 'Rock 'n' Roll Sound Tracks and the Production of Nostalgia', *Cinema Journal*, 38, no. 2 (1999): 36–51.

Siegert, Bernhard. *Cultural Techniques: Grids, Filters, Doors, and Other Articulations of the Real*. Trans. by Geoffrey Winthrop-Young. New York: Fordham University Press, 2015.

Silva, Jennifer M. *Coming up Short: Working-class Adulthood in an Age of Uncertainty*. Oxford: Oxford University Press, 2013.

Singer, Ben. *Melodrama and Modernity: Early Sensational Cinema and Its Contexts*. New York: Columbia University Press, 2001.

Singleton, Fred. *A Short History of Finland*. Cambridge: Cambridge University Press, 1998.

Smith, Damon. 'Aki *Kaurismäki, Le Havre*', *Filmmaker Magazine*, 19 October 2011. Available online: http://filmmakermagazine.com/32663-aki-kaurismaki-le-havre/#. VLqBtsZ3b_Q.

Smith, Murray. 'Darwin and the Directors: Film, Emotion and the Face in the Age of Evolution'. In *Evolution, Literature and Film: A Reader*, edited by Brian Boyd, Joseph Carroll and Jonathan Gottschall, 258–269. New York: Columbia University Press, 2010.

Soila, Tytti. 'The Landscape of Memories in the Films of the Kaurismäki Bros', *Film International*, 1, no. 3 (2003): 4–15.

'Sound Unseen: The Acousmatic Jeanne Dielman' (2016). Available online: http://www. filmscalpel.com/sound-unseen/ (accessed 12 March 2017).

Sontag, Susan. 'Spiritual Style in the Films of Robert Bresson', *Against Interpretation*, 177–195. London: Vintage, 1991.

Srnicek, Nick and Alex Williams. *Inventing the Future: Postcapitalism and a World Without Work*. London and New York: Verso, 2015.

Standing, Guy. *The Precariat: The New Dangerous Class*. London and New York: Bloomsbury, 2011.

Stavrakakis, Yiannis. 'The Return of "the People": Populism and Anti-populism in the Shadow of the European Crisis', *Constellations*, 21, no. 4 (2014): 505–517.

Stavrakakis, Yannis, Ioannis Andreadis and Giorgos Katsambekis. 'A New Populism Index at Work: Identifying Populist Candidates and Parties in the Contemporary Greek Context', *European Politics and Society*, 18, no. 4 (2016): 1–19. Available online : http://dx.doi.org/10.1080/23745118.2016.1261434

Stern, Lesley. 'Paths That Wind Through the Thicket of Things', *Critical Inquiry*, 28, no. 1 (2001): 317–354.

Stratton, David. 'Leningrad Cowboys Meet Moses', *Variety*, 21–27 February 1994. A clipping held in Leningrad Cowboys Meet Moses file at the National Audiovisual Institute, Helsinki.

Suárez, Juan Antonio. *Jim Jarmusch*. Urbana and Chicago: University of Illinois Press, 2007.

Sutcliffe, Tom. *Watching*. London: Faber and Faber, 2000.

Tan, Ed S. *Emotion and the Structure of Narrative Film: Film as an Emotion Machine*. New York and London: Routledge, [1996], 2011.

Thompson, Kristin. 'The Concept of Cinematic Excess'. In *Narrative, Apparatus, Ideology: A Film Theory Reader*, edited by Philip Rosen. New York: Columbia University Press, 1986.

Thompson, Kristin and David Bordwell. *Film History: An Introduction*. Boston et al.: McGraw-Hill, 2010.

Timonen, L. 'Päämme päällä ja sisällämme moraalilaki'. In *Suomen kansallisfilmografia, 1996–2000*, Vol. 12, edited by S. Toiviainen, 54–62, Helsinki: Edita, 2005.

Timonen, L. *Aki Kaurismäen elokuvat*. Helsinki: Otava, 2006.

Toiviainen, Sakari. *Uusi suomalainen elokuva*. Helsinki: SES, 1975.

Toiviainen, Sakari. *Levottomat sukupolvet: uusin suomalainen elokuva*. Helsinki: SKS, Finnish Literature Society, 2002.

Toiviainen, Sakari. 'The Kaurismäki Phenomenon', *Journal of Finnish Studies*, 8, no. 2 (2004): 20–45.

Toles, George. *A House Made of Light: Essays on the Art of Film*. Detroit, MI: Wayne State University Press, 2001.

Vacche, Angela Dalle. 'Surrealism in Art and Film: Face and Time'. In *Global Art Cinema: New Theories and Histories*, edited by Galt Rosalind and Karl Schoonover, 181–197. Oxford: University of Oxford Press, 2010.

Väliaho, Pasi. *Mapping the Moving Image Gesture, Thought and Cinema Circa 1900*. Amsterdam: Amsterdam University Press, 2010.

Valkola, Jarmo. *Landscapes of the Mind: Emotion and Style in Aki Kaurismäki's Films*. Saarbrücken, Germany: Lambert Academic Publishing, 2013.

Vandaele, Jeroen. 'Humour Mechanisms in Film Comedy: Incongruity and Superiority', *Poetics Today*, 23, no. 2 (2002): 221–249.

Vismann, Cornelia. 'Cultural Techniques and Sovereignty', *Theory, Culture and Society*, 30, no. 6 (2013): 83–93.

Von Bagh, Peter. 'Aki Kaurismäen elokuvat kertovat ankarasta arjesta ja ihmisarvosta', *Lapin Kansa*, 4, March 2002.

Von Bagh, Peter. 'Aki Kaurismäki ja suomalainen todellisuus'. In *Suomen kansallisfilmografia, 1986–1990*, Vol. 10, edited by S. Toiviainen, 138–145, Helsinki: Edita, 2002.

Von Bagh, Peter. *Aki Kaurismäki*. Paris: Cahiers du Cinema, trans. Anne Colin du Terrail, 2006.

Von Bagh, Peter. *Aki Kaurismäki*. Helsinki: WSOY, 2006.

Von Bagh, Peter. 'The Uncut Interview', *Film Comment*, September/October 2011: np. Available online: http://www.filmcomment.com/article/aki-kaurismaki/

Weber, Carl. 'Brecht's Concept of *Gestus* and the American Performance Tradition'. In *Brecht Sourcebook*, edited by Carol Martin and Henry Bial, 43–49. London: Routledge, 2000.

Werner, Jochen. 'Talking Without Words: Aki Kaurismäki's Rediscovery of the Virtues of Cinema', *Journal of Finnish Studies*, 8, no. 2 (2004): 63–76.

Werner, Jochen. *Aki Kaurismäki*. Mainz: Bender Theo Verlag, 2005.

Willemen, Paul. 'Through the Glass Darkly: Cinephilia Reconsidered', in *Looks and Frictions: Essays in Cultural Studies and Film Theory*. London: BFI, 1994.

Willett, John. *Brecht in Context*. London: Methuen, 1984.

Wilson, George. *Narration in Light: Studies in Cinematic Point of View*. Oxford: Oxford University Press, 1989.

Wilson, Lana. 'Aki Kaurismäki', *Senses of Cinema*, 51 (2009): np. Available online: http://sensesofcinema.com/2009/great-directors/aki-kaurismaki/76 (accessed 21 April 2016).

Withrop-Young, Geoffrey. 'The Kultur of Cultural Techniques Conceptual Inertia and the Parasitic Materialities of Ontologization', *Cultural Politics*, 10, no. 3 (2014): 376–388.

Yliruikka, Minna. '*The Man Without a Past*'. Available online: http://touchingcinema. com/themanwithout-a-past/ (accessed 19 April 2016).

Zuberi, Nabeel. *Sounds English: Transnational Popular Music*. Chicago: University of Illinois Press, 2001.

INDEX

Lightning Source UK Ltd.
Milton Keynes UK
UKHW020825250320
360829UK00008B/392